Women P

Ste

Women Pioneers in Twelve Step Recovery

Charlotte Hunter
Billye Jones
Joan Zieger

HAZELDEN

Hazelden
Center City, Minnesota 55012-0176

1-800-328-0094
1-651-213-4590 (Fax)
www.hazelden.org

Library of Congress Cataloging-in-Publication Data
Hunter, Charlotte.
    Women pioneers in twelve step recovery : Charlotte Hunter, Billye
Jones, Joan Zieger.
        p. cm.
    Includes bibliographical references.
    ISBN 13: 978-1-56838-163-3
    1. Women alcoholics—Rehabilitation—United States. 2. Twelve-
step programs—United States. 3. Alcoholics Anonymous. I. Jones,
Billye. II. Zieger, Joan. III. Hazelden Foundation. IV. Title.
HV5137.H86 1999
616.86'103'082—dc21   99-42780
                                                               CIP

08 07   9 8 7 6 5

Cover design by David Spohn
Interior design by Nora Koch / Gravel Pit Publications
Typesetting by Nora Koch / Gravel Pit Publications

We are grateful to the following individuals who donated funds
for the production of this book:

Patty Botes

Jo Ann and Don Browning, M.D.

Marc Cellier

Margaret Graves

Allison and William Cope Moyers

Judith and Bill Moyers

Judith Pew

Barbara and Joseph Pittman, M.D.

Mimi Shafer

Contents

Acknowledgments

We wish to thank the many individuals who assisted in this first volume on women pioneers. Especially to Bob P., past general manager of AAWS, for his wisdom and interviewing skills. And to Brigid Harmon, Karin Nord, and Alexis Scott for their final manuscript review.

Note to the Reader

The profiles contained within this book come from a variety of different sources; some are original pieces; some are transcriptions of speeches; others are reprints of articles. Please see the source notes at the end of each profile for this information. Sources with direct quotations are cited within the profiles themselves.

INTRODUCTION

*As we grow in wisdom, as we grow in understanding, as
we realize the promises of this program, we'll stand ready,
as women, to weather all our personal storms. Like the wil-
low in the wind, we'll bend rather than break. And we'll be
able to help our sisters become wise through our example.*
Each Day a New Beginning—June 17

ALCOHOLICS ANONYMOUS WAS FOUNDED IN 1935. FOUR YEARS
LATER THE FIRST EDITION OF THE BIG BOOK WAS PUBLISHED,
with twenty-nine personal stories from men but only one from
a woman. Many historians, and we at Hazelden, believe women
have not been given enough credit for their contributions to the
beginning of AA. Many feel there would be no AA if only men
had been exclusively involved. The men who wrote the book
Alcoholics Anonymous and shaped the principles of the Twelve
Step program were mostly married. Women supported their
spouses during the formative years of AA. There would have
been no AA without this support from the wives or the first
women to join AA. And probably the most important influence
on the AA program came from a woman, Anne Smith.

During the 1940s and early 1950s, women slowly began
attending and receiving help in the male-dominated program
of AA. Many of the following stories illustrate the difficulties
women had during the early years, including actually being
denied access to AA meetings. Although there have been dramatic, positive developments for women in Twelve Step programs in the past sixty-four years, women are still "pioneering"
today.

Marty Mann was one of the first women in AA. Her Big Book
story is "Women Suffer Too." She was a founding director of the
organization that would become the National Council on
Alcoholism and Drug Addiction. She began a nationwide

education program to stimulate public interest in providing diagnostic, counseling, and treatment facilities for alcoholics.

In the article "Women Alcoholics Have a Tougher Fight," published in the May 1945 issue of the *AA Grapevine*, Marty wrote:

> We women who have found the answer to our alcoholic problem in AA have learned also that there should be no stigma attached to this alcoholic disease that so many of us share. We have learned that it is nothing to be ashamed of, that it is an illness like any other, with a name and symptoms, and we have learned that we can get well. . . . Women alcoholics are today, in ever-increasing numbers, seeking the answer to their alcoholic problem in AA. It hasn't been easy for us to reach them, and it hasn't been easy for them to reach out to us—but it is getting easier all the time. We women are making it so.

Our recovery as women is closely aligned with our growth in decision making, our choosing responsible behavior and activities, our personal achievement. We do, each of us, need to discover our own wholeness. We need to celebrate our personhood. We need to cheer one another on as women recovering from an addictive past, as worthwhile women in full measure.

Each Day a New Beginning—January 12

An excellent example of the attitude toward women in AA during the 1940s appeared in the October 1946 issue of the *AA Grapevine*. An article entitled "Women in AA Face Special Problems" was written by a woman. Grace O. states in part of the article, "Here then, is a list of perplexities and snags. . . . But remember, as you read, that the faults and complaints apply only to some women—to many, perhaps—but not to all." Following is the list that Grace O. created:

FEMALE FRAILTIES

1. The percentage of women who stay with AA is low. Too many of them drop out after the novelty wears off; a few months to a year and a half.

2. Many women form attachments too intense—bordering on the emotional. Best-friends, crushes, hero-worship cause strained relationships.

3. So many women want to run things. To boss, manage, supervise, regulate and change things. Twenty want to decorate; one will scrub or mend what is already around.

4. Too many women don't like women.

5. Women talk too much. Gossip is a cancer to all AA groups and must be constantly watched. Men gossip far too much, too. But few men use it for punishment, or revenge, or cutting someone down to size. Once the news value has been absorbed, men generally drop a topic. But women worry the same dead mouse until it's unrecognizable.

6. Women are a questionable help working with men and vice versa. In Twelfth Step work, the intimate confidences often lead to the pity that's akin to love, and is often mistaken for same. The protective, the maternal, the inspirational interest often lands one or both in a broadside slip—and sometimes in extra-marital experiments, which, however clothed in the glory of "honesty," are disillusioning to many others, and frequently present a troubling question to those who are actually trying to live the Twelve Steps.

7. Sooner or later, a woman-on-the-make sallies into a group, on the prowl for phone numbers and dates. Oddly enough, perhaps, she does not wear a

placard and is not always easily recognized. Results of her operations can cause havoc.

8. A lot of women are attention demanders. Spotlight sisters. They want to be spoonfed, coaxed, babied, encouraged, teased, praised and personally conducted into recovery.

9. Few women can think in the abstract. Everything must be taken personally. Universal truths, to many women, are meaningless generalities. These women are impatient of philosophy, meditation and discussion. This is the kind of woman who figures, "Just let's have this bargain; we'll pay so much faith down and the rest in installments." Which is a deceiving deal, for such buyers are generally the ones who have to watch the collector come and take the piano back.

10. Women's feelings get hurt too often. They rapidly and frequently are misunderstood.

11. Far too many women AAs cannot get along with the non-alcoholic wives of AA members. They feel ashamed or defiant, and they show it. Often they unwittingly forbid overtures—and then feel snubbed! Lots of AA women feel they attend a meeting to be helped—and concentrate to the point of rudeness on non-AA contacts. If they behave superciliously toward the non-alcoholic wives of members, they should hardly complain of being treated coolly in return.

In this book, *Women Pioneers in Twelve Step Recovery*, we take a look back on the incredible contributions of women, the countless challenges faced, and the efforts of our current women pioneers. We dedicate this book to the women pioneers past, present, and future.

*We have changed. We will continue to grow. The past need
haunt us no more. The future can be faced with confidence.
Whatever strength is needed to fulfill our destinies will find
us. And our forward steps will make the way easier for the
women to follow.*

Each Day a New Beginning—September 16

Note: We present this book as a first volume about women pioneers. Many incredible women need to be added to the next book, for example, Sylvia K., Ethyl M., and Geneva V. If you know the story of a woman pioneer and would like to share it, please contact the HP Archives Press Editor at Hazelden (P.O. Box 176, Center City, MN 55012).

Anne Smith

"For some reason, we alcoholics seem to have the gift of picking out the world's finest women." So said Alcoholics Anonymous cofounder Dr. Robert Holbrook S. (Smith), better known to millions of AA's as Dr. Bob. Though couched in a generalized third person embracing Lois W. and the wives of other early members, Dr. Bob was speaking directly of his wife, Anne. He continues, "Why they should be subjected to the tortures we inflict upon them, I cannot explain.

"How my wife kept her faith and courage during all those years, I'll never know, but she did. If she had not, I know I would have been dead a long time ago."

Anne Smith was indeed a remarkable and beloved woman, known for her caring and concern, her kindness and love for others. She was also a woman of faith. She believed in reading her Bible and praying daily and sought to know and follow the will of God. Anne is generally credited with being first to recognize the spiritual force that passed between Bill Wilson and Dr. Bob, later embodied in the Twelve Steps. She attended Oxford Group meetings before Dr. Bob and then was the one who persuaded him to go. After battling her husband's alcoholism unceasingly in their own house, it was she who answered the call from Henrietta Seiberling telling her of "a man who might help Bob with his drinking problem." And it was she who took Dr. Bob, over his protests, to Henrietta's gatehouse to talk with Bill W.

Her home became a hostel for would-be AA members (the name did not exist yet) where she was an equal team member in getting them sober and helping them on the long road to recovery. In the early meetings that developed soon after, she and the other wives attended and participated; indeed, they organized and led them. At later meetings at King Street School, she was remembered for always looking out for the newcomers.

Bill W. once called Anne Smith "the mother of AA." This may have been not only because of her actions, but because of the direct influence of her thoughts and her writings on the Twelve Steps and other AA literature. Anne attended Oxford Group meetings from 1933 (two years before her husband's recovery) until 1939, during which time she kept a workbook, or "spiritual journal." Its notes on the Oxford Group principles and her own comments reveal a close, unmistakable similarity to the wording in the Big Book. For example, Anne writes of an Oxford Group prayer, "O Lord, manage me, for I cannot manage myself." Note the comparison in the Big Book, Step One (p. 59), the "pertinent ideas" (p. 60), and the Third Step prayer in *Twelve Steps and Twelve Traditions*, or Twelve and Twelve. Another example: Anne writes in her journal, "We can't give away what we haven't got." Recent scholars cite dozens of similar comparisons.

Anne was especially effective in counseling wives, helping rid them of their anger and despair, comforting them by showing them they were not alone, giving them hope. Although she died two years before the Al-Anon Family Groups began, its cofounder, Lois W., and the fellowship itself recognized that Anne Smith. exemplified the spiritual principles and ideals of Al-Anon.

Lois W. lived to be ninety-seven and a half, and fifty-four of those years were after Bill had sobered up. Anne Smith died at sixty-nine, with only fifteen years of Dr. Bob's sobriety behind her. Little wonder, then, that Lois W. is remembered more clearly, particularly in the East; but more's the wonder that Anne made such a profound impact on the fellowship in a relatively short span of time.

In 1898, nineteen-year-old Anne Robinson Ripley was

spending a holiday with a college friend in St. Johnsbury, Vermont, when she met Robert Holbrook Smith, the young man who was to become her husband. She was small in stature and reserved in temperament but had a cheerfulness, sweetness, and calm that were to remain with her throughout her years. She came from the Chicago suburb of Oak Park, Illinois, where she had been reared, one of four children. Her father worked for the railroad. Although the family did not have much money at that time, it was a comfortable, sheltered environment. Unusually bright in the Oak Park schools, Anne won a scholarship to Wellesley College—a prestigious achievement for a young woman from the Midwest in the late nineteenth century. (Anne, who abhorred ostentation and pretense, always took pains to explain that she attended Wellesley on a scholarship because her parents could not have afforded to send her otherwise.)

The occasion for the meeting of Anne and Bob was a dance in the gym of the St. Johnsbury Academy, where Bob was a senior. He was a handsome young man, over six feet tall with wide, athletic shoulders and big bones. His strong, classic features and lively personality attracted Anne almost immediately. What she did not know at that time was that he had a reputation for waywardness and rebellion against authority—despite which he had maintained a creditable grade average.

Their meeting was hardly the beginning of a whirlwind courtship. It was to culminate in marriage after seventeen years! During all that time they kept in touch, saw each other when possible, and corresponded regularly. The reasons for the long delay are not clear today, except that in those days more than now it was customary to be sure the groom could support his bride before entering into matrimony.

After graduating from college, Anne returned to Oak Park and taught school. Bob had ahead of him four years at Dartmouth College, three years of working unsuccessfully in business, followed by three years at the University of Michigan doing premed and medical school, finishing up at Rush

University, near Chicago. Throughout his varied college career, his drinking accelerated, sometimes disastrously. Consequently he didn't receive his M.D. degree until 1910, at age thirty-one.

At the end of his last year at Rush, Bob was able to stay dry, possibly because he was near enough to his sweetheart, Anne, to see her more frequently and was trying to impress her. In any case, his grades and deportment won him a coveted two-year internship at City Hospital, Akron, Ohio. There, hard work took the place of hard drinking, and with his internship behind him, the thirty-three-year-old doctor opened an office in the Second National Building. Soon, unfortunately, a combination of stomach trouble and a return to his worst drinking habits had him in and out of drying-out places, ending in a breakdown so severe that he spent two months back home in Vermont recuperating.

Resuming his practice in Akron and "thoroughly scared by what had happened, or by the doctor, or probably both," Dr. Bob said, he stayed sober for the rest of 1914 and into 1915. Anne Ripley may have had a healthy fear of entering into matrimony with a drinking man for the past seventeen years but now believed he was sober for good—or perhaps she was just tired of waiting. In any case, she consented to marry Dr. Bob. He went to Chicago, and the ceremony took place in the home of Anne's mother, Joyce Pierce Ripley, "at half past eight" (as the wedding invitation read) on January 25, 1915.

Anne came back to Akron by train with Dr. Bob to a house he had purchased at 855 Ardmore Avenue, a tree-lined street in the fashionable west end of town. It was a new, two-story clapboard house with large, airy rooms including a completely modern, well-equipped kitchen. In that day, the house cost four thousand dollars!

The first three years of their married life were ideal, free from any of the unhappiness that was to come later. Dr. Bob continued to stay sober, relieving Anne of any lingering worries on that score. They were, and continued always to be, an extremely devoted couple, deeply in love with each other. As Dr. Bob's reputation as a physician flourished and his practice grew, the couple acquired a wide circle of friends and became pillars of the community.

In 1918, a son, Robert Ripley Smith Jr. (later nicknamed "Smitty"), was born. When he was age five and Anne was in her mid-forties, she was advised that she could not have any more children. Not wanting to raise Smitty as an only child, they adopted a daughter, Sue, also age five. (The recollections of Smitty and Sue as adults are the richest and most authentic source of information about their parents and are used extensively in this chapter.)

The children were not aware of their father's drinking in their early years. They had a happy childhood. They remembered their parents' devotion and said they never heard them have an argument. "They spoiled us both rotten," said Sue. "Oh, we got spankings all right. Not often, but when we did, we really deserved it. We learned early that the louder we yelled, the sooner it was over."

Their memories of their mother show deep affection: "She was quiet and unassuming—a lady in the true sense of the word," Smitty wrote. "She was of medium build, always battling to keep her weight down. She had a delightful sense of humor and a melodious laugh. We kids played a lot of tricks on her, because she took it so well."

One practical joke they loved to tell about came after Anne started to smoke—at age fifty-six! All she ever did was take a few puffs on a cigarette before putting it down and lighting another. "If she ever inhaled, it was by mistake," declared Sue, who ascribed her mother's habit to tension over Dr. Bob's drinking. "She was broiling inside. She had to be," said her daughter. Smitty and Sue, on the sly, swiped not only occasional cigarettes from her pack, but her butts as well, as they were scarcely used.

In the middle of the depression, Anne decided to buy a roll-your-own device. "We kids volunteered to roll her some," chuckled Smitty, "and we mixed pencil shavings in with the tobacco. When she lit one, it flared up and she had to blow it out. The same thing happened with the next. Finally, she said, 'You know, these don't taste as good as the ones you get in a pack.'"

When Anne discovered that Smitty had begun to smoke, she chided him. "What about you, Mom?" he retorted. "You smoke."

"Don't you say anything to me about smoking now," Anne replied. "If you wait until you're fifty years old before you start, I won't say anything to you, either."

His wife's shyness and naïveté were a source of delight to Dr. Bob. He loved to bring home an off-color story just to watch her shocked reaction. "Later on, though," recalled Smitty, "after being exposed to a bunch of drunks, nothing seemed to shock or surprise her. No matter how bizarre their actions were compared to her sheltered upbringing, she just would not criticize. She would always seek to excuse whatever they did. Her extreme tolerance for others was one of her great qualities."

When Anne issued a directive or gave advice, she seldom did so on the spur of the moment. Her comments were reserved until she had time to pray and think about the problem. And then her words were given in a loving, objective way.

Smitty recalled, "Mother always had a very deep loyalty to our family, and later to A.A., which made no sacrifice too great. She just would not spend any money on herself, so the family could get the things she thought they needed.

"By nature a rather timid person, she would nevertheless rise to great heights if she thought the occasion warranted. I have personally seen her rise out of her quiet disposition in defense of Dad or myself. And later, when she thought the AA program was in danger in some way, Mother would be ready to do battle with anyone."

In the depression years in the early thirties, times were hard in Akron. It was a one-industry town, and when the rubber plants were idle, money was scarce for everyone. The Smith family somehow acquired a second car but lacked the money to license it. Only a federal mortgage moratorium saved their house. The children recalled, "We ate enough potato soup to float us." Anne had to pay household debts with money received for Christmas or birthdays.

In the face of these desperate financial straits, Dr. Robert Smith, once one of the most successful surgeons in town, now had almost no practice left. When a patient called him, he would be in hiding or at home and indisposed. Anne lied to his patients, and so did Lily, his office assistant.

This was just one more motivation for Anne's constant battle to keep her husband's worsening alcoholism in check. She tried again and again to extract promises from him that he would not drink. Dr. Bob would promise her—or the children, or the occasional remaining friend—to stop. "I was absolutely sincere when I made the promise," said Dr. Bob later, "but it would seldom keep me sober even through the day I made it." When he got on a real binge, he wouldn't even come home, which worried Anne sick.

She tried to frisk him for hidden bottles when he got to the door, wanting to keep him in shape for the next morning. But he usually outwitted her. Smitty recalled, "In the winter he wore heavy driving gloves, as car heaters worked poorly then. He would put a half-pint of medicinal alcohol in one of them and toss it up on the second-story sun porch. After Mother had frisked him, he would go upstairs and get his alcohol. When he came down again, it was obvious he had been drinking. She never did figure that one out."

Like many an alcoholic before and after him, Dr. Bob was an expert in maintaining his supply. He later confessed, "If my wife was planning to go out in the afternoon, I would get a large supply of liquor and smuggle it home and hide it in the coal bin, the clothes chute, over door jambs, over beams in the cellar, . . . in old trunks and chests, . . . and even in the ash container."

As the children grew older, they were more aware of their father's problem with alcohol. Although he was never abusive and seldom drunk enough to make a spectacle of himself, they remembered him as irritable and cross when he was under the influence. They were ashamed of his abject slavery to booze and sympathized with their mother, who was trying to hold the penniless family together, praying that her husband would somehow find an answer to his problem.

The seed of that answer was sown in 1933 with the introduction of the Oxford Group to Akron. It was a spiritual movement that sought to recapture the power of first-century Christianity in the modern world. Its members sought to achieve spiritual renewal by surrendering to God, making a rigorous self-examination, confessing their character defects to another person, making restitution for harm done to others, and helping others without thought of reward. Emphasis was placed on prayer and reading the Scriptures as ways of finding guidance from God in all matters. The Oxford Group thought all behavior should be guided by "four absolutes": absolute honesty, absolute unselfishness, absolute purity, and absolute love. (The absolutes became a part of the early AA program in the Akron/Cleveland area.)

A rubber company president, grateful because his son had found sobriety through the Oxford Group, brought thirty Oxford Group leaders and members to Akron in 1933 for a ten-day gathering, culminating in a dinner for four hundred prominent local residents. As a result, a number of weekly meetings were set up in Akron, and many new members were attracted. Among these was Anne Smith, who attended the West Hill meeting. Another was Henrietta Seiberling, Vassar graduate and mother of three, who was the daughter-in-law of the founder and president of the Goodyear Tire and Rubber Company.

Anne persuaded Dr. Bob to come with her to the Oxford Group meetings, hoping they would help him control his drinking habit. Anne herself, shy by nature and painfully sensitive about her husband's alcoholism, did not share at the meetings, nor did Dr. Bob. He nevertheless was attracted to the people "because of their seeming poise, health, and happiness. . . . They had something I did not have," he said. So he continued to attend Oxford Group meetings regularly. But he also continued drinking.

Henrietta took a personal interest in Dr. Bob's problem and felt guided to hold a separate meeting focused specifically on Dr. Bob, hoping to get him to open up. (The meeting was held at the home of Oxford Groupers T. Henry and Clarace Williams, where meetings continued to be held weekly—the first meetings attended by Akron alcoholics.) Anne was in attendance, of course. After everyone else had shared deeply about their shortcomings over which they had been victorious, there was a silence. Finally Dr. Bob spoke in his deep, sonorous voice, saying, "I am going to tell you something which may cost me my profession: I am a secret drinker, and I can't stop." The group knelt and prayed for him. But he still continued to drink.

This was the situation when early Saturday evening, May 11, 1935, Henrietta received a call from a total stranger. It was Bill W.

Bill had called out of his own desperation when, after pacing up and down the lobby of the Akron's Mayflower Hotel, he needed to talk to another alcoholic to keep from drinking himself. Instead of joining the crowd in the festive hotel bar, Bill found the directory of church services in the lobby, and he began to call the ministers listed. All were dead ends until he reached the Reverend Walter Tunks, who knew of Henrietta's efforts to help Dr. Bob. He gave the stranger her name. Bill told Henrietta, "I'm from the Oxford Group and I'm a rum hound from New York. I'm told you know a man with a drinking problem I may be able to help."

Henrietta immediately called Anne and invited her and Dr. Bob over to her house (she lived in the gatehouse of the Seiberling estate) to meet a new friend who might help Dr. Bob. Anne replied at first that she didn't think it would be possible for them to make it that day. But Henrietta persisted until Anne was forced to tell her that Dr. Bob was drunk and had passed out upstairs.

Anne Smith 9

Henrietta called again on Sunday and this time persuaded Anne to accept an invitation for dinner. Dr. Bob, suffering from a terrible hangover, agreed to meet the stranger who might help him but made Anne promise to get him away after fifteen minutes.

The two men ended up talking for more than six hours. What they said to each other during all that time is not completely known. Bill said he "had quit preaching." He talked about his own case and hammered home the seriousness of the disease, "the verdict of inevitable annihilation." He emphasized he was there as much to help himself as to help Dr. Bob.

For his part, Dr. Bob noted that here "was a man . . . who had been cured by the very means I had been trying . . . the spiritual approach. He gave me information about the subject of alcoholism which was undoubtedly helpful. *Of far more importance,*" he continued, "*was the fact that he was the first living human with whom I had ever talked, who knew what he was talking about in regard to alcoholism from actual experience. In other words, he talked my language.*"

What happened in the gatehouse that night was one alcoholic talking to another.

Daughter Sue, in retrospect, remembers that her father, upon his late return home that night, seemed sober and more at ease and "looked better all around." Anne's reaction is not recorded, but she probably did not dare be overly optimistic in view of broken promises in the past. But as the days passed with her husband not drinking, she did what she could to encourage the new friendship.

Henrietta was aware that Bill had no money, so she arranged through a neighbor to put him up for two weeks at the country club, to keep him in town. The two men continued to see each other frequently, as Anne invited Bill for dinner almost every night. Shortly, Bill and Dr. Bob started carrying the message to other prospects. Meanwhile, Bill's business partners back in New York sent him some money to enable him to continue the proxy fight that had brought him to Akron.

Anne, hardly daring to hope that her husband's newfound sobriety would be permanent, but determined to do what she could to protect it, invited Bill to come live with them. "There," said Bill later, "I could keep an eye on Dr. Bob—and Anne could keep an eye on me. I lived with these wonderful people for the next three months. I shall always believe they gave me more than I ever brought them."

Each day at the Smith residence began with devotion led by Anne; they called this "the quiet time," which came directly from the Oxford Group. Seated in her chair in a corner, she would begin by reading from the Bible, often from the book of James—her favorite and consequently the favorite of the first AA groups. She would usually conclude with her favorite quotation, "Faith without works is dead." Then one or more of those present would say a prayer. This was followed by a time of quiet. The meeting concluded with a general sharing of what each person had gotten from the meeting. These devotions ran from a half hour to an hour.

Around the last week of May, Dr. Bob broached the idea of his attending an annual American Medical Association convention, which he hadn't missed in twenty years, to be held in Atlantic City, New Jersey, the first week of June. Anne, knowing her husband's alcoholic predilections, cried out, "Oh, no!" But Bill was more agreeable, feeling that recovering alcoholics had to learn to live in the real world with all its temptations. The upshot was that Dr. Bob went to the convention. Predictably, he began drinking heavily almost from the moment he boarded the train and continued for five days, when he returned, rolling off the train dead drunk.

He was scheduled to perform an operation in three days, which were occupied with Anne and Bill tapering him off with canned tomatoes and sauerkraut, along with Karo corn syrup—and just enough beer to steady his nerves. Miraculously, he was able to go through with the operation, which was a success. That morning's beer was the last drink he ever had. The date was June 10, 1935, generally agreed as the date Alcoholics Anonymous began—though it had only two members and no name.

One of the first alcoholics Bill and Dr. Bob worked on was Eddie R., a "borderline manic depressive who was also a wild drunk," according to Smitty. When Eddie and his wife lost their house, they moved into Anne and Dr. Bob's home. In the brief intervals he was sober, Eddie gave them great hope, but when he went off again, he caused enough trouble to keep Bill and Dr. Bob too busy to drink even if they had wanted to. He repeatedly ran away, tried to commit suicide, beat his wife, and went berserk without warning.

Anne loved to tell of one such traumatic incident. As he was having a tuna fish sandwich lunch, out of a clear blue sky, Eddie jumped up, grabbed a large butcher knife, and chased Anne out of the kitchen and upstairs. "I didn't know what to do," she related later, "so I got down on my knees and started praying. Eddie was gibbering about what he was going to do with the knife, and I just prayed and prayed in a low monotone. I figured sooner or later it was going to bore him. Sure enough, he finally started to calm down, and Bill came up and took the knife from him."

After that, they decided Eddie R. was not the right person to work on.

To find the next alcoholic, Dr. Bob called City Hospital, where he was affiliated, and talked to Mrs. Hall, the admissions nurse. He explained that he and a man from New York had a "cure" for alcoholism and needed a prospect to try it out on. The nurse, who knew Dr. Bob all too well, asked, "Have you tried it on yourself, Doctor?" Dr. Bob, somewhat taken aback, said, "Yes, I sure have."

Mrs. Hall did have a prospect, a lawyer who had been in the hospital six times in the last four months and now lay strapped down to his bed because he had gone on a drunken rampage the night before and roughed up some nurses. Dr. Bob and Bill talked first with the lawyer's wife, Henrietta D., who described her husband as "the grandest man in the world when he's sober; but when he's drinking, he's the worst."

"Yes, I know," replied Dr. Bob.

The two men talked with the patient, Bill D. (Dotson), whom they found in a state of hopelessness and despair over his inability to stop drinking. He was ready, and they reached him with their message. He became "AA No. 3" and remained sober the rest of his life, a much-loved and respected member.

Immediately after Dr. Bob and Bill's second talk with Bill D., Dr. Bob said to Bill D.'s wife, "[Anne] wants to see you at our house." Reluctant at first, Henrietta D. nevertheless made the call. She related, "When Anne came to the door, I said, 'Are you Mrs. S.?' And she said, 'Anne to you, my dear.' That broke the ice. Anne was so sweet, everyone loved her. There was never anything to make you feel she was better than anyone else. She said, 'Let's you and me stay in the background.'"

Remembering how it was later on, Henrietta D. said, "Anne talked to the other wives a lot more than I did, because I never was a good talker. Anne would prod the other wives to talk to new women, to go to their houses if necessary. She would call me every single morning and ask, 'Did you have your quiet time? Did you get anything special out of it?' She was wonderful!"

J. D. H., one of the first dozen Akron AA members (he came in September 1936), told of the confusion of drunks and newly sober men in the Smith house: "Anne never knew who would be on her davenport when she got up in the morning. She was a sweet, motherly type of woman you couldn't help but love. She didn't care much for style. If she wanted to go anywhere, she went regardless of whether she had a new dress or she didn't. She'd pick up a hat whether it was five or ten years old, put it on, and go. I've heard her say she had only one pair of stockings.

"One thing I'm grateful for. Dr. Bob and Anne had planned to go to Vermont two days before I came into the group. But Anne woke up in the middle of the night and said she felt they shouldn't go, that they would be needed here. Thank God!"

A similar thing happened soon after that shows Anne's deep

belief in her guidance. A Sunday picnic was planned, and on Saturday night Anne announced firmly that she wasn't going. Something told her it wasn't right. Sure enough, about five o'clock Sunday morning, there was a call from Detroit saying they had a man they wanted to send down. He turned out to be Archie T., who stayed with Dr. Bob and Anne almost a year, because he was too frail and too broke to go out and hunt for a job. He eventually started the first AA group in Detroit. Later, Archie T. told of what happened:

"I was taken in off the streets and nursed back to life by Anne S——. I was not only penniless and jobless, but too ill to get out of the house and look for work. So great was Anne's love and so endless her patience with me, so understanding her handling of me, that ten months later, I left a new man, perhaps imbued with just a few grains of that love.

"Their love for each other and for their two children was of such a nature that it permeated the house, and if one lived in that house and were willing, that same love was bound to get under one's skin. In the ten months I lived in their home," Archie said, "young Bob and Susie treated me exactly as another member of the family. Neither of those kids ever, for so much as a single instant, did anything or said anything to make me feel 'out of the family.'

"Anne let me feel my way without interference, let me figure things out for myself, knowing with a wisdom not granted to many, that in that way I would learn and apply in my daily life what I had learned." On Archie's tenth AA anniversary, in Detroit, he introduced Anne to a crowd of fifteen hundred people and related the story of his rehabilitation with great emotion.

Another Akron early-timer, Bob E., who came in 1937 at age thirty-two, remembered that he, too, spent a lot of time with Anne. "She had a quiet, soft way of making you feel at home. I shared a good many of my life problems with her. She read the Bible to me and counseled me. She tried to keep things simple, too. I told her about being nervous and demoralized. She gave me a couple of phrases to say whenever I got downhearted or confused or frustrated. One I remember is: 'God is love.' And I used it a lot."

In November 1937, Bill W., on a business trip, was able to stop over to visit with Dr. Bob and Anne for the first time since he had left two years before. As the threesome sat in the living room counting up recoveries, they realized that (as Bill wrote later) "a hard core of very grim, last-ditch cases had by then been sober a couple of years. All told, upwards of 40 alcoholics were staying bone dry." Bill and Dr. Bob realized a "chain reaction" had started that "conceivably could one day circle the world." The three of them bowed their heads in silent thanks. (During this same visit, Bill, the visionary, proposed to a meeting of members such grandiose ideas as a chain of hospitals and missionaries. The Midwest conservatives knocked down these ideas, but after a long, hard-fought session, approved by a narrow margin the idea of a book.)

Back in New York, Bill met with John D. Rockefeller Jr. who was interested in principle but who forthwith dispatched a staff advisor, Frank Amos, to go to Akron, investigate what was going on, and report back. Amos made a thorough investigation indeed, talking to Henrietta Seiberling, the T. Henry Williamses, and many doctors and hospital officials. He met with Dr. Bob and Anne, attended meetings of the alcoholic group, and interviewed many of the recovering drunks.

He found enthusiastic support for Dr. Bob everywhere, and his report to Rockefeller was unstinting in its praise. In it he said, "Dr. Smith has a wife—a lovely, cultured lady who supports him to the limit in this work—and a son and daughter around the ages of 18 and 20. His modest home is mortgaged and he has not been able to keep it in proper repair. He needs a competent secretary. . . . Mrs. Smith has her hands full with the home and with her work with the wives and with an occasional woman alcoholic who turns up. . . . Men can rarely work satisfactorily with women alcoholics [so] Mrs. Smith and other wives must handle most of this, for which there is a growing need."

Rockefeller was apparently impressed with what Frank Amos had found. As one result, he agreed to put up five thousand dollars for the personal use of Bill and Dr. Bob. Three thousand of this went to pay off Dr. Bob's mortgage; the rest was parceled out to the two cofounders equally at thirty dollars a week.

Drunks were sent—or occasionally came on their own initiative—from other towns in the area to be "fixed" by Dr. Bob. One of these was Clarence S. (Snyder), who came over from Cleveland in 1938 with his wife, Dorothy, who had arranged to get him there. After the mandatory week's hospital stay, Clarence and Dorothy went directly to the meeting of the "alcoholic group" at T. Henry's house. Dorothy recalled, "Walking up the path to that door was one of the hardest things I've ever done. I didn't want to meet a bunch of drunks and I didn't want to meet their wives.

"I walked in there, and all these people came up to me. One of the very first was Anne S———. Somebody introduced her to me as Mrs. S——— and she said, 'Call me Anne.' Well, that did it. I could hardly even talk. It seemed to break the shell that I had been so careful to build up all those years.

"There were about 50 people there. The living room was packed. The thing that impressed me most was the *joy* that was there. Everybody seemed happy, and all these women I thought I hadn't wanted to meet—I just thought, 'If only I could be like them.' Life began for me that night."

(Clarence S. went on to found the first group in Cleveland, which was also the first group to be called "Alcoholics Anonymous" from the name of the book.)

With a burst of favorable publicity beginning with the publication of the Big Book, *Alcoholics Anonymous*, in the spring of 1939 and the accompanying reviews in major newspapers, AA began to grow at an alarming rate. That fall, a series of articles in the Cleveland *Plain Dealer* brought in scores of desperate calls for help in that city. At nearly the same time, a favorable article appeared in the major national magazine *Liberty* and was greeted with great elation. Several other breaks followed in newspapers, smaller magazines, and radio. The culmination was the Jack Alexander article in the March 1941 *Saturday Evening Post*, which opened the floodgates everywhere.

In Cleveland, newcomers with only a few days' sobriety were pressed into Twelve Stepping even newer prospects. In Akron, as many as seven prospects at a time occupied every available bed in City Hospital and other facilities. All this put a terrific strain on Dr. Bob and Anne, particularly as it came at a time when their finances were at an all-time low. A friend who dropped into their house for dinner discovered that "dinner" was bread and milk.

A milestone in AA history came in early 1940 when Dr. Bob gained permission to treat alcoholics at St. Thomas Hospital, where he and the legendary Sister Ignatia set up a program for treating drunks. (Between then and the time Dr. Bob died, 4,800 alcoholics were admitted to St. Thomas under his care.) Sister Ignatia recalled later, "Dr. Bob took a personal interest in all the alcoholic ward activities. He visited the patients daily without salary until his health failed.

"I had to learn from experience that it was a waste of time to force anyone to accept the program," said Sister Ignatia. "Many of these patients were a great source of worry to me. They would come with their complaints, imaginary or otherwise. I didn't like to bother Doctor too much, so I would call Anne. Anne's advice was of great value to me. Her calm, soothing tone and sympathetic understanding were a source of encouragement. She always found the correct answer. In her diplomatic way, she might present the problem to the doctor, then telephone me and advise."

As the alcoholic group that met at the T. Henry Williamses' as part of the Oxford Group acquired its own identity, it was inevitable that it would split off. That time came in early 1940. The alcoholics now had their own program set out in their own textbook. They had the precedent of the New York group breaking away from the Oxford Group there in 1937. The wives of the Akron alcoholics perhaps had less ties to the Oxford

Group than their husbands and may have been an influence.

The specific causes of the split are unknown, but Dr. Bob did go to talk with T. Henry to propose that the alcoholics meet on their own. The final meeting at the Williamses' came soon after, with praise and good wishes all around. Apparently the person most upset was Henrietta Seiberling who had brought about the joint meetings in the first place.

For two weeks the alcoholic group, numbering more than seventy, met at Dr. Bob and Anne's house, which was too small to handle such a crowd. They were able to move to King Street School, where the daughter of one of the members, Wally G., was a student. The meetings continued there on Wednesday nights for many years, with Anne and Dr. Bob in faithful attendance until their deaths. They are remembered as having "regular" seats toward the back. The leader almost always asked Dr. Bob to say something. His comments were simple, down to earth, and spiritually based.

The refreshment period was Anne's part of the meeting. She would make it her business to go from table to table and introduce herself. She told the new women they were in the same boat and that she and the other women there were their friends. Dan K., an early King Street School attendee, recalled: "[Anne] always looked to the newcomers. She'd spot you and after the meeting, she would go to your table and introduce herself. 'I want to welcome you and your lovely wife to Alcoholics Anonymous. We hope you'll keep coming back.' She'd give a bit of background on AA and then maybe she'd go on to another new member."

Anne's friend Dorothy S. said that she couldn't remember Anne in anything except the same old black dress. For Dorothy's first sober Christmas, her brother gave her a new dress, the first in a long time. Anne had also received a gift of three new dresses from someone. "We were going to a New Year's Eve party together," said Dorothy, "so I went by and asked Anne which of her new dresses she was going to wear. She looked at me and said, 'You know, Dorothy, there are some new people who won't have anything, and I can't bear to wear any of them.' Sure enough, she showed up in her old black dress."

That wasn't the only lesson Dorothy learned from Anne. Thrilled at the new friends she was making, Dorothy would rush up to them at meetings and engage in animated conversation. One night Anne called her over: "Dorothy, people have been awfully good to you, haven't they? You've been pretty lucky, and you made a lot of new friends." Dorothy agreed enthusiastically. "Don't you think you could pass that on, a little bit? There's a new woman sitting over there in the corner, and nobody's talking to her."

"That was a lesson from Anne I tried to remember ever afterward," said Dorothy S. "It's the new people that count. To really try and make them feel welcome and wanted—that's one way I can pay back what I have received. Anne always called everybody by their first names. She would remember them. She knew all the children they had. She took a terrific personal interest in everybody."

In 1940, Duke P., a salesman in Toledo with a drinking problem, was sent to Akron by his boss to try this new program for alcoholics he had read about. He was admitted to City Hospital with "acute gastritis" and was released that same night to attend an AA meeting at Wally G.'s. "I was amazed," he said, "—a dozen people sitting around calling each other rummies and alkies and not getting upset. The next morning, who should come to see me but Dr. Bob! He just radiated charm, love and confidence—all the things I didn't have. He said, 'Duke, everything's going to be all right.' And I knew it would."

Duke P. never had another drink. He and his wife, Katie, would drive from Toledo to Akron to attend the Wednesday night AA meetings. It was there he met Anne. "Anne gave us a feeling of stability," he recalls. "She always had the right thing to say, no matter what. You couldn't have a feeling of anger or animosity toward anyone when she was around. She always said that in order to know someone else's feelings you had to walk a mile in his shoes."

In September 1940, Duke and Katie, with other Toledo members, started the first AA group in that city.

In World War II, Smitty, in the army, was sent to Texas, where he met his bride-to-be, Betty. He chuckled as he remembered taking Betty to Akron to meet his parents for the first time. Dr. Bob looked her up and down slowly, then remarked, "She's all right, son. She's built for speed and light housekeeping."

"I loved both Mom and Dad S. very deeply," Betty said. "Dad S. and I had a thing going about gin rummy. We would shout ugly words at each other, and had a marvelous time. His sense of humor was always at peak." She summed up her feelings about Anne thus: "She truly treated me like a daughter. . . . She was a place of shelter for people in trouble. I doubt that any minister in any given week could have counseled more people, prayed with more people. In times of trouble, people rushed to her. She was a rock, a comforter with God's help—truly a person who went placidly amid the noise and haste."

The years of happiness following Dr. Bob's recovery were marred at last by Anne's loss of sight and subsequent illness. Beginning in the mid-1940s, she developed cataracts that covered both eyes. She could no longer drive a car and could not recognize a person without getting up close—although she acquired a remarkable ability to identify people by their voices. An operation for the removal of one of the cataracts failed, and she opted to retain the limited vision in the other eye rather than risk total blindness.

Dr. Bob began to be her eyes as best he could. They both continued their regular attendance at the Wednesday night AA meeting. But the demands of Dr. Bob's medical practice made it impossible for him to be with Anne all the time. They needed to find daily care, which came as the result of his help to another alcoholic. Lavelle K. and his wife, Emma, a registered nurse, had come to Dr. Bob in 1941. Lavelle joined AA, and the two couples struck up a close friendship.

Once when Dr. Bob and Anne were planning a trip, they

asked the K.'s if they would move into the Ardmore Avenue house to take care of the dog in the their absence. That was the beginning. For eight years Emma and Lavelle stayed at the Smith house from time to time. So when Anne needed more and more help, naturally Emma was there. She recalled, "Mrs. S. could see a little out of one eye, but not well. She was having a very hard time walking, and her hands were cramped and swollen with arthritis." Emma's presence at this time, 1947 to 1949, was a godsend for the future of AA as well, for Dr. Bob was in the center of the schism between New York and Akron over the conference idea, caught up in the dissension and controversy that accompanied it.

In May 1949, Dr. Bob and Anne flew down to visit Smitty, Betty, and their family. Though Anne felt weak and tired, she hid it and went because she knew it would make Dr. Bob happy. On the way home, when their plane was grounded by bad weather, Dr. Bob called ahead to Sister Ignatia to request a hospital bed for his wife. She had contracted pneumonia, which was followed by a severe heart attack. She lingered only a few days and died June 1, 1949. Sister Ignatia, in a letter to Dr. Bob, wrote that Anne, as a patient, had been a model of calmness and acceptance: "She was more concerned about the well-being of her visitors than herself. . . . Her great patience, courage, and strength were outstanding."

Smitty said later, "When Mother died, Dad was very much broken up. They had been such a devoted couple. Only after she was gone did it dawn on me that this deep, quiet, considerate person, who would do battle for what she believed or to protect her family, was the solid foundation which Dad needed to carry on his part of A.A." Emma K. recalled, "When Mrs. Smith died, Doctor didn't know what to do. I went home and got my husband and said we'd better go over and stay overnight." They stayed through the funeral. And then, while Dr. Bob was looking for a housekeeper without success, they stayed another three weeks. At about this time, Emma said that Anne appeared to her in a dream and said, "Emma, please don't leave Dad." When she mentioned her dream to Lavelle the next morning, he said, "I don't know whether it was a dream or not, but I had the queerest feeling that Anne was talking to me also. We can't leave him."

So the K.'s gave up their home and spent Dr. Bob's last year and a half with him. Smitty said gratefully, "They were a lovely couple. They were a wonderful inspiration to him and cheered him up when he was blue and took care of him and the house in a very efficient manner."

At about that time, the AA members in Akron were talking about erecting a monument in honor of Anne and Dr. Bob and had even started a collection for that purpose. When Dr. Bob heard of it, he let it be known in no uncertain terms that he was opposed to any memorials or monuments and was dismayed that they wanted to mention AA on it. When Bill W. revealed in a conversation that a similar memorial had been proposed for him, Dr. Bob told him, "Let's you and I get buried just like other folks."

Dr. Bob knew that his time was coming. He had discovered prostate cancer two or three years before, and it had spread to other parts of his body. As a physician, he followed the deadly progression of his disease, facing his imminent death with acceptance. When he was not in the hospital for surgery or forced to stay in bed at home, he tried to enjoy the balance of his time as much as possible. With a friend, Dick S., he flew to the West Coast and renewed old acquaintances. After a time back home, where he received a constant flow of visitors, he and Dick visited his old home in Vermont and then went on to Maine.

He bought his dream car, a black Buick convertible, which he drove around town like a teenager. Said Smitty, "The older he got, the wilder he drove." Every afternoon he was able, he would drive down to the City Club to play cards with his friends. He particularly loved bridge. He continued to go to the AA meetings at King Street School.

As his pain grew more severe and he was getting ready to die,

Dr. Bob's goal was to get to AA's First International Convention in Cleveland in July 1950. He made it, delivering his memorable and oft-quoted "last talk" to the thousands of people who were gathered. Smitty and Betty were present, as were Emma and Lavelle.

His final piece of official AA business was to meet with Bill W. at the Ardmore house about the decision whether AA should have a conference or not. Bill made the point that if the two of them took no action, their silence would in itself be an action. It would be interpreted as approving the status quo. Bill thought that a trial conference should be called, even if it was a failure at first. The movement's delegates could then decide whether they wanted to take the responsibility or not.

Finally, Dr. Bob looked up and said, "Bill, it *has* to be A.A.'s decision, not ours. Let's call that conference. It's fine with me."

As Bill left a few hours later, both men knew that this might well be the last decision they would make together. Bill related, "Bob stood in the doorway, tall and upright as ever. Some color had come back into his cheeks, and he was carefully dressed in a light gray suit. This was my partner, with whom I never had a hard word. The wonderful old, broad smile was on his face as he said almost jokingly, 'Remember, Bill, let's not louse this thing up. Keep it simple!' I turned away, unable to say a word. That was the last time I ever saw him."

A few days later, Dr. Bob was taken to City Hospital for yet another operation. He survived only a few days more. Dr. Bob passed away November 16, 1950, to join his beloved Anne in "a new horizon," as he put it. Crowds of their old friends, people they had helped, came to the funeral home. The funeral service was conducted in the old Episcopal Church by Dr. Walter Tunks, whose sympathetic and understanding answer to Bill W.'s phone call fifteen years before had set in motion the events leading to Alcoholics Anonymous. Anne and Dr. Bob lie side by side in Mt. Peace Cemetery. They are buried "just like other folks." No monument marks the spot, only a simple headstone.

Henrietta Seiberling

THE "ALCOHOLIC SQUAD OF THE OXFORD GROUP," AS EARLY
AKRON AA'S LIKED TO CALL THEMSELVES, WAS BLESSED TO
have three unusual ladies as spiritual instructors.

Each was highly intelligent, well educated, and spiritually
tuned in. The first was Anne Ripley Smith, wife of AA
cofounder Dr. Bob. Anne Smith was a Wellesley graduate, a
former teacher, and an ardent student of the Bible and
Christian literature of the 1930s. The second was Clarace
Williams, wife of T. Henry Williams, in whose home the very
first AA group met. Clarace had gone to a Baptist missionary
school in Chicago, specialized in religious education at Ottawa
University in Kansas, and then worked in Akron, Ohio, with
the young people in a church there.

The third is the subject of this story. She was Henrietta
Buckler Seiberling, the only child of Judge Julius A. and Mary
Maddox Buckler. Henrietta grew up in El Paso, Texas, where
her father was judge of the common pleas court. Henrietta
received a B.A. degree from Vassar College, majoring in music
with a minor in psychology. In Texas, she met and married John
Frederick "Fred" Seiberling, son of Akron's rubber industry
magnate, Frank A. Seiberling.

Each of the three women became dedicated in the 1930s to
helping deliver alcoholics from their dreadful disease. It all
started with a series of momentous events in Akron during the
earliest months of 1933. Rubber tycoon Harvey Firestone Sr.
had a seemingly hopeless alcoholic son named Russell. Russell
had miraculously recovered from his disease in 1931 with the

assistance of his Oxford Group friend Jim Newton and with the spiritual coaching of the Reverend Samuel M. Shoemaker Jr., an Episcopal rector from New York, who led Russell to Christ on a return train ride from Denver, Colorado, to Akron. Russell's deliverance followed a meeting of Oxford Group people at an Episcopal Bishop's Conference in Denver.

After his recovery in 1931, Russell Firestone began witnessing about his deliverance and became an enthusiastic Oxford Group adherent. His grateful father invited Oxford Group founder Frank Buchman and a team of thirty Oxford Group activists to Akron to tell the Oxford Group's life-changing story. Russell was their star speaker. For more than ten days, Akron newspapers were ablaze with Oxford Group testimonies. Oxford Group terms like *Bible study, quiet time, prayer, sin, self-centeredness, restitution, life-changing,* and *surrender* could be found daily in headline stories. They also were heard in Akron pulpits and schools. These words, and the shared spiritual experiences of the Oxford Group team, were finally tendered to a huge, overflow crowd at the Mayflower Hotel in Akron in January 1933.

Due to the Firestone name and support, the fur-clad elite of Akron were there. So were hundreds of others. And so were the three ladies we mentioned—Anne Smith, Clarace Williams, and Henrietta Seiberling—as well as a fourth companion, Delphine Webber. The four women attended the Mayflower Hotel event and were captivated. They began at once attending Oxford Group meetings, later at the T. Henry Williams home in Akron; and they soon interested AA's cofounder-to-be, Dr. Bob, in the Oxford Group program and meetings.

Henrietta Seiberling had a special and vital role in the ensuing founding events of AA that began to take place soon thereafter. First, however, a brief description of Henrietta's life, then of the part she played in early AA, and finally the particular resources she made available to the spiritually needy AA pioneers.

Henrietta was born in Lawrenceburg, Kentucky, on March

18, 1888. She married Fred Seiberling in Akron, Ohio, on October 12, 1917. The marriage took place at Akron's baronial Seiberling estate, known as Stan Hywet Hall. Fred and Henrietta Seiberling had three children, all of whom were involved in the early AA Oxford Group meetings, though neither Henrietta nor her children were alcoholics. The three offspring were John F. Seiberling, later a Harvard College and Columbia Law School graduate, then a United States congressman from Akron, and still later director of Akron University's Peace Studies Center; Mary Seiberling Huhn, who lives in Devon, Pennsylvania; and Dorothy Seiberling Stiber, who lives in Shelter Island, New York. Both of the daughters are graduates of Vassar College.

Quite possibly, Henrietta's son, John, who has taken a continuing interest in Alcoholics Anonymous, is the only person alive with an intimate recollection of the earliest AA meetings at the T. Henry Williams home in Akron. John was then sufficiently old and attended sufficiently often that he recalls a good many facts.

Henrietta was a Presbyterian from childhood but not particularly an avid churchgoer. She was, however, an ardent student of the Bible. In January 1933, Henrietta was distressed over family and financial problems. She was living separate from her husband at the Seiberling estate gatehouse, where she raised her three children. She was attracted to the famous Oxford Group/Firestone witness meetings in 1933. She read all the Oxford Group books of the 1930s, as well as many other religious books by Christian leaders of that day. She also began attending the Thursday West Hill Oxford Group meetings. She organized the Wednesday night meetings at the home of T. Henry and Clarace Williams where the alcoholic squad of the Oxford Group (AA's earliest group) met from 1935 to 1939. She was the leader at many of these meetings—eventually composed of about 50 percent Oxford Group people and 50 percent alcoholics and their family members.

Henrietta was a member of Westminster Presbyterian

Church in Akron on West Market Street, where Dr. Bob and Anne Smith were charter members. The minister was J. C. Wright, who became an Oxford Group adherent. Probably unknown to most AA's today is that the Reverend Wright kept in touch with the Reverend Sam Shoemaker, Bill Wilson's Oxford Group mentor in New York. Dr. Shoemaker was rector of Calvary Episcopal Church in New York, where Oxford Group meetings were being held (in the adjacent Calvary House) and that were being attended by AA's other cofounder, Bill Wilson, and his wife, Lois. Henrietta took her children to Dr. Wright's Presbyterian church, and the children were baptized there in their teens. For several years, she and her family often went to that church, attended Oxford Group meetings, and learned to have their own "quiet times" after the Oxford Group and early AA custom.

It was Henrietta who put Bill Wilson in touch with Dr. Bob Smith on Mother's Day, May 11, 1935, at a meeting in her home at the gatehouse of the Seiberling estate. It was she also who persuaded a neighbor, John Gammeter, to pay to have Bill lodged at the prestigious Portage Country Club in Akron shortly before Bill moved into the Smith home for the summer of 1935.

Bill resided with the Smiths at 855 Ardmore Avenue in Akron for three months. Henrietta, Bill, Dr. Bob, and Dr. Bob's wife, Anne, studied the Bible and Oxford Group literature, prayed, and had quiet times together during that period. They discussed spiritual principles extensively. They sought out alcoholics to help. They attended Oxford Group meetings at the Williamses' home. And Henrietta worked closely with Dr. Bob and Anne, helping many alcoholics to recover. Commenting on Henrietta's work during two different visits he made to Akron in 1936, Bill was prompted to say (in an April 1936 letter to Lois) that he had spent the weekend in Akron and was "so happy about everything there. Bob and Anne and Henrietta have been working so hard with [the alcoholics] and with really wonderful success. There were very joyous get-togethers at

Bob's, Henrietta's, and the Williamses' by turns." Then, when Bill again visited Akron in September 1936, he wrote his wife that his arrival was "a signal for a house party, which was very touching. . . . Anne and Bob and Henrietta have done a great job. There were several new faces since spring."

Just what were the contributions that Henrietta made and with which she was achieving such success along with Dr. Bob and Anne Smith? The facts can be pieced together from various remarks and writings. But first these accolades were written by Bill Wilson:

> Right here I want to set on record the timeless gratitude that AA's will always have for Henrietta Seiberling, she who first brought Dr. Bob and me together. Of the ten people to whom I had been directed by Clergyman Walter Tunks, Henrietta was the only one who had understood enough and cared enough. And this had been only the beginning of her mission. During the first summer at Akron she affectionately counseled many an alcoholic's family, just as Anne [Dr. Bob's wife] was doing. Despite the fact that she had no direct experience of alcoholism, Henrietta had a rare capacity for identification with us. Therefore she was eagerly sought out for her great spiritual insight and the help she could give. What Alcoholics Anonymous owes to her will always be beyond anybody's reckoning. And Dr. Bob's debt and mine are the greatest of all (*Alcoholics Anonymous Comes of Age*, p. 73).

Speaking of a few older Clevelanders, Bill said:

> They had met and listened to Henrietta Seiberling, the nonalcoholic who had brought Dr. Bob and me together in her house three years previously—one who had understood deeply and cared enough and who was already seen as one of the strongest links in the chain

of events that Providence was unfolding (*Alcoholics Anonymous Comes of Age*, p. 19).

After Bill and Dr. Bob's work with their first newcomer prospect had failed, Bill said:

> Then came a lull on the Twelfth Step front. In this time, Anne and Henrietta infused much needed spirituality into Bob and me" (*The Language of the Heart*, p. 357).

And what are the specifics that Dr. Bob and Bill learned? As with so many of his words of praise, Bill did not get into details. But there are other factual sources and records. They cover the Oxford Group meetings of 1933 and Henrietta's immense study of the Bible, Oxford Group books, and other religious literature.

The leading Oxford Group books that Henrietta read and discussed with early AA's were *Life Changers*, by Harold Begbie; *Children of the Second Birth* and *If I Be Lifted Up*, by Samuel M. Shoemaker; *For Sinners Only*, by A. J. Russell; *Soul-Surgery*, by Howard A. Walter; *Inspired Children*, by Olive Jones; and *Discipleship* and *Psychology and Life*, by Oxford Group admirer Dr. Leslie Weatherhead. Henrietta made a present to Bill of the two Weatherhead books—inscribed with Bill's name and hers. She studied and shared a number of other important Christian books of the day. Dr. Bob and his wife read and recommended them to, and they were read by, early AA's. They included *Love: The Law of Life*, by Toyohiko Kagawa; *Modern Man in Search of a Soul*, by Dr. Carl Jung; *The Soul's Sincere Desire* and *I Will Lift Up Mine Eyes*, by Glenn Clark; *Practicing the Presence of God*, by Brother Lawrence; *The Meaning of Prayer*, by Harry Emerson Fosdick; *My Utmost for His Highest*, by Oswald Chambers; many books by E. Stanley Jones; and the quarterly Bible devotional known as *The Upper Room*. There were also many other such materials.

Henrietta's interest in the Bible was substantial. She studied the teachings and story of Jesus, as did Dr. Bob and Anne. Henrietta also found useful James Moffatt's modern translation of the New Testament, published—along with the King James Version in parallel columns—by Harper Brothers in 1922. She clung to the inspiring version of First Century Christianity (a name the Oxford Group and early Akron AA's used to describe themselves) as it paralleled Christ's own methods. She stressed Jesus' teaching on forgiveness—forgiving seventy times seven if that need be. Jesus' sermon on the mount (Matthew 5–7) was something she loved. The guidance of God was most important to her. Her Bible readings and daily quiet times were an effort to let God guide her life. Her attitude about guidance paralleled that of the Oxford Group: "Speak, Lord, for thy servant heareth" (I Samuel 3:9). The Gospel of John and I Corinthians 13 were a large part of her reading. Finally, but not exclusively, she emphasized, "Thy will be done"—a phrase from the Lord's Prayer—that can be found in various forms in Alcoholic Anonymous's own basic text, *Alcoholics Anonymous* (the Big Book).

Recent research has established some twenty-eight Oxford Group ideas that substantially influenced the language and program of Alcoholics Anonymous's Big Book and its Twelve Steps. When Henrietta's son, John, heard and read these, he said, "I would have had to be deaf not to have heard them" in the early Alcoholics Anonymous days. He said his mother talked about the principles a great deal. These concepts really provide the structure for the Big Book's life-changing program—its "design for living." Many historians today have noted the degree to which Alcoholics Anonymous borrowed from these specific Oxford Group concepts. Here, therefore, arranged for convenience in eight groups, are the Oxford Group ideas early AA's heard so often, just as John Seiberling did from his mother:

God:

    (1) He is creator, maker, father, spirit, and living God.

    (2) God has a plan—His universal will as revealed in the Bible.

    (3) Humanity's chief end is to do God's will.

    (4) The path toward God being by belief that God is.

Sin:

    (5) Sin is the self-centeredness that blocks humans from God and others.

Finding God:

    (6) Surrender is the turning point that occurs when as much of a person is surrendered to God as is understood.

    (7) Soul-surgery is the art by which that person cuts away sin.

    (8) A conversion of life change is the result.

The path to a relationship with God:

    (9) A decision to surrender marks the beginning.

    (10) Self-examination to discover the blocks is the next step.

    (11) Confession of the sins to God and another human being follows the inventory.

    (12) Conviction of a need to change is the next step.

    (13) Conversion—a change to a God-directed life—is next.

    (14) Restitution—clearing away the wrongs sin has caused—must follow.

Jesus Christ:

    (15) There is, and can be, no change or conversion without the transforming power of Christ—Christ in you.

Spiritual Growth—Continuance:
Conversion is just the beginning of a changed life. Spiritual growth must continue by

(16) conservation, a process by which the relationship with God grows.

(17) daily surrender, which continues the surrender process.

(18) guidance, the continuing process of seeking God's will in all matters.

(19) the Four Absolutes—Absolute Honesty, Absolute Purity, Absolute Unselfishness, and Absolute Love— representing the absolute standards believed to be the heart of Jesus Christ's teachings and toward which people are to progress in their daily lives.

(20) quiet time, a special time for communing with God, particularly in the mornings.

(21) Bible study, a vital part of quiet time.

(22) prayer—talking to God, also a vital part of quiet time.

(23) listening to God and writing down thoughts received—the second part of "two-way" prayer.

(24) checking with Scripture and the Four Absolutes to make sure the thoughts received have come from God and not self-deception.

The Resultant Spiritual Experience:
When a person has gone through the life-changing process through surrender, receiving the power of Christ, taking stock of and being rid of sin, cleaning up the past, and daily communing with God, the person will

(25) know God's will, as John 7:17 promises.

(26) be God-conscious—conscious of the power and presence of God in his or her life.

Fellowship and Witness:
Oxford Group leader Sam Shoemaker of New York often taught that no spiritual experience or awakening is complete without

(27) fellowship—the corporate experience of meeting, praying, and believing together—as described in the Book of Acts in the Bible.

(28) witnessing to the delivering power of God by passing on the message—as AA's and Oxford Group people say, "You have to give it away to keep it." They were paraphrasing (they thought) the teachings of Jesus, Paul, and other New Testament writings that command believers, as ambassadors of Christ, to "go and tell!"

The foregoing twenty-eight principles can be found frequently in the writings of Sam Shoemaker, whom Bill Wilson said was his teacher and whose books Dr. Bob and Anne Smith, Henrietta, and the other Akron pioneers widely read. The principles can be found in many other Oxford Group books. And they can be found in detail in the spiritual journal that Anne Smith assembled and wrote between 1933 and 1939 and also shared with alcoholics and their families. Each concept embodies an Oxford Group idea extracted from the Bible. Henrietta was thoroughly conversant with, and taught about, all the principles in her work with alcoholics and their families. The principles embody the heart of Alcoholics Anonymous's Twelve Steps—even to the point that the Big Book today contains some two hundred phrases almost directly derived from these ideas.

Now for the specifics about Henrietta's early Alcoholics Anonymous role. Several of the details were covered in a tape of a telephone conversation Henrietta had with her son shortly after Bill Wilson's death. The occasion was an Alcoholics Anonymous Founders' Day in Akron in 1971.

As recorded, the first event followed a concern someone expressed to Henrietta over Dr. Bob Smith's drinking. Henrietta decided to gather together some Oxford Group people at the T. Henry Williams home in Akron and have them use the Oxford Group idea of "sharing for confession and sharing for witness." The people were to share some costly things about their lives and thereby, she hoped, help Dr. Bob to lose his pride and share what he thought would cost him a great deal. They believed his sharing would necessarily be about his alcoholism. Henrietta warned Dr. Bob's wife, Anne, that there would be an Oxford Group meeting that she and Dr. Bob should attend. She said, "Come prepared to mean business. There is going to be no pussyfooting around."

The Smiths attended. The Oxford group people shared their shortcomings and how they had achieved victory over them. Silence followed their confessions. Then Dr. Bob said, "Well, you good people have all shared things that I am sure were very costly to you, and I am going to tell you something which may cost me my profession: I am a silent drinker, and I can't stop." The group asked Dr. Bob, "Do you want us to pray for you?" And he said, "Yes." Then someone said, "Do you want to go down on your knees and pray?" And he said, "Yes." So they knelt together and prayed. And for many years thereafter, T. Henry Williams often would point to the place on his carpet where Dr. Bob knelt down to pray. T. Henry then would say, "It [the fellowship of Alcoholics Anonymous] started right there."

An extraordinary event occurred the next day. Henrietta knew nothing about alcoholism. She thought a man should drink like a gentleman, and that's all. She said a prayer for Dr. Bob. She declared, "God, I don't know anything about drinking, but I told Bob that I was sure that if he lived [the Oxford Group way], he could quit drinking. Now you have to help me." Henrietta said she then received guidance from God. She said it was like a voice in the top of her head. The message was, "Bob must not touch one drop of alcohol." And she said, "I knew that was not my thought."

Coincidentally, Bill Wilson had learned from his physician in New York, Dr. William Silkworth, about the disease of alcoholism—involving the so-called allergic reaction that occurs when an alcoholic takes just one drink, the first drink. That first drink for the real alcoholic, Dr. Silkworth had said, creates the phenomenon of craving that overcomes all mental and physical control and thus causes the alcoholic to lose control over the amount taken and to experience all the trouble that excessive drinking inevitably causes. Silkworth then had told Bill, from the medical perspective, that the alcoholic, if wishing to quit, could not touch the first drink. Henrietta knew none of this medical information. She firmly believed she had received the vital words of wisdom and knowledge by divine revelation.

She called Dr. Bob and said she had important guidance for him. He came to visit her, and she told him her guidance was that he mustn't touch one drop of alcohol. Dr. Bob, though himself a doctor, said, "Henrietta, I don't understand it. Nobody understands it. Some doctor has written a book about it, but he doesn't understand it. I don't like the stuff. I don't want to drink."

The next event in this remarkable sequence involved the encounter that Bill Wilson soon had with Henrietta. According to her, Bill arrived in Akron, was virtually broke, and had been confronted with a business failure. Bill had been tempted to drink and forget it all. But Bill prayed. Then, instead of drinking, he went to a church directory and called an Episcopal rector, Dr. Walter Tunks. Tunks had been deeply involved in hosting the Oxford Group/Firestone events of 1933. Tunks gave Bill a list of names, one of whom was Norman Sheppard, a close friend of Henrietta's who knew what she was trying to do for Dr. Bob. Bill reached Sheppard but was told that Sheppard was on his way to New York. Sheppard recommended that Bill call Henrietta Seiberling. Bill was down to his last nickel but used it to phone Henrietta.

Bill said to Henrietta, "I'm from the Oxford Group, and I'm a rum hound." Having prayed so fervently for and with Dr. Bob, Henrietta thought, "This is really manna from heaven." She told Bill, "You come right over here." And, though Dr. Bob was then drunk, she was able to get Bill and Dr. Bob together the next day for six hours. Bill had been out to get help for himself, by seeking out another to help. But, as Henrietta said, "That is the way that God helps us if we let God direct our lives."

After meeting with Dr. Bob, Bill stayed on in Akron, but he had no money. Henrietta had a friend named John Gammeter, who had seen the change in her life that the Oxford Group had brought about. And Gammeter arranged for Bill to stay at the Portage Country Club for two weeks or so. The purpose was to keep Bill in town. After that, Bill went to live with Dr. Bob and Anne Smith for about three months during the summer of 1935. It was at that time that Bill learned the vital principles of the Bible from the Smiths, T. Henry Williams and his wife, and Henrietta—biblical principles that formed the basic ideas AA's use for their recovery program. And Alcoholics Anonymous's own basic spiritual tools of recovery then began to be developed.

Henrietta's role in this process was continuous. Every Wednesday the little group of alcoholics and Oxford Group people would meet. She would speak on some new experience or spiritual idea she had read. There was great stress, in and out of the meetings, on guidance and quiet times.

By 1940, Bill had begun to rely for spiritual sponsorship on a Roman Catholic Jesuit priest named Father Ed Dowling. Dowling came to Akron to see the alcoholic squad leaders there. Commenting on Alcoholics Anonymous, Dowling said to one of the squad, "This is one of the most beautiful things that has come into the world. But I want to warn you that the devil will try to destroy it."

Henrietta was later to observe that one of the most destructive weapons the devil would use was having money, sanitariums, and other expensive things Bill was planning. Henrietta staunchly proclaimed, "No, we'll never take any money." And, except for the large sum of money it later derived from book publishing, the Alcoholics Anonymous fellowship never did receive or solicit significant outside money. Henrietta also believed the devil could destroy Alcoholics Anonymous through having prominent members. She felt this would be destructive because "no one is on top spiritually all the time." She said, "We'll never have any names."

As the years rolled by in Alcoholics Anonymous, Henrietta declared, "I tried to give to the people something of my experience and faith. What I was most concerned with [was] that we always go back to faith." She found to her dismay that the devil was moving destructively in that arena. She said that Dr. Bob and Bill had both said to her, "Henrietta, I don't think we should talk too much about religion or God." Henrietta would have none of it. She proclaimed to the founders:

> Well, we're not out to please the alcoholics. They have been pleasing themselves all these years. We are out to please God. And if you don't talk about what God does, and your faith, and your guidance, then you might as well be the Rotary Club or something like that. Because God is your only source of power.

She said Bill and Dr. Bob finally agreed with her position and that "they weren't afraid anymore."

But Henrietta began to believe that Alcoholics Anonymous was slipping away from faith in God's power. For example, she went to a New York Alcoholics Anonymous dinner attended by more than three thousand people. She was sorely disappointed and commented:

> There were two witnesses there, a man and a woman; and you would have thought they were giving you a description of a psychiatrist's work on them. Their progress was always on the level of psychology. I spoke to Bill afterwards, and I said that there was no spirituality there or talk of what God had done in their lives. They were giving views, not news of what God had done. Bill said, "I know, but they think there are so many people that need this and they don't want to send them away." So there again has come up this same old bugaboo—without the realization that they have lost their source of power.

Henrietta stood for God. To the end, she believed strongly in His guidance, His love, and His power. Of the New York dinner, she said, "This makes me think of the story of the little Scotch minister who was about to preach his first sermon, and, as his mother hugged him, she said, 'Now, Bobbie, don't forget to say a word for Jesus. . . .' And then there is one other thing I'd always like to stress, and that is the real fact of God's guidance. People can always count on guidance, although it seems elusive at times." In other words, AA's were enjoined to remember that it was God who had done for them what they could not do for themselves.

Henrietta's children all had admiring comments about their mother's staunch principles and beliefs. Dorothy Seiberling Stiber wrote:

> She was a seeker, and it took the form of Christian belief. She had aspirations toward spiritual and moral improvement. By observing and trying to live by the standards of the Oxford Group, she achieved greater humility and surrendered her ego and fears to God. There is no question that mother was concerned about the spiritual core of Alcoholics Anonymous. She always feared its secularization into a kind of how-to-do-it.

John Seiberling wrote:

> Henrietta made a constant effort to lead a life of Christian spirituality and to help others do the same. She was insistent on following the OG Four Standards of Absolute Honesty, Purity, Unselfishness, and Love. Also important to her were the OG practices of daily surrender to God, "quiet times," witnessing, and making restitution to those you may have hurt. She was also firm that when one witnessed, he or she should talk "news, not views," i.e., tell what had happened in one's

life, not what one thought about things. Humility and the belief that people are more important than things were uppermost in her messages. Also the importance of being right on the inside, not just the appearance of being right. Her Bible reading and her daily quiet times were an effort to let God guide her life.

Mary Seiberling Huhn wrote:

> Mother became intensely interested in the teachings and story of Jesus. She turned to them for help in her own problems and then was able to use the insights gained as she nurtured the developing AA. Mother was always quoting from the Bible to teach us how to get along better. When we were quarreling or angry and said spiteful things, she would say, "If you don't love your brother whom you have seen, how can you love God whom you haven't seen?" Most of what she taught us reflected the original OG ideas about returning to the roots and not getting hung up on institutional baggage.

The foregoing, then, are some of the important ideas Henrietta infused into early AA's, their families, and leaders. She died in New York City on December 5, 1979. She is buried at Lawrenceburg, Kentucky. On her gravestone is an inscription familiar to many people, and certainly to Oxford Group adherents and to the fellowship of Alcoholics Anonymous: "Let go and let God."

Sources: *

Dick B. *The Akron Genesis of Alcoholics Anonymous.* Seattle: Glen Abbey Books, 1992.

Dick B. *Anne Smith's Journal, 1933–1939.* 3d ed. San Rafael, Calif.: Paradise Research Publications, 1999.

Dick B. *The Books Early AAs Read for Spiritual Growth.* 5th ed. San Rafael, Calif.: Paradise Research Publications, 1997.

Dick B. Interviews, phone calls, and letters with or from John F. Seiberling, Dorothy Seiberling Stiber, and Mary Seiberling Huhn. November 1997.

Dr. Bob and the Good Oldtimers. New York: Alcoholics Anonymous World Services, Inc., 1980.

Origins of Alcoholics Anonymous

Turning Point: A History of Early A.A.'s Spiritual Roots and Successes. San Rafael, Calif.: Paradise Research Publications, 1997.

Seiberling, Henrietta. Interview by T. Willard Hunter. January 1955.

*Additional sources are cited within the profile itself.

Sister Ignatia

SISTER MARY IGNATIA, ONE OF THE FINEST FRIENDS THAT WE OF AA SHALL EVER KNOW, WENT TO HER REWARD FRIDAY morning, April 2, 1966. Next day, the Sisters of Charity of St. Augustine opened their Mother House to visitors. More than one thousand of them signed the guest book in the first two hours. These were the first of many who during the two days following came to pay their respects to Sister.

On Monday at high noon, the Cathedral at Cleveland could barely seat its congregation. Friends in the city and from afar attended the service. The Sisters of Charity themselves were seen to be seated in a body, radiant in their faith. Together with families and friends, we of AA had come there in expression of our gratitude for the life and works of our well-loved Sister. It was not really a time for mourning; it was instead a time to thank God for his great goodness to us all.

In its affirmation of the faith, the Mass was of singular beauty; the more so to many, since it was spoken in English. The eulogy, written and read by a close friend of Sister's, was a graphic and stirring portrayal of her character and of her deeds. There was a most special emphasis upon the merits of AA, and upon the part co-founder Dr. Bob had played in Sister's great adventure among us. We were assured as seldom before that those who dwell in the fellowship of the spirit need never be concerned with barriers or with boundaries.

For those thousands of men, women, and children whose lives had been directly touched and illumined by Sister, it would perhaps not be needful to write this account of her. Of

Sister, and of the grace she brought to all these, they already know better than anyone else. But to the many others who have never felt her presence and her love, it is hoped this narrative may be something for their special inspiration. Born in 1889 of devout and liberty-loving parents, Sister entered into this world at Shanvilly, County Mayo, of the Emerald Isle. The famed poet Yeats, born nearby, once remarked that the strange beauty of County Mayo had been specially designed to raise up poets, artists, heroes, and saints. We can little doubt that even when Ignatia was aged six, and her parents had emigrated from Ireland to Cleveland, she was already beginning to manifest many a sterling virtue.

Soon the child began to reveal unusual musical talents, both for piano and voice. A few years later she was seen giving lessons at the home of her parents. During 1914, she became possessed of a great desire to become a religious. In this year she joined the community that many of us AAs know so well: the Sisters of Charity of St. Augustine. There she continued her musical education and her teaching.

But even then, as ever since, Sister was frail, exceeding frail. By 1933 the rigors of her music teaching had become too great. She had a really serious physical breakdown. Her doctor put to her this choice: "You will have to take it easy. You can either be a dead music teacher or a live Sister. Which is it going to be?"

With great good cheer, so her community says, Mary Ignatia accepted a much quieter and less distinguished assignment. She became the registrar at St. Thomas Hospital in Akron, Ohio, an institution administered by her order. At the time it was wondered if she could manage even this much. That she would live to the age of seventy-seven was not believable; that she was destined to minister to 15,000 alcoholics and their families in the years to come was known only to God.

For a considerable time Sister serenely carried on at the admissions desk in St. Thomas. It was not then certain she had ever heard of AA. Though Group One at Akron and Group Two in New York had been in slow and fitful growth since 1935, neither had come to public notice. However, in 1939, the scene changed abruptly. In the spring of that year the AA Book was first printed, and *Liberty* magazine came up with an article about our Society in the early fall. This was quickly followed by a whole series of remarkable pieces which were carried by the Cleveland *Plain Dealer* on its editorial page. The newspaper and the mere two dozen AAs then in town were swamped by frantic pleas for help. Despite this rather chaotic situation, the Cleveland membership burgeoned into several hundreds in a few months.

Nevertheless, the implications of this AA population explosion were in some ways disturbing, especially the lack of proper hospital facilities. Though the Cleveland hospitals had rallied gallantly to this one emergency, their interest naturally waned when bills often went unpaid, and when ex-drunks trooped through the corridors to do what they called "Twelfth Step" work on sometimes noisy victims just arrived. Even the City Hospital at Akron, where Dr. Bob had attended numerous cases, was showing signs of weariness.

In New York we had temporarily got off to a better start. There we had dear old Dr. Silkworth and, after a while, his wonderful AA nurse Teddy. This pair were to "process" some 12,000 New York area drunks in the years ahead, and so they became, as it were, the "opposite" numbers to the partnership of co-founder Dr. Bob and Sister Ignatia at Akron. Much concerned that, hospital-wise, his area might be caught quite unprepared to cope with a great new flood of publicity about AA, Dr. Bob in 1940 decided to visit St. Thomas and explain the great need for a hospital connection that could prove permanently effective. Since St. Thomas was a church institution, he thought the people there might vision a fine opportunity for service where the others had not. And how right he was!

But Bob knew no one in authority at the hospital. So he simply betook himself to Admissions and told the diminutive nun in charge the story of AA, including that of his own recovery. As this tale unfolded, the little sister glowed. Her compassion was deeply touched and perhaps her amazing intuition had already begun to say, "This is in." Of course Sister would try to help, but what could one small nun do? After all, there were certain attitudes and regulations. Alcoholism had not been reckoned as an illness; it was just a dire form of gluttony! Dr. Bob then told Sister about an alcoholic who then was in a most serious condition. A bed would simply have to be found for him. Said Mary Ignatia, "I'm sure your friend must be very sick. You know, Doctor, this sounds to me like a terrible case of indigestion." Trying to keep a straight face, Dr. Bob replied, "How right you are. His indigestion is most terrible." Twinkling, Sister immediately said, "Why don't you bring him in right away?"

The two benign conspirators were soon faced with yet another dilemma. The victim proved to be distressingly intoxicated. It would soon be clear to all and sundry that his "indigestion" was quite incidental. Obviously a ward wouldn't do. There would have to be a private room. But all the single ones were filled. What on earth could they do? Sister pursed her lips and then broke into a broad smile. Forthwith she declared, "I'll have a bed moved into our flower room. In there he can't disturb anyone!" This was hurriedly done, and the indigestion sufferer was already on his way to sobriety and health.

Of course the conspirators were conscience-stricken by their subterfuge of the flower room. And anyhow, the indigestion pretense simply couldn't last. Somebody in authority would have to be told, and that somebody was the hospital's Superior. With great trepidation, Sister and Dr. Bob waited upon this good lady, and explained themselves. To their immense delight she went along, and a little later she boldly unfolded the new project before the St. Thomas trustees. To their everlasting credit they went along too—so much so that it was not a great while before Dr. Bob himself was invited to become a staff physician at St. Thomas, a bright example indeed of the ecumenical spirit.

Presently a whole ward was devoted to the rehabilitation of

alcoholics, and Sister Ignatia was of course placed in immediate charge. Dr. Bob sponsored the new cases into the hospital and medically treated each, never sending a bill to any. The hospital fees were very moderate and Sister often insisted on taking in patients on a "pay later" basis, sometimes to the mild consternation of the trustees.

Together Ignatia and Dr. Bob indoctrinated all who cared to listen to the AA approach as portrayed by the book *Alcoholics Anonymous*, lately come off the press. The ward was open to visiting AAs from surrounding groups who, morning to night, told their stories of drinking and of recovery. There were never any barriers of race or creed; neither was AA nor church teaching pressed upon anyone.

Since nearly all her strenuous hours were spent there, Sister became a central figure on the ward. She would alternately listen and talk, with infinite tenderness and understanding. The alcoholic's family and friends received the very same treatment. It was this most compassionate caring that was a chief ingredient of her unique grace; it magnetically drew everyone to her, even the most rough and obstinate. Yet she would not always stand still for arrant nonsense. When the occasion required, she could really put her foot down. Then to ease the hurt, she would turn on her delightful humor. Once, when a recalcitrant drunk boasted he'd never again be seen at the hospital, Sister shot back, "Well, let's hope not. But just in case you do show up, please remember that we already have your size of pajamas. They will be ready and waiting for you!"

As the fame of St. Thomas grew, alcoholics flocked in from distant places. After their hospitalization they often remained for a time in Akron to get more firsthand AA from Dr. Bob, and from Akron's Group Number One. On their return home, Sister would carry on an ever mounting correspondence with them.

We AAs are often heard to say that our Fellowship is founded upon resources that we have drawn from medicine, from religion, and from our own experience of drinking and of recovery.

Never before nor since those Akron early days have we witnessed a more perfect synthesis of all these healing forces. Dr. Bob exemplified both medicine and AA; Ignatia and the Sisters of St. Augustine also practiced applied medicine, and their practice was supremely well animated by the wonderful spirit of their community. A more perfect blending of grace and talent cannot be imagined.

It should never be necessary to dwell, one by one, upon the virtues of these magnificent friends of AA's early time—Sister Ignatia and co-founder Dr. Bob. We need only recollect that "by their fruits we shall always know them."

Standing before the Cleveland International Convention of 1950, Dr. Bob looked upon us of AA for the last time. His good wife Anne had passed on before, and his own rendezvous with the new life to come was not many months away.

Ten years had slipped by since the day when he and Sister had bedded down that first sufferer in the St. Thomas flower room. In this marvelous decade, Sister and Dr. Bob had medically treated, and had spiritually infused, five thousand alcoholics. The greater part of these had found their freedom under God.

In thankful recollection of this great work, we of AA presented to the Sisters of Charity of St. Augustine and to the staff of the St. Thomas Hospital a bronze plaque, ever since to be seen in the ward where Sister and Dr. Bob had wrought their wonders. The plaque reads as follows:

> In Gratitude: The friends of Dr. Bob and Anne S. affectionately dedicate this memorial to the Sisters and staff of St. Thomas Hospital. At Akron, birthplace of Alcoholics Anonymous, St. Thomas Hospital became the first religious institution ever to open its door to our Society. May the loving devotion of those who labored here in our pioneering time be a bright and wondrous example of God's grace everlastingly set before us all.

Visitors at St. Thomas today often wonder why this inscription says not a word about Sister Ignatia. Well, the fact was, she wouldn't allow her name to be used. She had flatly refused; it was one of those times when she had put her foot down! This was of course a glowing example of her innate and absolutely genuine humility. Sister truly believed that she deserved no particular notice; that such grace as she might have could only be credited to God and to the community of her sisters.

This was indeed the ultimate spirit of anonymity. We who had then seen this quality in her were deeply affected, especially Dr. Bob and myself. Hers came to be the influence that persuaded us both never to accept public honors of any sort. Sister's example taught that a mere observance of the form of AA anonymity should never become the slightest excuse for ignoring its spiritual substance.

Following Dr. Bob's death, there was great concern lest Sister might not be allowed to continue her work. As in other orders of the church, service assignments among the Sisters of Charity were rather frequently rotated. This was the ancient custom. However, nothing happened for a time. Assisted by surrounding AA groups, Sister continued to carry on at St. Thomas. Then suddenly in 1952, she was transferred to St. Vincent Charity Hospital at Cleveland, where, to the delight of us all, she was placed in charge of its alcoholic ward. At Akron a fine successor was named to succeed her; the work there would continue.

The ward at Charity occupied part of a dilapidated wing, and it was in great need of repair and rejuvenation. To those who knew and loved Sister, this opportunity proved a most stimulating challenge. The Charity trustees also agreed that something should be done. Substantial contributions flowed in. In their spare hours, AA carpenters, plumbers, and electricians set about redoing the old wing—no charge for their services. The beautiful result of these labors of love is now known as Rosary Hall.

Again the miracles of recovery from alcoholism commenced

to multiply. During the following fourteen years, an astonishing 10,000 alcoholics passed through the portals of Rosary Hall, there to fall under the spell of Mary Ignatia and of AA. More than two-thirds of all these recovered from their dire malady, and again became citizens of the world. From dawn to dark Sister offered her unique grace to that endless procession of stricken sufferers. Moreover, she still found time to minister widely to their families and this very fruitful part of her work became a prime inspiration to the Al-Anon Family Groups of the whole region. Notwithstanding her wonderful workers within the hospital, and help from A.A.s without, this must have been a most exacting and exhausting vocation for the increasingly frail Sister. That she was providentially enabled to be with us for so many years is something for our great wonder. To hundreds of friends it became worth a day's journey to witness her supreme and constant demonstration.

Toward the close of her long stewardship there were brushes with death. Sometimes I came to Cleveland and was allowed to sit by her bedside. Then I saw her at her best. Her perfect faith and her complete acceptance of whatever God might will were somehow implicit in all she said, be our conversation gay or serious. Fear and uncertainty seemed entire strangers to her. On my leave-taking, there was always that smiling radiance; always her prayerful hope that God might still allow her a bit more time at Rosary Hall. Then a few days later I would learn that she was back at her desk. This superb drama would be re-enacted time after time. She was quite unconscious that there was anything at all unusual about it.

Realizing there would come the day which would be her last, it seemed right that we of AA should privately present Sister with some tangible token that could, even a little, communicate to her the depth of our love. Remembering her insistence, in respect of the Akron plaque, that she would not really like any public attention, I simply sent word that I'd like to come to Cleveland for a visit, and casually added that should her health permit, we might take supper together in the company of a few of her stalwart AA friends and co-workers. Besides, it was her fiftieth year of service in her community. On the appointed evening, we foregathered in one of the small dining rooms at Charity Hospital. Plainly delighted, Sister arrived. She was barely able to walk. Since we were old-timers all, the dinner hour was spent in telling tales of other days. For her part, Sister regaled us with stories of St. Thomas and with cherished recollections of Anne and co-founder Dr. Bob. It was unforgettable.

Before Sister became too tired, we addressed ourselves to our main project. From New York, I had brought an illuminated scroll. Its wording was in the form of a letter addressed by me to Sister, and it was written on behalf of our AA Fellowship worldwide. I stood up, read the scroll aloud, and then held the parchment for her to see. She was taken by complete surprise and could scarcely speak for a time. In a low voice she finally said, "Oh, but this is too much—this is too good for me." Our richest reward of the evening was of course Ignatia's delight; a joy unbounded the moment we assured her that our gift need not be publicized; that if she wished to stow it away in her trunk we would quite understand.

It then seemed that this most memorable and moving evening was over. But there was to be another inspiring experience. Making light of her great fatigue, Sister insisted that we all go up to Rosary Hall, there to make a late round of the AA ward. This we did, wondering if any of us would ever again see her at work in the divine vocation to which she had given her all. For each of us this was the end of an epoch; I could think only of her poignant and oft-repeated saying, "Eternity is now."

The scroll given to Sister may now be seen at Rosary Hall. This is the inscription:

> In gratitude for Sister Mary Ignatia on the occasion of her golden jubilee: Dear Sister, We of Alcoholics Anonymous look upon you as the finest friend and the greatest spirit we may ever know. We remember your tender ministrations to us in the days when AA was very

young. Your partnership with Dr. Bob in that early time has created for us a spiritual heritage of incomparable worth.

In all the years since, we have watched you at the bedside of thousands. So watching, we have perceived ourselves to be the beneficiaries of that wondrous light which God has always sent through you to illumine our darkness. You have tirelessly tended our wounds; you have nourished us with your unique understanding and your matchless love.

No greater gifts of grace than these shall we ever have.

Speaking for AA members throughout the world, I say: "May God abundantly reward you according to your blessed works—now and forever."

In devotion,
Bill W.

SOURCES:

This profile is reprinted with permission from *AA Grapevine* (August 1966).

FURTHER REFERENCES:

Darrah, Mary C. *Sister Ignatia: Angel of Alcoholics Anonymous.* Chicago: Loyola University Press, 1992.

Lois Wilson

LOIS W.—FOR FIFTY-THREE YEARS WIFE OF ALCOHOLICS ANONYMOUS COFOUNDER BILL WILSON AND HERSELF THE founder of Al-Anon—was beloved by millions. And since her death in 1988 at age ninety-seven, recognition of her importance to both fellowships has grown, not diminished.

Michael Alexander, attorney for Bill and Lois and past chairman of the General Service Board of AA, put it this way: "In the early days, the future of A.A. and hence the lives of countless alcoholics hung on the thread of the determination and efforts of Bill's and Dr. Bob to put the fellowship on firm ground. Without Lois W., her husband could not have succeeded in that crucial work. Bill called her 'a full partner' in the struggles and joys of those early days. Indeed, many A.A.s today feel their lives are owed to Lois as well as to Bill, Dr. Bob and Anne S."

Alexander also spoke of Lois's many talents and many sides: "Writer, artist, poet, musician, much sought-after and effective speaker, lover of nature, homemaker, tireless hostess, devoted wife to Bill." Throughout her long life she was known for her indomitable spirit, sharp mind, sense of humor, and feistiness. Ralph B., writer of some of AA's first pamphlets and frequent visitor to Stepping Stones (Bill and Lois's home), says she was "a *force* that kept everything going while Bill was thinking or writing or visualizing. I would sometimes stand up to Bill," he adds, "but I wouldn't *think* of arguing with Lois."

John B., general manager of AA's General Service Office, caught her spirituality when he called on her in the hospital just five days before she died. Looking heartbreakingly tiny in her bed, suffering from terminal pneumonia, and unable to speak because of the tubes in her throat and the oxygen mask she wore, Lois could communicate only by writing on a pad. John expressed his personal gratitude and that of the fellowship because, he told her, "We in A.A. owe our lives to you."

A ghost of a smile crossed Lois's features and she wrote on her pad, "Not to me, to God."

John replied, "But you were His servant."

Lois wrote, "So are you."

Lois summed up her life thus, in the preface to her memoirs, *Lois Remembers:*

> Bill's recovery came about in spite of me. Although it was what I had been working for all our married life, I had gone about it the wrong way. My love, deep as it was, was also possessive; and my ego was so great I felt I could change him. . . . Bill *was* my life. . . . For the first 17 years of my recovery and Bill's, there was no fellowship for the family of alcoholics. The ideas of Al-Anon germinated during this period, but Al-Anon did not take its own shape until 1951. A.A. was therefore my first love. Although not an alcoholic, I feel even today as much a member of A.A. as of Al-Anon, at least in spirit.
>
> The big lesson I have learned is that we cannot change another human being—only ourselves. By living our own lives to the best of our ability, by loving deeply and not trying to mold another to our wishes, we can help not only ourselves but that other also.

Lois Burnham was born March 4, 1891, in Brooklyn, New York, the oldest of six children, from a distinguished and affluent family. Her father, a gynecologist and surgeon, came from Lancaster, Pennsylvania, where *his* father had practiced law and medicine and was also minister of the Swedenborgian church. After medical school, Dr. Burnham came to Brooklyn to practice because his uncle owned a department store there and knew many people. The young doctor boarded at a fine old brick townhouse at 182 Clinton Street, where he rented a room for both sleeping and an office. In 1888, he leased the whole house and brought his bride there.

Lois's father had met her mother, Matilda Hoyt Spelman, at her coming-out party. The oldest of four, Matilda had gone to Miss Prentiss' Finishing School, where she made all A's. Her father, William Chapman Spelman, had come from Granville, Massachusetts. He was a cousin to Laura Spelman Rockefeller, wife of John D. Sr. Lois recalls being taken as a youngster for a weekend visit to the Rockefeller estate at Pocantico Hills. Lois's maternal grandmother, Sarah Hoyt Spelman, had come from a lovely home in Manchester, Vermont. When Lois was still young, her father purchased the Manchester house, which the whole family enjoyed enormously as a summer home. (The George Thacher family from Albany were also regular summer visitors and became Burnham family friends. The youngest Thacher son, Edwin, nicknamed "Ebby," a pal of Lois's brother Rogers, was to play a crucial role in her life—and Bill's.)

A measure of the Burnhams' relative affluence was their lifestyle. All six children were sent to private schools and colleges. To staff the two homes in those days required a children's nurse, a cook, a maid, and a coachman to drive a smart, yellow-wheeled, horse-drawn rig. (The coachman later became the chauffeur when the family acquired a touring car.)

Lois's mother liked dramatics and belonged to a literary club as well as a choral club. Lois remembers her as "absolutely without self-consciousness and totally selfless. Mother loved people and people loved her. Everyone told us that Mother was the loveliest person they knew. Her features were somewhat plain, but they were framed by curly, burnished-blond hair, and her outgoing spirit charmed everyone and made her beautiful."

Lois began her schooling at the well-known Pratt Institute in Brooklyn, and went on to Friends School for eight years and to Packer Collegiate Institute for five. Her closest girlhood friend, Elise Valentine, sat next to her for those thirteen years. Lois's education included reading the best literature, taking dancing and music lessons, and enjoying classical concerts, musical comedies, and dramas at the theater.

Her happiest memories were of her summers in Vermont with her parents and grandparents. She was a tomboy, joyfully going barefoot, riding her bicycle, climbing trees. With her chums, she swam and boated on the lake, and as she grew up, enjoyed Manchester's tennis, golf, and dances.

"My childhood was an extremely happy one," Lois wrote.

In their teens, Lois and her friend Elise developed a healthy interest in boys. Indeed, "young men now occupied quite a bit of our thoughts and conversation." Nevertheless, the girls adhered to the family rules that forbade premarital necking or petting. "There were several young men to whom I was attracted physically, yet I knew I didn't love them," she wrote.

After graduation from Packer, Lois attended the New York School of Fine Art, where she learned to draw in charcoal with live models—a skill that she enjoyed the rest of her life, illustrating her Christmas cards and her book, *Lois Remembers*. She worked several years for the YWCA and a small private school in New Jersey. During this time, on family vacations in Vermont, she met Bill W.

Her brother Rogers kept talking enthusiastically about his friend Bill. When Lois finally met him, she wasn't particularly impressed with the tall, lanky lad. For one thing, he was four years younger, still a teenager, whereas Lois was a sophisticated young lady of twenty-two. And Bill was a Vermonter, a "local," whereas Lois was from New York City, one of the privileged "summer people." Finally, in contrast to the large, close-knit Burnham family, Bill's parents were divorced; he and his sister, Dorothy, lived with their maternal grandparents, whom they dearly loved, in East Dorset. Nevertheless, they felt abandoned. After divorcing, Bill's father, of whom Bill was especially fond, left for the West to take a quarry job in British Columbia. His mother, a brilliant, independent woman, had become an osteopath in Boston, returning to East Dorset, Vermont, for vacations.

In the summer of 1913, Bill, his mother, and his sister camped at one end of nearby Emerald Lake; the Burnhams occupied cabins at the other end. Lois and Bill had fun sailing together. The following summer Rogers and Dorothy were going together, and the foursome had a glorious time hiking, picnicking, boating, and, above all, talking. "Long before the end of the season," Lois wrote, "I thought Bill the most interesting, the most knowledgeable, and the finest man I knew. I forgot all about the difference in our ages." Their summer courtship became more serious, and in 1915 they declared their love for each other.

The couple carried on a romance by mail—she on a daily basis, he more sporadically. Bill was in and out of Norwich University, a military college in Northfield, Vermont. When the United States declared war on Germany in 1917, his class joined the army reserves, and Bill was sent to officers training camp at Plattsburg, New York. By this time, Bill and Lois's engagement was official. During the preceding two and a half years, Bill had made several visits to Brooklyn, and Lois had spent weekends with Bill's grandparents, mother, and sister in East Dorset. In August, Bill was commissioned as a second lieutenant in the Sixty-sixth Coast Artillery Corps and stationed in New Bedford, Massachusetts, where Lois visited him several times.

When it was rumored that Bill's regiment might be ordered overseas, he and Lois were married on short notice on January 24, 1918. Her old friend Elise Valentine Shaw was her matron of honor; two of her sisters and two schoolmates, her bridesmaids. Rogers was best man. The couple left almost immediately for New Bedford, where they were welcomed with flowers, congratulations, and parties.

Bill had not touched alcohol during their courtship. His mother had divorced his father largely because of his dad's drinking; his paternal grandfather also had had bad drinking episodes. So Bill had been warned that if he began, he, too, might get into trouble. He had believed this and decided not to drink. Now, however, he occasionally drank at New Bedford parties—and on at least one occasion got drunk and passed out, to Lois's great shock. "I was only slightly unhappy about his drinking," Lois remembered later, "because I felt confident I could persuade him to return to his former abstinence. I could 'fix' him."

In August, Bill and his regiment were shipped overseas to join the war in France. Lois worked at Walter Reed Hospital in Washington, D.C. Bill was apparently a good officer in active duty, recommended for promotion and honored by the men in his battery, which touched him deeply. After the armistice, Bill returned on a troop ship; Lois resigned her Walter Reed job just in time to meet him at the dock.

The couple stayed temporarily with Lois's mother and father in Brooklyn. Shortly, Rogers also returned from overseas, and to celebrate, he and Bill went down into the cellar, where Dr. Burnham stored the liquor given to him by his grateful patients. They both got roaring drunk, made a shambles of the cellar, and became deathly sick. Although this upset the household, the returning war heroes were readily forgiven.

Bill had no vocational training and didn't know what to do in civilian life. He had great dreams about the future but had a hard time holding the only jobs he could get: a clerk in an exporting firm; a laborer on the docks. "To think things over," Lois said, "we decided to take an extended walking trip through Maine, New Hampshire and Vermont. This started a lifelong habit. When we were unable to solve some problem, we would go off by ourselves in the woods or by the sea. We were then better able to think clearly."

Such trips also kept Bill temporarily away from booze.

On their return, Bill was still restless and unable to keep jobs. Lois was able to capitalize on her Walter Reed experience and went to work as an occupational aide at the Brooklyn Naval Hospital. With her income, they were able to move to a small apartment around the corner from her parents. Bill's drinking increased. Again they decided to "get away from it all"—this time hiking over the Green Mountains in Vermont. And this trip did help Bill make a decision to study law, as his grandfather had always wanted him to do. He enrolled in a night course at the Brooklyn Law School and kept at it conscientiously for four years. But at the time of his graduation in 1924, he was too drunk to go and pick up his diploma.

During this period and the years that followed, Bill's drinking grew steadily worse. Although they had dreamed of having children, Lois suffered three ectopic pregnancies, each with accompanying surgery and long recuperations. Although Lois said that Bill took the disappointment and worries over her health "with grace and kindness to me," Lois blamed herself for Bill's increasingly frequent bouts with alcohol.

After learning they could never have children of their own, they applied to the Spence-Chapin adoption agency. When there were no results even after their continued inquiries, Bill was sure the real reason was his drinking. (He was right. Years later, Lois discovered that one of their references had reported to Spence-Chapin that Bill drank to excess.)

After finishing his law course, Bill worked as a fraud investigator for the United States Fidelity and Guarantee Company. This took him to Wall Street, where he made contacts with several brokerage houses. There, he developed a strong personal theory that brokers and their customers should know more about the companies in which they invested, rather than gambling blindly. Lois explained: "When Bill's grandfather wanted to purchase a cow, he went to look at the cow, feel its legs, find out how much milk it gave, its age and so on. Why shouldn't the same precautions be applied to buying stocks? Bill wanted to do this kind of investigating. Though none of his Wall Street friends encouraged him, . . . he decided in 1925 to take a year to test his theory.

"I wanted to get away, too. I was so concerned with Bill's drinking, I wanted to get him away from New York and its bars. I felt sure that during a year in the open I would be able to straighten him out. So in April 1925, in spite of advice from friends and family, we gave up our jobs and our apartment and made [a Harley-Davidson motorcycle with sidecar] our home for a year."

The trip turned out to be a highlight of both their lives. Bill researched and investigated many industries large and small across the East and Midwest. His conscientious reports back to Wall Street were a financial success. Between these working intervals, as they "vagabonded," they had adventures and new experiences, met new people, and had a wonderful time. Bill's drinking bouts were infrequent.

The next eight years, however, were a different story—a story of descent into the hell of acute alcoholism. In the beginning and on the surface, Bill's new career was an exciting success. He was, in effect, the first "security analyst." He received a stream of assignments to investigate industries from his old friend and Wall Street investor Frank Shaw and others. For these he was paid a weekly retainer and given options on the stocks he recommended. He often exercised these options, buying stocks for himself—on margin, of course. Friends and relatives frequently asked his advice about investing.

With their newfound affluence, Bill and Lois were able to buy their first car, a fairly new Dodge, which made travel easier than by motorcycle, so Lois was able to continue to accompany Bill on trips. She wrote: "We traveled to Washington, D.C.; Holyoke, Mass.; Rochester, Clifton Springs, Syracuse, Messina, New York; Houston, Dallas, Texas; New Orleans, La.; Birmingham, Ala.; and many places in Canada." In the main, these excursions were ventureful and fun for Lois.

During the winter Bill sometimes made the investigations himself, by train. "When he didn't call me to tell me where he was," said Lois, "I knew he had been drinking."

In their new prosperity, they were able to rent a large apartment on Livingston Street in Brooklyn. Bill bought Lois a grand piano. But as their prosperity grew, Bill's drinking kept pace, and behind the facade was a growing nightmare for Lois. One big change was that Bill knew he had to control his drinking—but was unable to do so. In depression and despair over his own behavior, Bill cried out in 1927, "I'm halfway to hell now and going strong."

Even Bill's most important business dealings were punctuated with disastrous drunken sprees. Frank Shaw, for whom he made many investigations, was extremely tolerant of Bill's behavior and remained a good friend. Another supporter was Wall Street operator Joe Hirshorn, who amassed a considerable fortune and became famous as a collector of fine art, which now resides in the Hirshorn Museum, a part of the Smithsonian Institute in Washington.

But back in their apartment, Lois waited night after night when her husband didn't come home until the wee hours—and then arrived dead drunk. One such night in 1927, after walking the floor for hours, Lois poured out her feelings in writing:

"Come home to me. My heart is breaking. How can we go on like this? What's to become of us? I love you so, and yet my love doesn't seem to do you any good. Still I have faith that it must, someday. God grant that that day may be soon. . . . It seems each night as though I couldn't stand another, and yet another comes, and still another until my heart is like a stone. A great dullness spreads over me until all things, good and bad, seem to taste alike."

In the depression that followed the great stock market crash in 1929, Bill lost a lot of money. He and Lois had to leave their fine Livingston Street apartment; however, he had made some good business connections in Canada, which had not been hit as hard by the crash as the States, and so he was invited to join the staff of Greenshields & Company, an investment firm in Montreal. For Lois, this was a pleasant respite, despite her concern over her husband's increased drinking. At the end of several months, the depression hit Montreal, and Bill was fired. The couple had to borrow money and sell their car—a Packard they had purchased in prosperous times—to finance their move back to the United States and to Clinton Street.

Again in this period, Lois, trying to analyze what to do in her desperate situation, wrote her thoughts on paper: "What is one to think or do after so many failures? . . . If I should lose my love and faith, what then? I see nothing but emptiness, bickering, taunts. . . . I love my husband more than words can tell, and I know he loves me. He is a splendid, fine man . . . everybody loves him . . . a born leader . . . so bighearted he would give away his last penny . . . a compelling talker . . . remarkable memory . . . His mind is of the farseeing, long-perspective kind. . . . He continually asks for my help, and we have been trying to find an answer to his drinking problem."

Soon after their return to Clinton Street, on Christmas Day 1930, Lois's beloved mother died. Bill was drunk that day and for days before and after.

Lois found a job clerking in a department store to buy food for the table. Twice, she put Bill into Towns Hospital on Central Park West to be dried out, and twice took him to the country, to Vermont, to nurse him back to health herself. Nothing was of any lasting help. Finally, he virtually stopped eating and drank around the clock. In Lois's words, he "became a drunken sot who didn't dare leave the house." Lois went numbly about her duties on her job and at home. "Not daring to let myself think or feel, I plowed ahead like an automaton."

One day in the fall of 1934, Lois came home from the department store to find their old friend Ebby T. (Thacher)—sober, to Lois's surprise—talking to Bill in the kitchen. Ebby was a childhood friend of Lois's brother Rogers. Bill had been drinking all day, yet seemed absorbed in what Ebby told him. After his friend departed, Bill told Lois excitedly how Ebby had come to the Oxford Group and had quit drinking. Although Lois felt that Ebby's newfound sobriety was indeed a miracle, she passed off Bill's enthusiasm as just one more false hope.

Sure enough, Bill continued his drinking, ending with a several-day bender that took him to the Calvary Mission on East Twenty-third Street and finally once again to Towns Hospital, on his own volition. There, Bill called for Ebby to visit him again, after which he had his transforming spiritual experience.

For Lois's part, upon learning that Bill had taken himself to

Towns Hospital, she was angry and upset: "Why hadn't he consulted me? What good would it do anyway? He would get drunk again the minute he left. Who was going to pay the bill? The money I made was barely enough to keep us going—including Bill's liquor. . . . We would have to sell some wedding presents. What possible permanent good could it do for Bill to go to the hospital again?

"I soon found out. The minute I saw him in the hospital, I knew something overwhelming had happened. His eyes were filled with light. His whole being expressed hope and joy. From that moment on, I shared his confidence in the future. I never doubted that at last he was free."

Upon leaving Towns, Bill tried to sober up all the alcoholics at the hospital, in missions, and anywhere else he found them—without success. Meanwhile, he and Lois were constantly attending Oxford Group meetings at Calvary Episcopal Church at Twenty-first and Park Avenue South. Eager to get a new toehold in Wall Street, Bill was hired in May 1935 to go to Akron, Ohio, with several other men to help with a proxy fight to gain control of a rubber company there. The attempt failed, the other men returned to New York, and Bill was left stranded with only ten dollars in his pocket.

Discouraged and tempted to drink, he undertook to find another alcoholic to help, as he had in New York. Through a series of miraculous "coincidences," he was put in touch with an alcoholic physician, Dr. Robert S. (Smith). The following after-noon, on Mother's Day, May 12, 1935, the two men met. They were immediately drawn to each other, needed each other, and shared the same disastrous drinking and the same yearning for sobriety. June 10, 1935, the day Dr. Bob stopped drinking, is now marked as the beginning of Alcoholics Anonymous—though at the time there were only two members and no name.

Bill stayed on in Akron for three months, living at the home of Dr. Bob, his wife, Anne, and their two teenage children, Robert Jr. and Sue. Bill and Dr. Bob almost immediately found in Akron City Hospital a nearly hopeless alcoholic who wanted

to get well. He was Bill D., a lawyer, who became "AA No. 3."
They were soon working on other prospects.

Back in New York, Lois had been promoted to assistant
buyer of furniture at the department store, but when she
received an invitation from Anne and Dr. Bob to visit them in
Akron on her week's vacation, she was "tickled to do so, and
traveled there by bus in June," she wrote. "I loved Annie and
Bob from the moment I saw them. They were so warm, so gra-
cious, so good." She found Bill not only excited over the new
friends he was making in the Akron Oxford Group and his
work with alcoholics, but still pursuing the proxy fight, which
had been refinanced from New York.

Back home after her vacation, Lois missed her husband: "I
nagged and nagged him to return. He finally explained in a
long letter that he wanted to finish the work to reorganize the
rubber company, to prove to himself that he could succeed at
something now that he was sober. When I realized this, I
became more patient."

True to his word, after he had maneuvered a showdown
between the two sides in the proxy fight, he rushed home.

The months that followed in New York were happy times for
Bill. He was enjoying success in helping other alcoholics, making new friends, gaining spiritual inspiration from regular
attendance at the Oxford Group, attending to a small business
he had started in New Jersey with Hank P. (Parkhurst), and
doing occasional investigations for his Wall Street contacts. It
was a harder transition time for Lois. She felt left out and
unneeded. Although she was joyous over Bill's recovery, she
missed their companionship, their outdoor weekends. She went
with him to Oxford Group meetings because "that's what a
devoted wife should do, but now that Bill was well I felt I didn't
need the meetings."

As a young girl, she had daydreamed of changing bad people
into good. "Is it any wonder, then, that I thought I could inspire
Bill to stop drinking—and that I kept trying for seventeen
years? Even after Bill's spiritual awakening, it didn't occur to

me that I needed to change!" That is, not until a fateful Sunday morning when her husband said to her casually, "We'll have to hurry or we'll be late for the Oxford Group meeting."

"I had my shoe in my hand," related Lois, "and before I knew what was happening, I had thrown it at him and cried out, 'Damn your old meetings!'"

She was shocked at her own anger, her violent reaction to a natural, even trivial, remark. As she began to look at herself analytically for the first time, she realized she had never put her reliance on God, but had been trying to do it all herself. She had faith in her power to change Bill and stop his drinking. Even when his drinking got worse, she had prayed to God to help her to "cure" Bill of his alcoholism, never submitting her will to God's. "When Bill sobered up," she realized, "it was a great blow to me that he didn't need me in the way he had before. My primary aim in life was gone. . . . My ego had been nourished during the drinking years by the important roles I had to fill: mother, nurse, breadwinner, decision maker.

"God, through the Oxford Group, had accomplished in a twinkling what I had failed to do in (seventeen) years. I resented it! So one minute I would get down on my knees and thank God, and the next minute I would throw things at Bill and cuss the Oxford Group."

As Bill worked with alcoholics, he began bringing many of them home to Clinton Street. "We used to have as many as five in the house at once," he wrote in *Alcoholics Anonymous Comes of Age,* "and sometimes they would all be drunk at once." Russ B., one of the "Clinton Street Boys," who was one of Lois's favorites and who stayed for more than a year, described it thus: "All of us were living rent-free, food-free, everything-free . . . and Lois was doing all the work. She was working in a department store during the day and cooking for us and providing all the money the whole house had." There were fights and one suicide—after the victim had sold hundreds of dollars worth of Bill and Lois's clothes and luggage.

As Alcoholics Anonymous began to take hold and grow, as

the Big Book was written (by Bill, dictating to secretary Ruth Hock at the New Jersey office of Honor Dealers) and published, and as an office was acquired and groups sprang up in other cities, Lois's life, along with Bill's, was filled with furious activity. "It was a hectic and fruitful time," she recalled.

It was also a time when they had no money at all. Lois's father had remarried and left Clinton Street in 1933. When he died three years later, the mortgage company took over the house, allowing Bill and Lois to live there for a tiny rental. In April 1939, the property was sold, and Bill and Lois had to move out. For the next two years they literally lived off the charity of friends. They jumped around from Green Pond, New Jersey, to various apartments on short loans in Manhattan, to Connecticut, to Brooklyn, and back to Greenwich Village. During 1939 and 1940, they moved an incredible fifty-one times!

In February 1940, as they were going through Grand Central Station, Lois suddenly sat down on the stairs and burst into tears, wailing, "Will we ever have our own home?" They ended up living for several months in a tiny room above the old Twenty-fourth Street Clubhouse for AA's with only a borrowed bed and two orange crates for furniture.

Their wanderings ended in April 1941, when through an AA friend, the owner of a house in Bedford Hills, New York, made it possible for them to buy the house on terms they were able to eke out. Later named Stepping Stones, it was a lovely, brown-shingled, hip-roofed, seven-room house standing among trees on a hill, overlooking a valley. It was not only their home as long as they lived, but also became a mecca for countless AA's and Al-Anons until the present day.

The day they moved into their new home was also the day Lois embarked on a long-anticipated six-week cruise to South America as guest of a friend, Fan Williamson, connected indirectly with the Moore-McCormack Steamship Line. Lois and Fan were the only passengers on a freighter that stopped at a succession of fascinating cities, ending up at Rio de Janeiro. On her return, she learned Bill had had a miserable time trying to make order out of the chaos of the move. She began the task of fixing up the house, which needed a lot of work.

The decade of the 1940s was a period of fantastic growth for AA. In 1939, just after the Big Book was published, there were AA groups in (besides Akron and Brooklyn) New York; Cleveland; Philadelphia; Greenwich, Connecticut; Washington, D.C.; Boston; Chicago; Milwaukee; Minneapolis; and a very few other cities.

But forces were at work—the cumulative effect of publicity in newspapers, magazines, and radio, and public endorsement by such popular figures as Harry Emerson Fosdick and Norman Vincent Peale—that lighted the fuse of AA growth. The explosion came in the form of a *Saturday Evening Post* article on March 1, 1941. Within about a week, 150 were present at the AA meeting in the Twenty-fourth Street Clubhouse, and within a month the South Orange group had doubled in size. It was the same everywhere. Groups outgrew their meeting places and had to be divided. Older members worked frantically with newcomers, who were sent out, barely sober, on Twelfth Step calls. It is estimated that six thousand AA's owe the beginning of their sobriety to the *Post* article, and nobody knows how many more thousands were sparked by them. New groups were springing up faster than the AA office could keep track of.

For Lois, it was a decade of extensive travels around the country with Bill, not only to visit the AA groups but also to enjoy new experiences themselves, as they had back in their motorcycling days. Their first tour was in 1943 to 1944 to the West and South, including their first view of the Grand Canyon. After visiting AA gatherings in Chicago, Omaha, and Denver, they took the scenic train to Los Angeles, where more than a thousand were present at the AA meeting. They visited Bill's mother in San Diego and continued on to San Francisco, Portland, and Seattle, returning via Tucson, Houston, Oklahoma City, Little Rock, and New Orleans.

Two years later they drove to many beautiful spots in the Northwest, ending up visiting Bill's father and his wife in British Columbia. In 1948, they made a similar trip through Canada, stopping at Toronto, Winnipeg, and Calgary. There were also many shorter trips: Quebec and Nova Scotia; Virginia, South Carolina, and Hawaii; cruises through the Panama Canal and the Caribbean and to Spain and Portugal.

During the 1940s, AA had been forming in many overseas countries. So, in the spring of 1950, the AA office laid out a ten-week trip for Lois and Bill to tour the groups in eight countries: Norway, Sweden, Denmark, Holland, France, England, Ireland, and Scotland.

On the trip around the country in 1943, Lois "usually spoke briefly at the large open meetings, thanking the AA's for giving me such a wonderful program to live by. But at teas and luncheons for the families, I made more personal talks, telling how important it was for me to live by the spiritual principles of AA, and how I came to discover this" with her shoe-throwing incident. Between 1939 and 1951, she made no fewer than sixty-two talks and found that in some places the families of AA's had already formed their own groups. In Toronto in 1948, four hundred turned out to hear Lois speak at a meeting put on by the Wives Group. In Seattle, forty attended a similar meeting, and in San Francisco, eighty-five.

On several occasions, Lois and Anne S., Dr. Bob's wife, spoke together at meetings for AA families. Anne, a compassionate, caring person of deep personal faith and an active member of the Oxford Group, spoke movingly of her need for her own spiritual growth. Looking back, Lois explained what had happened:

"In the beginning A.A. was a family affair. Mates, parents and children attended the meetings, usually held in homes. Many of the wives tried to live by the program themselves, but this was in a general way only. There was little sharing of experience. . . . It wasn't until 1940 that constructive gatherings for the families of A.A. began to evolve. Soon after the 24th Street Clubhouse opened, the A.A.s felt they needed meetings for alcoholics only, which took place in a ground-floor room; a handful of us wives got to know each other in the studio above. At first we played bridge or gossiped, but soon began to discuss our own problems and what to do about them. I told my story. It was great to find out that because others had gone through similar experiences, each of us no longer had to be alone with our troubles."

The publication of the Big Book in 1939 gave a boost to the family groups by providing a mutually acceptable codification of the spiritual principles of AA, for use by anyone. Another stimulus to organization was provided by Ruth G., wife of a San Francisco AA, who conceived the idea of linking newly formed family groups through a twelve-page monthly magazine produced on her own initiative. Called *The Family Forum*, it was filled with editorials, correspondence from families of alcoholics, and helpful quotations from the Bible, Marcus Aurelius, St. Francis, Friedrich Nietzsche, and other philosophers.

In 1950, Bill went by himself to AA groups throughout the country to explore their feelings about establishing a General Service Conference. He was surprised to run into so many family groups. Upon his return, he told Lois of this budding fellowship and suggested she open a service office in New York where they could register, receive helpful literature, and become more unified. It would also be a place where any desperate wife could call for help and from which information could be spread to the public.

At first the idea did not appeal to Lois, who was excited about having a home and garden of her own; however, at the close of the 1951 General Service Conference of AA, she asked the wives of the delegates to meet at Stepping Stones for lunch with local family group members. All but two of them belonged to family groups in their hometowns. Now convinced of the need, Lois decided to open a Family Group service office, asking a friend, Anne B., to help her. They worked upstairs at Stepping Stones, beginning with a list furnished to them by the AA General Service Office of family members or groups who had written requesting help or asking to be registered. The two women sent a letter to this list of eighty-seven and received forty-eight replies from groups eager to affiliate. Soon they had more work than they could handle alone.

The two women moved their activities in early 1952 to the second floor of the Twenty-fourth Street Clubhouse, where they could more easily enlist volunteers to assist. The number of Family Groups served had now grown from forty-eight to two hundred. And thus Al-Anon was formed. The second AA General Service Conference, which met in April 1952, passed a resolution by standing vote, thanking those who had fostered the Al-Anon Family Groups. "We were quite moved and grateful," said Lois. By 1957, the fellowship was financially able to move to a suitable office of its own at 125 East Twenty-third Street, and three years later the Al-Anon members present at the AA International Convention in Long Beach, California, approved a plan to have an annual conference of delegates of their own.

Cofounder Anne B. later moved to California, became less involved in Al-Anon, and passed away in 1984 at eighty-four years of age. But Lois continued to take an active leadership role her entire life. She wrote the organization's basic book, *The Al-Anon Family Groups* (with the help of volunteer Margaret B. and AA writer Ralph B.), spoke at every annual convention of Al-Anon, attended all of its Service Conferences, led in founding Alateen in the late 1950s, and was the point person in obtaining publicity for the fellowship via magazine articles and radio interviews. "Undoubtedly the most effective publicity came in columnist Ann Landers's articles," Lois wrote. "From one in 1962, 4,000 letters poured in!" Every year, she was hostess at a huge Al-Anon picnic at Stepping Stones—an event that is still held.

In early 1970, while doing a chore on the roof of his studio, Bill fell to the ground. It marked the beginning of a decline in his health. His emphysema took a marked turn for the worse, so that at the AA International Convention in Miami in July, he was able to make only a surprise appearance at the spiritual meeting on Sunday—in a wheelchair, from which he rose to make a brief but immensely moving talk to the more than ten thousand AA's and Al-Anons present. After Bill spent a month's recuperation in Miami under the care of their doctor, Ed B., Bill and Lois returned to Stepping Stones.

Within weeks, Bill began to fail; he was constantly bedridden and made several emergency trips to Westchester Hospital. At first Lois did all the nursing, but soon day and night nurses were called in. On January 24, in a chartered plane, Bill was flown back to Miami, accompanied by Ed B., Nell Wing, and Lois. Bill died in the night, on their fifty-third wedding anniversary.

Lois was overwhelmed by literally thousands of letters of sympathy and support that poured in. *The New York Times* carried a front-page, nine-column obituary. Memorial services were held in many cities in the United States, Canada, overseas, and around the world. "Thank God for A.A. and Al-Anon," Lois wrote. "I still have a purpose in life even with Bill gone."

That year with an Al-Anon friend, Evelyn C., as a companion, she circled the globe. The Al-Anon and AA offices contacted the fellowships everywhere to arrange meetings and hospitality. They toured Africa completely, went on to Australia, New Zealand, Hong Kong, and Japan, and finished in Hawaii. They were welcomed with tumultuous meetings at every stop. Almost every year thereafter, Lois made other trips, often with Nell Wing accompanying her: to view the 1972 eclipse from the sea, to London, to Ireland, Switzerland, South American countries, Mexico, and elsewhere.

Lois had attended all AA International Conventions (held every five years), beginning with Cleveland in 1950. At the "Coming of Age" Convention in St. Louis in 1955, she was the first speaker after the vote approving the Conference and General Service Structure. At Long Beach, Toronto, Miami, Denver, and New Orleans, she was featured on both the AA and Al-Anon programs. A symbolic culmination of Lois's life was her appearance in July 1985 at the Fiftieth Anniversary Convention in Montreal. At age ninety-four, she addressed a hushed audience of more than forty-five thousand. The very appearance of her tiny figure on the stage in the center of the vast Olympic Stadium brought the huge crowd to its feet in a tumultuous standing ovation that went on and on.

In her book, *Lois Remembers*, written in 1979, she wrote, "I hope I understand correctly A.A. and Al-Anon members' special devotion to me. As the only living survivor of the A.A. founders and their wives and as Bill's widow, I am a symbol to A.A.s of their beloved Fellowship. . . . At conventions, I never know whether I'm A.A. or Al-Anon. A.A. was my first love. It was in A.A. that I started my own spiritual striving. So I feel allegiance to both Societies."

From the time of Bill's death, Lois was concerned that Stepping Stones continue to be maintained and kept open after her own death for the benefit of AA and Al-Anon members. She also wanted to use a substantial portion of the money that had come to her from Bill's estate (largely from the royalties on AA books he had written) for alcoholism and prevention. Therefore, in 1979, she formed the Stepping Stones Foundation for these purposes.

Until her late eighties, Lois insisted on living independently, with only her housekeeper, Harriet, to help. And in these years, Lois continued to entertain with open houses, picnics, and other events. One event grew out of an idea she had to gather AA old-timers from everywhere for a reunion and celebration at Stepping Stones. She wrote a personal letter of invitation to every member she knew who had sobered up before 1950. The response was tremendous. She acted as hostess throughout, addressing every guest by name.

Then, after suffering several falls and fractures, she surrounded herself with aides and helpers who enabled her to live comfortably and graciously during her last years. This staff was supplemented by constant attention from devoted friends, especially Nell Wing and Ann Burnham Smith, Lois's second cousin. She was far from an invalid even then. When she was ninety-four, she was a speaker at the Desert Roundup in California. As Ron S. pushed her wheelchair across the hotel parking lot, she spied a huge, gleaming Harley-Davidson motorcycle, which she asked to go over and admire. Once there, she asked to be photographed alongside it. When she was introduced the next day, the motorcycle group of AA's made her an honorary member, to the cheers and whistles of the enormous crowd. "She loved it," declared Ron.

At ninety-seven and a half, she finally contracted pneumonia, was hospitalized, and died on October 5, 1988. On October 20, a memorial service was held at the beautiful, historic Marble Collegiate Church in New York. The large church was nearly filled, causing the minister, Dr. Arthur Caliandro, to comment on how unusual it was for such a huge crowd to turn out for the funeral of a ninety-seven-year-old person and how they symbolized the larger family of millions who lived new lives because of Bill and Lois.

Lois had written an epitaph of sorts for herself in the closing pages of her book nearly a decade earlier. She said, "I deeply believe it is love that makes the world go 'round. God is love and love is the creative force, the force that ties family and friends together. . . . The more one gives of love, the more one has to give. . . . This force, embodied in God's love, kept Bill and me together and finally, through various channels, sobered him up. The wonder and beauty of Bill's regeneration still fill me with awe. I used to believe that *thinking* was the highest function of human beings. . . . I now realize that *loving* is our supreme function. The heart precedes the mind."

Lois's devoted day nurse for the last four years of her life, Ethyl Dumas, whom she dubbed "Eternal Ethyl," recalls that "this lady always knew what she wanted." She relates that in the hospital on the afternoon of October 5, Lois wrote on her pad, ". . . want to go to sleep."

"And, you know," says Ethyl, "that's just what she did."

Ruth Hock

IN THE OPENING CHAPTER OF THE CLASSIC AA BOOK *Alcoholics Anonymous Comes of Age,* COFOUNDER BILL WILSON REMINISCES about the early days of the movement. He said, "We thought of Ruth Hock, the devoted nonalcoholic girl who had taken reams of dictation and had done months of typing and retyping when the book *Alcoholics Anonymous* was in preparation. She often went without pay, taking the then seemingly worthless stock of Works Publishing instead. I recall with deep gratitude how often her wise advice and her good humor and patience helped to settle the endless squabbles about the book's content. Many an old timer also remembered with gratitude those warm letters Ruth had written to him when he was a loner struggling to stay sober out there in the grass roots."

Although Ruth served for only five years as national secretary, her unique role in helping write the Big Book and helping AA put down its first roots earned her immortality in the minds of countless members of Alcoholics Anonymous. Almost a half-century later, in 1985, she was invited as guest of honor at the Fiftieth Anniversary International Convention of AA, held in Montreal, Canada. At the opening ceremonies in the Olympic Stadium, she received a standing ovation from the crowd of nearly fifty thousand as she was presented with the five millionth copy of the Big Book.

She said that at that climactic moment, all she could do was look skyward and murmur silently, "What do you think about this one, Willie?"[1]

1. Only seconds before, someone on the stage realized they did not have an actual five millionth copy of the Big Book, which was just coming off the

Elsewhere in *Alcoholics Anonymous Comes of Age*, Bill W. pieced together the background of Ruth Hock's involvement. He said, "Henry 'Hank' P. (Parkhurst) [was] my partner in Works Publishing and the book enterprise. Among all the prospects Dr. Silkworth had pointed out to me at Towns Hospital in 1935 [when Bill had returned from staying with Dr. Bob in Akron], Henry was the first one to sober up. He had been a big-time [Standard Oil] executive and salesman and [had] really prodigious enthusiasm. . . . At 17 William Street, Newark, New Jersey, Henry had an office which was the head-quarters for a rapidly failing business [called 'Honor Dealers,' based on pooling together service station dealers to enable them to purchase tires, batteries, and accessories by the car-load]. He also had a secretary named Ruth Hock, who was to become one of AA's real pioneers. The other assets consisted of a huge desk and some plush furniture."

In the fall of 1937, Bill had revisited Akron, where he and Dr. Bob were able to count some forty sober alcoholics between their two locations. Aware that they were on to something of tremendous significance to humanity, they gathered the Akron alcoholics. They obtained the members' approval (over consid-erable reluctance) to write and publish a book to codify the recovery program that, up to that time, had been carried only by word of mouth. Returning to New York, Bill had contacted (through his brother-in-law, Dr. Leonard V. Strong) several individuals on the staff of John D. Rockefeller Jr. who were sympathetic and helpful. The result was the formation of the Alcoholic Foundation to direct and manage the affairs of the budding society, but money for a book was not forthcoming. Discouraged but determined, Hank P. and Bill W. formed Works Publishing, Inc., with shares at twenty-five dollars each to be sold to members and others (frequently on the installment plan). In April 1938, Bill began work on the book.

press. So they scrambled to grab an available copy of the book to present to her temporarily. Ruth was vastly amused at this byplay and pro-nounced it "typically alcoholic."

"Each morning I traveled all the way from Brooklyn to Newark," he related, "where, pacing up and down in Henry's office I began to dictate rough drafts of the chapters. As we seemed unable to come up with any genuine outline, I worked from a hastily drawn-up list of chapter headings. Week after week, Henry raced around among the stock subscribers, prodding them for their installments."

Ruth's recollections of the process were this: "Although I was good at shorthand, Bill hated to dictate that way. He came in daily with a yellow legal pad on which he had scribbled notes. I sat at an old-fashioned typewriter, and Bill would stand behind me or pace up and down while he talked. As each page or two came out of the typewriter, I gave them to him to look over as he sat with his long legs up on the big desk. He wanted the typed pages right then while his thoughts were working in the same vein." Later, when objections and comments came in from the New York members and the Akron group, Ruth and Bill would work together on the draft to incorporate them, yet keep the text reading smoothly. Ruth said that the work would have gone much quicker if Bill had not dropped everything to talk to every visitor who dropped in, trying to help them in their time of need.

Ruth's parents, of German descent, had been brought to the United States as small children. Ruth Eva Miller was born to them on November 12, 1911, in Newark, New Jersey. She attended local schools, graduating from high school in 1928.

She was married to George Hock in 1929 at the age of eighteen. Although they had a son, Gene, born in 1932, she described the marriage as "disaster"; they separated in 1935 and were divorced in 1941. Looking back later, she said that the difficulty of rearing a child as a single mother, without child support, and relying on a series of small, boring jobs during the depth of the depression, helped her to accept whatever life had to offer. Her own defeats and hurts gave her not only an understanding of what Bill and Hank were trying to do, but also an empathy and concern that enabled her to reach other unfortunates. She gave her loving parents much credit for supporting her during her bad marriage and tough divorce. But, she said, "Bill and Hank put me back together and gave me a purpose for life."

After drifting from one unrewarding job to another, Ruth was referred to Honor Dealers by an employment agency in 1937. Her starting salary was fifteen dollars a week. She sat at a desk in an outside room, while Hank and Bill had large desks in a private office. She had no idea at the time what kind of business she had fallen into. "I was confused, to say the least," she recalled, with a chuckle. "There was very little business coming in, and as it was during the depression it didn't look as if it were going to get better. Hank was forceful, demanding and energetic; Bill was more of a listener, with a deep belly-laugh with which he often laughed at himself. Both men seemed extremely busy: they were out of the office a great deal, and had frequent visitors who talked long with the bosses in the inside office. I assumed the visitors were on business, but I came to find out Bill and Hank were involved in alcoholism and the visitors were often terribly distraught and desperately seeking help."

She told of one visitor during her first week—a well-dressed man wearing a bowler hat, who said he *had* to see Bill. Both Bill and Hank greeted him heartily with "*Hello*, Bob! Glad to see you!" and ushered him into the inner office. Ruth couldn't help overhearing Bob telling a sad tale of terrible things that had happened to him, punctuated by gales of laughter from the other two. Her first thought was, "What hard-hearted persons they are!" She also thought it was a shame they were wasting so much time. To top it all off, when she peeked in a while later, all three men were kneeling beside the desk, praying. Ruth, then only twenty-five, was shocked and worried. When she went home and told her father about the strange occurrence, he wasn't sure she should stay.

"But after a few months," she said, "you couldn't have paid me to leave!" Her father became so interested in what was going on that when the business finally went bankrupt due to the principal owners' devotion to their fellow alcoholics, he purchased shares in Works Publishing. That helped to pay his daughter's salary and to keep the office open.

As the recovering drunks reentered the outside world, word of the success of the new movement spread beyond the fledgling groups meeting in Brooklyn and Akron. Salesmen in the fellowship carried the good news on their business trips. As a result, letters were beginning to trickle into the Newark office asking for help and guidance.[2] Bill was simply too busy to answer them all, so after Ruth had written dozens of replies under his direction, he would say to her, "Answer this, Dutch, you can handle it." (His nickname for her, Dutchess, came partly from her German extraction and partly because of her bossiness in keeping him working on the Big Book.) Eventually, she handled all the routine queries, signing her letters *R. Hock.* "I now felt a part of all this," she said, "and I was completely accepted by those who knew me, but it was thought that letters written and signed by a female would not be accepted by the male alcoholics." Even over the phone, Ruth's rich contralto voice disguised her gender. So "R. Hock" became a familiar name to thousands of AA members. She accompanied Bill to many AA meetings and "sat up with many men at all hours of the night and day, doling out coffee and sympathy."

Ruth played a major part in introducing the Serenity Prayer to the fellowship. Jack C. (Carney), a New York newspaperman and recovering drunk, brought a newspaper clipping to the office. It was an obituary that closed with these words: "God grant us the serenity to accept the things we cannot change, courage to change the things we can, and the wisdom to know the difference." Bill and Ruth agreed with Jack that "never had we seen so much AA in so few words." And Ruth began at once to tuck the prayer into the letters she was sending out. Not long afterward, Horace C. (Crystal), an older member and friend of

2. Following favorable publicity, including articles in *Liberty* magazine in 1939 and *The Saturday Evening Post* in March 1941, the trickle swelled to a flood.

Bill, came in with the suggestion to print the prayer on cards that could be included with all outgoing letters. Everyone thought it was a wonderful idea, but they had no money to implement it—so Horace personally paid to have the cards printed. "In an amazingly short time," said Bill, "the Serenity Prayer came into general use"—and remains so to this day.

Ruth Hock remembered vividly how the Big Book acquired its title—which became the name for the fellowship itself. From the inception of the book idea, choosing a suitable title was a hot issue, not only among those who had had a hand in it, but among everyone else as well. "We considered more than a hundred titles, all told," according to Bill. Ruth remembered *100 Men* as being the first possibility. *The Broken Glass* was another. The favorite of the Akron group was *The Way Out*.

After the book's text, including the stories, was completed, it was decided to reproduce four hundred multilithed (photo copies) copies to send to members, doctors, ministers, and any-one else concerned with alcoholism, to make sure it would be acceptable before it was officially published. Bill arbitrarily slapped on a working title, *Alcoholics Anonymous,* that had been discussed as a possibility since about October 1938. Bill explained its origin thus: "After we New Yorkers had left the Oxford Group in 1937 we often described ourselves as a 'name-less bunch of alcoholics.' From this phrase it was only a step to 'Alcoholics Anonymous.' That was its actual derivation."

Not everyone liked the working title as well as Bill, but according to Ruth, its greatest proponent was one Joe W., the former editor of a popular and respected magazine, who had only recently been "scraped out of the Bowery." When Joe W. saw the title *Alcoholics Anonymous,* he cried "That's it!" and ral-lied a number of other New Yorkers around him.

To resolve the dilemma, Bill had a bright idea: "I sent a wire to good old Fitz M. then on his farm in Maryland. I asked him to go to the Library of Congress in Washington and find out how many books in publication were entitled 'The Way Out' and how many 'Alcoholics Anonymous.' Two days later we got this reply: The Library of Congress shows twelve books titled 'The Way Out.' No book listed there is called 'Alcoholics Anonymous.'" That did it. They left the title *Alcoholics Anonymous* on the manuscript that went to the printer. "And that," declared Bill, "is how we got the title for our book and that is how our society got its name."

Ruth was in the midst of another last-minute event "of great significance for AA's future," that took place in the Newark office. Bill described it in these words: "Present were Fitz [M.], Henry [P.], our grand Secretary Ruth, and myself. We were still arguing about [the religious tone of] the Twelve Steps. When I wrote them, I had consistently used the word 'God' and in one place the expression 'on our knees.' I had refused to budge on this. Fitz, a minister's son and deeply religious himself, agreed, as he wanted a powerfully religious document. Henry, a former atheist, fell into a hot argument with him. He was positive we would scare off alcoholics by the thousands when they read those Twelve Steps, and he quoted a newcomer named Jimmy B. [Burwell] who emphatically shared that view. Little by little both Fitz and Ruth came to see merit in Henry and Jimmy's contentions."

At last they arrived at a compromise on the words, which are well know throughout the length and breadth of AA today—words that apparently were from Jimmy B. In Step Two, they used "a Power greater than ourselves." In Steps Three and Eleven they used "God *as we understand Him.*" And in Step Seven the phrase *on our knees* was deleted. The wording embodying these concessions, declared Bill, "widened our gateway so that all who suffer might pass through regardless of their belief or *lack of belief.*" [Bill's emphasis.]

Ruth followed the book she helped create right up to its publication. Through a lot of hustle, begging, and wheedling, Hank had rounded up enough sales of Works Publishing shares to make a five-hundred-dollar payment for the printing, which was to be done by the Cornwall Press, one of the country's largest book printers. So the day came when Bill, Hank, Ruth, and a good friend, Dorothy S. (Snyder) from Cleveland, wheeled up to Cornwall, New York, to deliver the master multilith copy, with all the corrections, to the printing plant.

When the manager saw what a mess the manuscript was in, he almost sent them back to Newark to type a clean copy. But Hank persuaded him to begin setting the type in galley proofs, on the condition that the party would correct them on the spot, as they came off the press. So they all checked into the town's only hotel, where they spent the next several days proofreading galleys.

Ruth said that the hotel bill amounted to more than all the cash they could raise among them. The shareholders had been wrung dry, so, wracking their brains, they thought of putting the arm on Charlie Towns of Towns Hospital. Bill drove back to New York and borrowed enough from Towns to cover the hotel bill and about a hundred dollars to spare.

Ruth was extremely fond of Dorothy, and the two of them thoroughly enjoyed the excitement of the whole adventure. She remembered on night that she and Dorothy, who shared a double bed in one hotel room, stayed awake talking. Bill couldn't sleep either, so, hearing them chatting, he appeared at the door, plunked himself down in the middle of the bed, and joined the palaver until 1:30 in the morning.

When the first of five thousand copies of the Big Book came off the Cornwall presses in April 1939, the problem was to sell them.

Hank and Bill had pinned their hopes to a keenly anticipated article on this new society of recovered drunks in *Reader's Digest*, only to have their hopes dashed when the article failed to materialize.[3] Ruth remembered it as a bleak and discouraging time. The bank had foreclosed on Bill and Lois's family house on Clinton Street in Brooklyn, throwing them on the generosity of friends for lodging. The sheriff had also evicted

3. Since that time, no publication has been more generous to AA than *Reader's Digest*. Over the years, it has run many favorable and supportive articles.

the bankrupt Honor Dealers from the office in Newark. Ruth was living at her parents' home with only promissory notes and worthless Works Publishing shares for salary. No one had any money at all.

A ray of hope came when a newly sober Irish member, Morgan R., who had been in the advertising business, said that he knew Gabriel Heatter, a popular network radio commentator with a large following, who might be willing to help. His idea appealed immediately to Heatter, who set a date to interview Morgan on his program. Everyone was bursting with excitement, and Hank, with borrowed money, sent a postcard notice of the forthcoming broadcast to twenty thousand doctors across the country. The only fly in the ointment was the distinct possibility that Morgan, fresh from a mental asylum, might be caught drunk on the night of the program. So, for the three days and nights before the appointed date, Morgan was kept locked up in a room at the Downtown Athletic Club, with someone with him round the clock.

Heatter's radio interview with Morgan was a complete success but brought in only twelve replies to the doctor mailing, of which just two were book orders! Morgan R. himself, however, made an unforgettable impression on Ruth Hock—who then, remember, was a pretty, warmhearted girl in her twenties. More than forty years later she said with throaty emotion, "Morgan was one of the best looking men on earth. He was maybe 30 years old, tall, well-built—a beautiful man!" They had a couple of romantic dinners together, but Ruth realized the charming Irishman was emotionally immature and insecure in his sobriety.

Hank P. also became one of Ruth's suitors. After the eviction from the Newark office, Hank found a job that took him to western New Jersey. Bill and Ruth found temporary office space in a tiny cubicle in Newark. They had also rented a post office box in downtown Manhattan to provide a more central address in the New York area to receive orders for the book. Now, in late 1939, Bill and Ruth (backed by the Works Publishing shareholders) decided to move to an office at 30

Vesey Street, next door to the post office box. Hank objected violently. "He wanted to take the book business wherever he went, and me with it," said Ruth.

She explained that Hank had broken up with his wife just prior to the Cornwall Press trip and soon thereafter began making overtures to her. "I thought highly of Hank," she said. "After all, it was his promotional ability that made possible the publishing of the Big Book. He tried to dissociate me from Bill and AA. He wanted me to marry him, but I had already been through all that. I soon realized that he had begun drinking again, but never, when he was with me, did he lose control. Shortly after that, feeling separated from Bill and the other early New York members, and feeling he was entitled to more, he just fell apart and went on a terrific bender. He never again really recovered and kept on drinking until he died a few years later."

In September 1939, *Liberty* magazine ran the first major magazine article about AA entitled "Alcoholics and God." Related Bill, "*Liberty* received 800 urgent pleas for help which were promptly turned over to Ruth and me. She wrote fine personal letters to every one of them, enclosing a leaflet which described the AA book. The response was wonderful. Several hundred books were sold at once. More importantly Ruth struck up a correspondence with alcoholics, their friends and their families all over the country. Ruth could at last draw a few dollars a week for herself."

Shortly after this, the Cleveland *Plain Dealer* ran a series of articles on AA that led to virtually an explosion of activity in that city. That brought new book orders and new problems by the score. "Alcoholics Anonymous was on the march, out of infancy and into adolescence," said Bill. Meanwhile, back in New York, John D. Rockefeller Jr., who had been following the progress of the movement with great interest for two years, decided to host a dinner for his friends on February 8, 1940, to introduce them to Bill, Dr. Bob, and the other sober alcoholics. The alcoholics' hopes of large-scale financial support were dashed by Rockefeller's announcement that "this is a work of good will, its power lies in each member carrying the message without thought of financial reward, and so we believe it should be self-supporting." He did, however, order four hundred books to send to the guest list along with a favorable letter; and, most important, the news wires carried a story of the Rockefeller dinner all over the world.

So, in February 1940, Bill and Ruth moved into the office at 30 Vesey Street, where, Bill wrote, "Ruth and I set about answering the mass of inquiries that came in." Groups began springing up all over. Sales of the AA book increased steadily. It was also possible now to pay Ruth a fair salary. A decision was made to buy up all the shares of Works Publishing and turn the publishing over to the trustees of the Alcoholic Foundation that is, to AA itself.

Having come to work for Bill and Hank before AA even had a name and when the total number of recovered alcoholics between Akron and New York was fewer than fifty, Ruth Hock knew most of the pioneers personally. For example, she remembered that Ebby T. (Thacher), "who started Bill in the direction we all came to, even today," became sober in 1937 through going to the Oxford Group at New York's Calvary Church. This was where Bill was working with the alcoholics in the group, thus offending the other Oxford Group members, which led to the alcoholics breaking away on their own.

Ruth remembered the priceless help given by nonalcoholic friend Willard "Dick" Richardson, Rockefeller's aide, who was Bill's primary contact with the Rockefeller group. "One day Bill was going to bring Mr. Richardson to the Newark office," she said. "Before they arrived a well-dressed young man appeared, absolutely blotto, so I stuck him in the back office. Well, Bill arrived talking up a storm to his guest, bragging on their success in helping drunks and the work of the office. As he said, '. . . and this is my private office' he threw open the door and there was the drunk. Bill and Richardson absolutely roared with laughter. Bill was always able to laugh at himself."

Ruth was in constant touch with Clarence S. (Snyder), the person who had broken away from the Akron Oxford Group to found the first group in Cleveland—the first group to use the name Alcoholics Anonymous—and who contributed one of the first stories to the Big Book, entitled "Home Brewmeister." "Clarence was always arguing," declared Ruth, "disagreeing over things that didn't really matter much in the long run." Although the Cleveland pioneer later became extremely antagonistic toward Bill and highly controversial himself, he and his wife, Dorothy, were warm friends of Ruth.

Ruth was thrilled when Marty M. (Mann), from Greenwich, Connecticut, became the first woman member of Alcoholics Anonymous, in May 1939. She had been sent to the meeting at Bill and Lois's Brooklyn home by famed psychiatrist Dr. Harry Tiebout, medical director of Blythewood Sanitarium, where the alcoholic Marty was a patient. Marty, aided by Dr. Tiebout, founded AA group No. 3, in Greenwich. Marty became very active in New York AA. Ruth said, "I admired her a great deal, though I didn't see her often." Another early benefactor to whom Ruth was grateful was Bert T. (Taylor), who literally mortgaged his tailor shop in mid–Manhattan to enable the Big Book to be printed.

Of course it was Bill Wilson himself whom Ruth knew best and about whom she had the richest memories. "He had his faults," she conceded, "but he had unbelievable patience and understanding. He was a great listener, always willing to incorporate whatever the other person was trying to tell him. He was absolutely whatever the other person was trying to tell him. He was absolutely single-minded in striving to bring about his vision of what Alcoholics Anonymous could be." She chuckled as she said, "He always over estimated how many sober members there were. I always corrected him, and he would say, 'It doesn't really matter, Dutchess.'

"He [was] against idolization, though he did say once, 'I believe in anonymity, Dutchess, but it is nice to be appreciated!' He tried eventually to keep his ego in check over how far he had come. He constantly turned credit away from himself and toward others, always saying 'we' this and 'we' that."

Perhaps Ruth's—and AA's—greatest challenge came in March 1941 when *The Saturday Evening Post*, the largest and most prestigious publication in America, ran Jack Alexander's marvelous article about Alcoholics Anonymous. Bill wrote, "By mail and telegram a deluge of pleas for help and orders for *Alcoholics Anonymous*, first in hundreds and then in thousands, hit Box 658. . . . Pawing through the incoming mountains of heartbreaking appeals, Ruth and I found ourselves laughing and crying in turn."

They were swamped. They rounded up every AA woman and AA wife who could use a typewriter and set up emergency head-quarters on the upper floor of the Twenty-fourth Street Clubhouse, under the direction of Ruth. Every appeal received a warm, personal letter. Even after the peak of the flood had passed, the volume of correspondence at the office remained so great that two regular workers were added to the staff. The pins in the U.S. map on the office wall showed scores of new groups springing up every week. At year's end, AA had grown from two thousand members to eight thousand.

Bill wrote in *Alcoholics Anonymous Comes of Age*, "In early 1942, nonalcoholic secretary Ruth Hock left us to be married, carrying the affectionate wishes of thousands of members. The work of that little pioneer on the book *Alcoholics Anonymous* and AA's first Headquarters set us an example that will never be for-gotten."

The exact date of Ruth's marriage was February 28, when she was wed to Philip Crecelius, a Cleveland developer and presi-dent of a small coal company. At the church wedding, her father gave her away. Bill and Lois were present, of course, along with a crowd of other AA friends. The couple moved to Cleveland, where two daughters were born: Ellen in 1943 and Laurie in 1945. In 1946, the family moved to a farm near Marietta, Ohio, where Ruth was absorbed in motherhood and her hobbies of gardening and bridge. When her husband's business hit a bad time, he asked her to take over financial management of the company, which she did with verve and enthusiasm.

In 1952 the Creceliuses built a lovely home near Lowell, Ohio, on a site with woods and meadows and a breathtaking view of the Muskingum River. There, Ruth enjoyed a busy, happy life for the next fifteen years. Her two daughters grew up, graduated from college, and married. Her son, Gene, was married and living in Alaska. Then one day in 1966, he was killed in a plane crash. A few months later, the coal company was sold, so Ruth no longer had a demanding job. "I wasn't cut out to be a retiree," she said, and began looking around for part-time work. She found her niche as a court investigator in divorce cases where children were involved, reporting to the County Common Pleas judge.

By 1976, a new judge who had taken over decided to establish a support bureau with the responsibility of following up on all child-support orders the court made. Ruth Hock Crecelius was the obvious choice to head up the new bureau, a full-time job, much needed and eminently worthwhile. Her husband, Philip, died of cancer in 1982. Ruth continued working almost to the time of her own death.

Her younger daughter, Laurie, joined Alcoholics Anonymous in 1976, and so it was especially meaningful for her to accompany her mother to the great Fiftieth Anniversary International Convention of AA nine years later. Laurie said that after they returned from Montreal, her mother was so buoyed up by the experience that no one realized she was not feeling well. By fall, she had resigned her support bureau job and sold the family house. Her cancer was diagnosed in January 1986.

Always strongly maternal, she enjoyed listening to her grandchildren. "She was amazingly open-minded and understanding," Laurie recalled. "My sister, my niece Dion, and I stayed with her, and she always wanted us to be honest about our feelings. So when one of us would fall apart in hysterics, mother would say, 'It's okay.'" Ruth passed away May 4, 1986.

Wherever she is, she must have enjoyed the reprise of the Montreal experience when Laurie was invited to tell about her mother on the "AA Pioneers" program at the 1995, AA International Convention in San Diego. She told what is told in this chapter, simply, sweetly, with humor, and, above all, movingly. When she sat down, the audience of several thousand rose with tears in their eyes and gave her a standing ovation.

Sources:*

Hock, Ruth. Personal memories. 1985.

Hock, Ruth. Taped interview by Mel Barger. 1985. Made available by Laurie Lukens.

Hock, Ruth. Taped speeches. 1985. Made available by Laurie Lukens.

Lukens, Laurie. Speech on "AA Pioneers" program. AA International Convention in San Diego. 1995.

Schwab, Patricia. *Ruth.* Theme paper. Based on interviews with Ruth Hock. November 1979.

*Additional sources are cited within the profile itself.

Nell Wing

NELL WING, THOUGH A NONALCOHOLIC, PROBABLY KNOWS MORE ABOUT ALCOHOLICS ANONYMOUS THAN ANY OTHER living person. A key employee of AA's General Service Office from 1947 to 1982, she served cofounder Bill Wilson as executive secretary and assistant for twenty-five years, and in addition was, at different times, secretary of the AA World Services board, and editor of service publications including the annual General Service Conference report. During the last ten years before retirement, she was the archivist for AA.

A pretty girl, Nell had a perky, outgoing personality, always full of bright chatter. Although she had a couple of serious romances, she never married. So, during her decades of AA service, she was a regular weekend guest at Stepping Stones, Bill and Lois Wilson's residence in Bedford Hills, New York—sometimes in a working capacity with Bill, but more often as a friend and surrogate daughter. "They were my family," she says.

Following Bill's death in 1971, Nell remained for seventeen years a close friend and companion to his widow, Lois, cofounder of Al-Anon. From these professional and personal vantage points, Nell knew every pioneer and historic figure in both fellowships. An enthusiastic, perceptive observer of the excitement and turbulence of AA's growth and development, she was frequently a participant as well.

Nell Wing was born near Rochester, New York, in 1918, the second of four children of William Frank Wing, a teacher and local judge, and Daisy Sheppard Wing, a teacher and nurse. Both parents were of English lineage, and Nell has continued to attend regular Wing reunions attended by several hundred.

She remembers her childhood as a happy one, though her father was a tough, demanding tutor when she lagged in her lessons. "Dad had lots of friends in Rochester, most of them respectable professionals, but it seems to me almost every one was a heavy drinker. The state troopers would appear at our door in the middle of the night dragging a drunk to my father, the judge. Dad would post bail if necessary, as well as passing sentence. In this way, I learned early on what an alcoholic was like and how their problem affected other people. And I was curious about what alcoholism was."

Thus, later, in her senior year at Keuka College in Central New York State, she discovered the existence of something called Alcoholics Anonymous. She has a clear memory of sitting on the bed in her room reading an article in *Liberty* magazine entitled "Alcoholics and God" in which AA was described most favorably. "I was in my agnostic phase then," Nell recalls, "so I thought the program's emphasis on a Higher Power was a fatal mistake. I wasn't terribly optimistic about its survival." Still later, Nell also read the landmark article on AA in the March 1941 *Saturday Evening Post* and two other pieces in *Reader's Digest*. The seeker in the young lady was obviously intrigued.

After graduation from college, Nell took a fling at teaching in a Mexican high school in her mother's hometown of San Antonio, Texas. Deciding that a teaching career was not for her, she returned to Rochester to hold some secretarial jobs while living at home. By now the country was in the thick of World War II, and in 1944 Nell enlisted in the SPARS, the female branch of the U.S. Coast Guard. After boot camp at Lake Worth, Florida, she was stationed at the 13th Naval District in Seattle, Washington. It was an exciting time with lots of drinking and partying with the sailors—a period of growing up.

Discharged after the end of the war, she found herself at loose ends. Recalls Nell: "I was a bit of a nonconformist. You have to realize there was a lot of movement around the country in the immediate postwar years. Disrupted by the war, people's lives were unsettled. Ideas changed, especially for women, who had taken over a lot of jobs normally suited to men. New vistas opened up for women, and a spirit of travel hit a lot of people, including me."

Not involved in any serious relationship and having a talent for art and sculpture, she decided to head for Mexico to study under a famous sculptor who taught at the American University there and to live a bohemian life with the international set. To do so required a lot more money than she had from her coast guard severance pay, so she headed for New York by train. At the first employment agency she encountered, the woman interviewer studied Nell's resume and then leaned across the desk and whispered, "How would you like to work at Alcoholics Anonymous?" She almost fell off her chair at Nell's enthusiastic "Yes, I'd love to!"

"So it was," Nell says, "on Monday morning, March 3, 1947, a new life began for me when I knocked on the door of A.A.'s 'headquarters' (as it was called in those days) on the eleventh floor of 415 Lexington Avenue, across from Grand Central Station."

The next day, Tuesday, she met Bill Wilson. His usual pattern then, and to the end of his life, was to spend one or two days a week in town at the New York office. Staff member Bobbie Berger took Nell over to his desk and left her, saying, "And this is Bill." She remembers the occasion vividly: "I expected the usual amenities, but he didn't even say hello. He eased his long, lanky frame onto a straight-backed chair, leaned way back (a habit I was to become familiar with over the years, as we shared the same office), crossed his legs, and launched into a long monologue. He talked about how the trustees were trying to keep him isolated in an ivory tower, suggesting he ought to concentrate on just writing for the Fellowship. He went on about the need for something called the Traditions and for a general service conference made up of people from all over the country who would come to New York and help make decisions. I listened with all the interest I could muster, but I didn't really have the vaguest idea of what he was talking about and escaped as soon as I could."

Nell later observed that this first meeting exemplified two important characteristics of Bill. One, his lack of small talk—unless you introduced a subject in which he was interested, in which case it was hard to make an exit. Second, his tunnel vision, thinking far ahead, envisioning future needs. If Bill had not possessed these traits, she maintains, there might not be an AA as we know it today.

Nell Wing joined the AA office at a particularly exciting and propitious time—and as receptionist (her first assignment), she was in the midst of it. There were about 1,250 groups at that time, with an estimated 40,000 members, and new groups were forming at a rapid rate. Nell was often the first to learn from a visitor that a group had formed in a new area, and she helped him place a colored pin in the appropriate location on a big U.S. map (which can now be seen in Bill's studio at Stepping Stones). In just three years, she watched AA spread abroad to Australia, Mexico, Ireland, Scotland, England, continental Europe, and South Africa. She was acquainted with Captain Jack S., a merchant marine skipper who carried the AA message to foreign ports around the world and helped establish the Loners and Internationalists. During Bill and Lois's frequent trips, she and the rest of the small office staff handled the flood of publicity—from newspapers, magazines, and especially radio—stimulated in part by the box office success of the movie *The Lost Weekend*. She dealt with frequent visits by Ebby Thacher, the man who first brought the Oxford Group message to Bill, but who was unable to achieve any lasting sobriety himself. Nevertheless, Bill always called Ebby his sponsor and was a loyal friend.

The early groups and members usually had no one with whom to communicate except the office. So they wrote long letters, and the office staff was their only source of help in staying sober. Besides Bill and Dr. Bob, there were lots of local "founders" who made up their own rules and regulations, leading to resentments and confusion. Clubhouses for AA members were being formed in many areas, leading to still more problems and confusion. There was even heated disagreement between the trustees and Bill regarding their respective roles in the total AA picture, and Bill was pushing hard among the groups for a general service conference to provide a structure for self-government. In the mid-forties, Bill was writing long, thoughtful memos that he called "Codes," which became the Twelve Traditions, accepted in 1950.

Marty Mann, the first woman to get sober in Alcoholics Anonymous, had founded the National Committee for Education on Alcoholism (later the NCA). Both Bill and Dr. Bob were so supportive of what she was trying to do that they allowed their names to be put on the NCEA letterhead. When Marty sent a letter to AA groups soliciting funds, it raised a tremendous hullabaloo from outraged members, and AA's cofounders withdrew their names.

Meanwhile, the office was growing too, and because of Bill's frequent absences, the trustees appointed a "general service committee" to oversee its operation. The chairman of this committee, Hank Grieme, began to serve as part-time volunteer manager of the office. (It eventually became a full-time salaried position, and Nell had the unique experience of serving under four general managers after Bill.)

As a result of all these growing pains and momentous events that exerted enormous demands on Bill Wilson, he needed someone to be his secretary/aide/assistant, and in early 1950 Nell was tapped for that job. "By this time, I had obviously given up any idea of going to Mexico," she says, with a wry smile. That same year, the office moved to larger quarters around the corner at 141 East Forty-fourth Street.

Among Nell Wing's most significant contributions to Alcoholics Anonymous over her first two decades was her involvement with Bill's writing projects and with other publications of the office. Bill perceived the need for a hard-cover book about the Twelve Steps: "To broaden and deepen them, both for newcomers *and oldtimers* . . . and to avoid distractions, distortions and the certain prejudices of all who may read [them]," as Bill explained in a letter to Father Ed Dowling in St. Louis, which he dictated to Nell. The book was also to include essays on the Twelve Traditions, adapted from a series Bill had written earlier for the *AA Grapevine.*

The immediate and continuing success of the resulting book *Twelve Steps and Twelve Traditions* encouraged Bill to form in 1954 a "writing and research team" consisting of himself and Nell Wing, plus, briefly, Ed B., a writer and editor whose career had been ruined by alcoholism; and later, also briefly, Tom P., a brilliant editor and speaker, active in early AA. However, for most of the four years of its existence, the "team" consisted of Nell by herself in a space that had been set up in a loft building at 305 East Forty-fifth Street, adjacent to the shipping department which had also been moved there.

Bill's announced program for the writing and research team was

1. A second edition of the Big Book, *Alcoholics Anonymous.* As Bill traveled around, he taped personal stories of old-timers for an updated story section, but the transcribing, editing, and production were the task of Nell with her sometime help. It was published in 1955.
2. The full-length, definitive history of Alcoholics Anonymous. Bill's debilitating depression precluded his undertaking this commitment, and his project ended up as *Alcoholics Anonymous Comes of Age,* This moving volume, treasured by AA members, consists primarily of reprints of the talks made at the seminal St. Louis International Convention in 1955—talks not only by Bill, but also by Father Ed Dowling; the Reverend Sam Shoemaker; Dr. W. W. Bauer of the American Medical Association; Bernard Smith, chairman of the General Service Board; and psychiatrist Dr. Harry Tiebout. Nell describes *Alcoholics Anonymous Comes of Age* as a vast canvas on which Bill paints a panorama of everything that had happened in AA

since its birth and a portrait of its place in the world at that time. However, Bill still hoped until his death to write a true history. (A full history of the fellowship's first fifty years was compiled and written in 1987, but for various political reasons has not yet been published.)

3. A book that would show how Bill and others applied the AA program spiritually and practically. The working title was "In All Our Affairs." This project eventually evolved into *The AA Way of Life*, later retitled *As Bill Sees It*. Nell says that *The Language of the Heart*, containing all of Bill's writing that appeared in the pages of the *AA Grapevine*, presents what Bill originally expected from "In All Our Affairs."

When the General Service Conference was initiated "on a trial basis" in the mid-1950s, it was Nell's task to take notes of the proceedings and then write and produce the conference report. Bill told her once that since she had helped him through the arduous years of going out to the groups to sow the seed of the conference idea, it was only fitting that she be in on the harvest. Later, as the conference grew in length and content, the stenographic and conference report duties were taken over by others, but Nell Wing attended at least part of every General Service Conference for a quarter-century.

From the writing and research team and the conference reports, it was a short step for Nell to be made responsible for all the stream of service materials—i.e., The *AA Service Manual*, *Box 459* newsletter, guidelines, and so on, which poured out of the General Service Office (GSO). In this capacity, she worked with the legendary (albeit anonymous) writers at the GSO: Al Steckman, Ralph Bugli, Barry Leach, and others. All this while, Nell continued her role as secretary/aide/assistant to Bill Wilson—in his office on his days in town and at Stepping Stones when he was working there. She assisted him at every five-year AA International Convention. Of what transpired at the "coming of age" convention in St. Louis in 1955, Nell says,

"It's hard for people today to realize the enormity of the decision to accept a General Service Conference plan on that Sunday morning in St. Louis. Bill had pushed through the idea largely by campaigning for it personally and relentlessly. But many members, particularly in the Midwest, still opposed the idea. After Bill presented his resolution, Bernard Smith, the chairman, asked for a moment of silence for the crowd to invoke the Guidance of God. I sat there with bated breath in the hushed silence. Then Bern called for the vote and a roar of approval went up. Tears came to my eyes."

Nell is somewhat awed today as she remembers the many figures important to AA's formative years whom she met in St. Louis. Of those mentioned above in *Alcoholics Anonymous Comes of Age*, she was particularly impressed with lawyer Bernard Smith, chairman of the General Service Board at the time. She recalls, "Bern Smith was the only trustee—almost the only *person*—who supported Bill when he was pushing the conference idea, and it was he who finally brought a majority of the other trustees around to accept the conference on a trial basis. He also helped Bill put together the conference structure." Ebby was also there. And one of Nell's duties was to escort another special guest; namely, Bill's mother, Dr. Emily Strobell. Nell kept her company through the day when Bill and Lois were busy at meetings, and the two became fast friends. Their mutual affection continued to blossom when Bill and Lois later brought his mother home to live with them at Stepping Stones for two years before she passed away in 1961.

Nell Wing's personal reminiscences of the time she was Bill's secretary and aide show her continual, close involvement with AA history. For example, she recalls the excitement of Bill and Lois's 1950 trip to visit AA in Europe, stopping at cities in Norway, Sweden, Denmark, Holland, France, England, Ireland, and Scotland. The trip was the first step in creating service structures in those countries, with the encouragement of letters she wrote for Bill. One of these said, "We are anxious here that New York never be regarded as the world capital of

A.A. . . . . We want to be known as the senior service center of longest experience. . . ." Nell observes, "That thinking was later incorporated in Bill's proposal for the first World Service Meeting in 1969." She recalls in the single decade of the sixties, the passing of Father Ed Dowling, the Reverend Sam Shoemaker, Ebby Thacher, Sister Ignatia, and Dr. Harry Tiebout—all of whom she knew.

The International Convention that ushered in the decade was held in Long Beach, California. Hank Grieme, who had been supervising it, was suddenly stricken with appendicitis and hospitalized. Herb Morse, his successor as General Service Office manager, stepped in, only to suffer a heart attack. Another capable trustee, Allen Bachman, took over at the last minute and flew to Long Beach with Bill, Dennis Manders, and staff member Hazel Rice, leaving Nell to follow with Lois Wilson.

Due to the distractions and confusion, Bill had not found time to prepare the major talk he had planned to make on the Saturday night of the convention on the how and why of the Twelve Traditions. So he and Nell spent all Saturday afternoon preparing his outline and notes. That night, at the open-air stadium right on the ocean, despite a record cold spell that came in unexpectedly, Bill went on for over two hours. Bill himself used to call it his "Deep Freeze Talk." Nell recalls, however, that amazingly almost everyone stayed, shivering and shaking, until the end.

Five years later, Nell was again helping Bill and Lois at the great thirtieth Anniversary Convention in Toronto, Ontario. She tells of Bill's meeting there with his bête noire, Clarence Snyder, the "Home Brewmeister" in the Big Book. Clarence was the first person to break away from the Akron meeting and start a group in Cleveland using the initials *AA*. On this slender basis he forever claimed to have founded AA and was the leader of a small group of dissidents who were anti-Conference, anti-GSO and who forever bad-mouthed Bill. So Nell was shocked to see Bill and Clarence reminiscing and chatting together.

In early spring of 1969, Bill fell from the roof of his studio at Stepping Stones. He never fully recovered. By the following April his health had failed to the point that he was unable to finish his opening talk at the General Service Conference. And three months later, he was unable to keep his scheduled appearances at the AA International Convention in Miami Beach. It was a hectic time for Nell at Bill's side, as Lois, Dr. Jack Norris, and Bob Hitchins, the general manager at GSO, scrambled to keep the program going for the 13,000 attendees and to cover for Bill's absentia.

Unexpectedly, at the big closing meeting on Sunday morning, AA's cofounder was wheeled onto the stage in a wheelchair, hooked up to oxygen tanks. The whole hall simply exploded into prolonged applause. Finally Bill heaved himself up to his full height at the podium. His voice clear and strong, he spoke for perhaps five minutes on what AA's growth had meant to him and ended with these moving words: "As I look out this morning on this vast crowd, I know in my heart that Alcoholics Anonymous will surely last a thousand years—if it is God's will!"

They were Bill's last public words.

Nell returned to New York while Bill returned to the hospital with Lois, remaining there another five weeks before returning to Stepping Stones. Hardly had they done so when Bill's condition took another downturn. He was on oxygen constantly now, with three nurses taking turns around the clock, and his hallucinations became worse. Nell spent more and more time at Stepping Stones.

Nell's mother died in mid-January 1971, so she flew home to Rochester. On her return, still recovering from her own family tragedy, she found Bill's condition was in a final, fatal decline. On the morning of January 24—the fifty-third anniversary of Bill and Lois's marriage—Nell found herself in a Lear jet chartered by Bill's friend Brinkley Smithers, accompanying Bill and Lois and their doctor to the Miami Heart Clinic in Miami, Florida. She recalls that as Bill moved about in his hallucinations, his left arm kept slipping off the narrow stretcher on which he lay. Nell repeatedly lifted it back, murmuring, "Hold fast. Hold fast," one of his favorite expressions.

In Miami, Lois and Nell checked into a motel close by the hospital. There, at 11:30 that same night, Nell was awakened by a call from the doctor, telling her Bill had passed away. She was almost immediately plunged into the posthumous duties of informing AA's throughout the United States and the world, helping arrange the innumerable memorial services, and dealing with the press. As she cleared out the office she and Bill Wilson had shared for so many years, she organized his papers, talks, and files. This was the beginning of her job as archivist for Alcoholics Anonymous, a position she held until her retirement at the end of 1982.

Says Nell, "Bill's death was also the beginning for me of an even closer companionship with Lois, which lasted until her death seventeen years later. My every-other-weekend visits to Stepping Stones continued, and my relationship with Lois grew into one I shall always cherish." Lois enjoyed travel, and she often invited Nell to accompany her for companionship. Their trips included a cruise to see the July 1972 solar eclipse off Nova Scotia; sightseeing in London, England; a 1974 Irish AA convention in Cork; Bermuda in 1980 as guests of early Oxford Group members; and a twenty-fifth anniversary AA convention in Switzerland in 1981.

Lois loved her home at Stepping Stones and was concerned that it be preserved and maintained primarily for use by the AA and Al-Anon fellowships. When she formed the Stepping Stones Foundation for this purpose in 1979, she appointed Nell Wing one of four directors. Nell continued as an active board member until the mid-1990s and in an emeritus capacity after that time.

Nell's unique overview of AA's history together with her personal knowledge of people, places, and events made her the perfect choice as AA's first archivist. After all, she had been actively collecting and organizing old documents and records ever since

1957, as a member of Bill's "writing and research team." Bill explained that his intense interest in preserving historical material was to ensure that "the basic facts of A.A.'s growth and development can never become distorted." For fifteen years, Nell continued to perform this chore along with her many other duties—sometimes working literally seven days a week.

In early 1972, prodded by a beloved old-timer and past trustee from Florida, Tom Sharp, who had a keen personal interest in preserving AA's history, GSO General Manager Bob Hitchins appointed Nell Wing official archivist. When the GSO expanded its space at 468 Park Avenue South by leasing the eighth floor, the archives were given choice space: a large, carpeted corner office for Nell, flanked on one side by a workroom and on the other by a sizeable storage room. She also acquired a much needed secretary/assistant. A Trustees Archives Committee was added to AA's service structure in 1975.

Under Nell's direction, the archives included displays of photos of pioneer people and places, and a wide variety of historical memorabilia and artifacts. Not only did the archives become a kind of mecca for tens of thousands of visitors to the GSO, but Nell herself began to receive invitations to share AA history and her personal memories of Bill and Lois at countless AA conventions, conferences, and get-togethers throughout the United States and Canada and even abroad.

"Because I, too, practice the Steps," says Nell Wing, "I have been able to cope with unforseen realities such as a heart murmur, cancer, several broken bones and other ailments instead of running away." Indeed, as she enters her eighties, she seems as perky as ever, still filling her speaking commitments and keeping in touch with countless friends throughout the world. "From the beginning," she adds, "I was caught by the caring in the A.A. Fellowship, the one-on-one caring, the love for one another without thought of any reward. The members' instant, unspoken communication is unique. This reaching out, this loving recognition is the essence of spirituality, the root of the Being in all of us. That's how I interpret A.A."

Sources:

Wing, Nell. *Grateful to Have Been There.* 2d ed. Park Ridge, Ill.: Parkside Publishing Corporation, 1992.

Sybil C.

THE FIRST WOMAN "LUSH" WEST OF THE MISSISSIPPI TO SOBER UP IN ALCOHOLICS ANONYMOUS RECENTLY CELEBRATED her fifty-sixth AA birthday. She came in on March 23, 1941, in Los Angeles, California. Her name then was Sybil Maxwell, though she later opened her talks by saying, "My name is Sybil Doris Adams Stratton Hart Maxwell Willis C., and I'm an alcoholic." This always drew whoops and applause from her audience.

AA had several false starts in Los Angeles between 1938 and 1941. The first began when Bill Wilson, on a trip to Cleveland, had given a prepublication multilith (Xeroxed) copy of the Big Book to a lawyer friend. A wealthy young client of the lawyer, Ty M., who had moved to Los Angeles, was drinking himself into one predicament after another. So the lawyer sent him the manuscript of the Big Book. Ty gobbled it up, saying it was the "first time he'd ever seen something that understood him—who he was and why he drank." However, lacking face-to-face contact with another alcoholic and without meetings, he didn't stop drinking. Although his wife, Kaye, did not read the book, she was impressed with her husband's reaction and wired the New York office for the location of an AA meeting. They replied, "There is no group west of Akron, Ohio."

So Kaye and Ty took off to Akron, where Ty put himself under the tutelage of Dr. Bob and the group there. Kaye went on to New York to meet Bill W., who gave her a copy of the newly published Big Book. She also attended her first AA meeting, which so impressed her that she returned to California determined to "beat the drum for Alcoholics Anonymous." The time was early December 1939.

Through probation officers who themselves had been trying to help alcoholics, Kaye rounded up the names of a handful of prospects. In addition, two New York AA members who had been given Kaye's phone number by Bill W., were visiting Los Angeles. Kaye decided to have an AA meeting, which took place in her home on Benecia Street in Westwood on December 19, 1939. Present were four nonalcoholics (Kaye and three social workers), the two New York visitors (Chuck and Lee T.), and nine alcoholic prospects—fifteen in all. Kaye wired news of the meeting to Bill W. in New York.

But there was still no alcoholic-to-alcoholic language of the heart; and several subsequent meetings were rather disorganized, so the alcoholics attending did not stay sober. Kaye finally gave up, feeling she was a failure. In the words of Bill W., "That first candle at Los Angeles was flickering, but it never quite went out."

The man who set it blazing again was at that time living in Denver: Mort J., a stockbroker and "a violent drunk, a blackout drunk, a geographic drunk." On one of his repeated hospitalizations, his doctor had shown him a copy of the Big Book. He had ordered a copy for himself but never sobered up enough to read it. Instead, he embarked on a traveling binge that lasted several weeks, ending up in Palm Springs, California. In a hotel room there, rum-sick and shaking, he finally picked the book out of his suitcase and read it all the way through in one sitting. Then he fell into a deep sleep. On awakening, he ate a hearty breakfast (his first in weeks) and read the book a second time. He never had another drink.

Mort moved from Denver to Los Angeles. From Ruth Hock at the AA office in New York, he obtained the name and phone number of Kaye M. as a contact. Calling on her, he asked, "When is the A.A. meeting?"

"There aren't any meetings anymore," she replied bitterly. "The A.A. members are all drunk."

"Well, I want to get in touch with them," Mort exclaimed. "Do you have their names?"

"You're wasting your time," Kaye said, "but there they are." She pointed to her wastebasket, where she had just thrown her index cards of inquiries and prospects. Mort fished them out and departed. He noticed that one address was in the vicinity, so he walked there and rang the bell. It was answered by Cliff W., whose wife, Dorothe, had read of AA and written to New York for help. Although Cliff had no desire to stop drinking, he listened as his visitor told of his last roaring drunk and of the need to carry the message to stay sober. Would Cliff W. come to a meeting if one could be organized? Cliff, fascinated by now with this Harvard-educated, soft-spoken, well-dressed person, said he would.

For five dollars, Mort rented a large room on the mezzanine of the Cecil Hotel on Main Street in the skid row district. He then got in touch with the men who had failed to sober up at Kaye's meetings and also got the L.A. *Daily News* to mention the meeting, which was held on a Friday night in March 1940. Besides Mort and Cliff, about ten men showed up. Mort didn't know how an AA meeting should be conducted. There were no coffee or doughnuts. After Mort opened the meeting and shared his own experience (he had not had a drink in five months), he thought it might be helpful to read from the chapter in the Big Book entitled "How It Works." He opened the book and began reading, "Rarely have we seen a person fail. . . ." And thus began the practice of reading a portion of chapter 5 at all AA meetings in southern California, which later spread to the rest of California and subsequently throughout the West, and then to AA gatherings throughout the world. From this tiny root, AA slowly began to grow in Los Angeles. As the word spread and tireless, diligent Twelfth Step work produced results, the Friday night meeting at the Cecil Hotel increased in attendance and eventually branched out.

It was to this meeting that Sybil Maxwell came.

She was born Sybil Doris Adams on May 20, 1908, in the

small oil town of Simmons, Texas, which didn't consist of much besides a store, a hotel, a schoolhouse, and a church. Her parents, though quite poor, were hardworking, kind people who were against drinking or smoking. She also had a brother, ten years older, named Herman but called Tex, whom she adored. As a young child, Sybil was timid and easily frightened. She remembered a tornado when she was about five, which tore through the town and blew her house away. Her mother and father threw a blanket over her head and ran through the storm to shelter in another house. "We were running through a forest of mesquite brush, and all I could see was my mother's feet," she recalled. "I was scared."

They put the children on pallets on the floor, with a quilt for the smaller babies. Sybil lay there shivering and shaking, with little comfort from her mother, who was near hysterics herself. "She was a saintly, sweet woman," mused Sybil, "but nervous and emotional." The tornado experience had such a lasting impact on the young girl that years later, living in California, when the wind blew the trees, she would run to her mother and ask, "Is the big wind going to blow again." And her mother would say, "No, honey, you don't have to worry."

Her older brother, Tex, was a source of strength for young Sybil. When she was five and he was fifteen, he would hold her and rock her to sleep. Tex had joined the army in World War 1 and was reported missing. After a year without word, the family concluded he was dead. But when Sybil was thirteen, her mother got word that her son was alive and living in Los Angeles. The family immediately pulled up stakes and moved to California.

Sybil felt she was a misfit in California. As a young teen, she affected the flapper makeup that was the rage among her peers: heavy white powder on her face, with two big red spots of rouge, lots of lipstick, and black eyebrows. Her hair fell to her knees. "I must have looked like a circus freak or something like that," wailed Sybil. "I was in eighth grade out there in Los Angeles, and the other kids laughed at me. I had trouble making friends, being shy and timid by nature, but also my papa wouldn't let boys even walk home with me, let alone go to parties. I just wasn't allowed to do anything, and I knew I didn't belong anywhere.

"So naturally I started drinking at a very early age, against my better judgment, full of shame and remorse because of Papa's teachings. He was a good man. When I was fifteen, I got drunk one night, passed out, and had to be carried home and put to bed in my mother's bed. I cried the next day and promised that it would never happen again—and I meant it. But I didn't know myself, I didn't know the disease of alcoholism. The next Saturday night the kids handed me a bottle and I drank it. And I continued to do that through a couple of semesters of high school, and I stayed drunk through seventeen years of failed marriages and more jobs than I can count."

As her parents were still poor, Sybil went to work at an early age. Dropping out of high school, she took a secretarial course and was hired as a secretary. It was the first in a long list of jobs. At various times and not necessarily in order, she was a real estate broker, a taxi driver, a bootlegger, an itinerant farm worker picking fruit in northern California, the editor of a magazine for pet owners, and a salesperson several times. "I didn't mind working," she asserted, "but I never seemed to get anywhere. I was just on a treadmill because of booze."

Sybil's first marriage was to a sailor—"not a bad man"—with whom she had a child, a baby girl. She said to herself, "I've got a *real* reason now not to drink. I have a baby! A pure, innocent little baby! I will never drink again!" But she drank worse than ever. The result was that her parents took the child from her.

She and her sailor husband hitchhiked out of town, up toward Bakersfield where grapes were to be picked. They dreamed that if they got away from their city friends, they would quit drinking and stay sober; they would go back and get the baby from her parents, find an apartment, and have a happy home.

They located a grape-picking job near the little town of Arvon. At sundown, after working hard all day, they gathered around a campfire with fifteen or twenty college students who had summer jobs in the vineyards.

It was a happy crowd, and Sybil felt real hope. They began singing and harmonizing as they toasted hot dogs and marshmallows over the fire, and soon two or three jugs were passed around the circle. As Sybil saw one of the bottles approaching, she knew she was going to drink it and get drunk all over again. What am I doing here? she cried to herself. However, she did take a pull from the jug, and another, and another. Not being able to help herself or stand herself, she rose and ran down the long row of grape arbors, unable to stop crying.

Nearby, she heard the sounds of heavenly music, which at first she thought must be a hallucination. But as she ran toward it, she realized it was real singing coming from a revival tent. She had been taken to revivals as a child in Texas. "Just as I parted the flap of the tent," she related, "the music stopped. The hymn was finished. There was a deadly hush as the preacher looked back at me—and so did the two hundred or so other people, probably everybody in that little town, staring at me as I swayed back and forth, dirt on my face, tearstains on my cheeks. The preacher broke the silence, saying, 'Turn to page 239 and start singing. If anyone here wants to be saved, you come forward and I will pray for you.' Well, that was me. I went all the way down while the people were singing. The preacher put his hand out and placed it on my head, and I threw up all over him. It was so terrible! I was so ashamed, I couldn't bring myself to tell anyone about it until I got into Alcoholics Anonymous eleven years later."

The next morning, Sybil hitchhiked back to Los Angeles, back to her mother's house, back to her baby. That was the end of her marriage to the sailor. Her brother, Tex, had a speakeasy down on skid row, and to make some money to take to her mother to support the child, she went into the bootlegging business with him. That lasted until the police raided the speakeasy and put it out of business. So she went across the street to a taxi-dance hall where she went to work.

One night a rich, handsome stranger walked in and bought dance tickets with Sybil for the whole night. During intermission he bought several pitchers of beer (the girls got a dollar for every pitcher their partner bought), and she told him her sad story. At the end, he said, "Little girl, you don't belong in a place like this. You say you want to quit drinking and you want to have a home and you want to take care of your child. Well, marry me! And I will take care of all of this. If we get married and providing you don't drink any more, I will adopt your child and be a good father to her."

And that is what happened. Sybil had a lovely home and a housekeeper and a car, and she grew to love her husband dearly, for he was a fine man. She had everything she had ever dreamed of, but being an alcoholic, she found herself drunker than ever within a week or two. She didn't know why she continued to drink, and her shame and remorse over it were terrible.

In 1939, while visiting her mother-in-law in San Diego, she picked up a copy of *Liberty* magazine with the words *Alcoholics and God* on the cover, referring to an article about AA inside. She read it and found it fascinating, but did nothing about it. As she continued her downward spiral of drinking, she thought back many times and wished she had the magazine she had left at her mother-in-law's apartment, but it was too late.

God gave her another chance eighteen months later. Sybil got roaring drunk and drove alone on the ridge route to Fresno and beyond. To this day she has no idea why. As she turned around and started back to Los Angeles, she realized she was too drunk to drive. Ahead she spotted a hitchhiker with his thumb out. So she stopped to let him in and asked, "Can you drive?" He said he could, so she said, "Well, get behind the wheel and take me to Los Angeles. I'm going to lie down in the back seat and grab some sleep."

Her driver woke her when they arrived in the city at Sixth and Hill Streets and turned her car back to her. She thought a Turkish bath might straighten her out before she headed home to the inevitable explanations and excuses, so she stopped at a newsstand to pick up a magazine before heading for the Turkish bath. Afterward, as she was cooling off, she picked up the magazine and looked at it. It was *The Saturday Evening Post* dated March 1, 1941, containing Jack Alexander's famous article about Alcoholics Anonymous. Although Sybil didn't read it all, she was intrigued with the photos of real alcoholics, with whom she identified. On impulse, she asked the attendant for writing materials and composed a letter to the AA office in New York. In it, she told them she was a woman alcoholic who desperately needed help and if, by any chance, she could obtain it from them, she would catch the next plane back. She mailed the letter immediately and then headed for home to face the music.

A short time later, she received a reply from Ruth Hock, who told her she didn't have to come back to New York to get help because a small group in California now met in the Elks Chapel across from Westlake Park (later renamed MacArthur Park) every Friday night. She told Sybil that there was a gal (Marty M.) back East who was sober in AA but there were no women members yet in California, so she should go down there and meet the AA's.

On Friday, March 23, Sybil got her nonalcoholic husband, Dick Maxwell, to drive her down to the meeting. She had no idea what to expect, of course, but was excited about the prospect. Having been drunk almost continuously, she shook so hard she couldn't comb her hair, so she had tucked it under a big red turban.

At the meeting, ten or twelve men were seated at a table, and three or four women were seated against the wall, which puzzled her. A man at the end of the table stood up and said (Sybil swore she remembered his exact words): "This is the regular meeting of Alcoholics Anonymous in California. We are a band of ex-drunks who have gathered together to obtain and maintain our sobriety on an all-time basis with no mental reservations whatsoever." (Sybil thought, "What an order! I can't go through with it.") Then the speaker added, "As is our custom before the regular meeting starts, we have to ask the women to leave." The other women rose and went out to the lobby, and Sybil followed them, holding her hands over her face and crying.

Her husband, Dick, remained in the meeting, where the members, assuming *he* was the alcoholic prospect, focused on him with advice and slogans. Dick was completely confused, as he had scarcely had more than a beer in his life. Meanwhile, Sybil cooled her heels in the lobby with the other women for literally hours. (As some of the men had driven long distances to attend the only AA meeting, it ran long, with no set closing time.) In her booze-clouded mind, she pictured the group discussing her case and deciding what medicine to give her, so when Dick appeared, she said, "Well, give me my prescription." He replied, "They don't know you're alive. They just went on and on bragging about their drinking until I was about to walk out, when they jumped up and said the Lord's Prayer, and here I am."

Sybil headed immediately for the nearest bar and got drunk. As she left about 2:00 A.M., scarcely able to stand up, she remembered that at the bottom of her letter, Ruth Hock had written, "If you need help call Cliff W." and had given his phone number. So she found a phone and called him in the middle of the night, saying, "Send your A.A. ambulance and pick me up!"

"You're drunk," he said.

"Of course I am," she replied.

"You didn't tell us you were an alcoholic. We thought you were one of the wives. If you had identified yourself as an alcoholic, you would have been welcome as the flowers in May." He told her he couldn't come to get her, but told her to come back next week. "I'll call Frank and Mort," he added, "and pave the way so they'll know they have a woman alcoholic. Believe me, Sybil, we need you all right."

The next Friday, she learned why. The leaders of the meeting were Mort J., who had originally brought the Big Book, and

Frank R., a dedicated and tireless Twelfth Stepper. After opening the meeting, Frank disappeared for a moment and returned with a carton full of letters bundled into bunches of twenty to fifty envelopes each. He explained that these were all inquiries and calls for help from people in southern California who had written to Alcoholics Anonymous in New York as a result of the same Jack Alexander article in *The Saturday Evening Post*. Ruth Hock had sent them to the Los Angeles group to make the Twelfth Step calls. Frank cried out, "Here they are! Here they are! If any of you jokers have been sober over fifteen minutes, come on up here and get these letters. We've got to get as many of these drunks as we can in here by next Friday, or they may die!"

With that, Frank began to parcel out the bundles by area. Those from Riverside County went to Kent H.; The Beaches were taken by Corny O'N.; Orange County was Mel T. area; and so on. When he reached the bottom, Frank held up the final bundle and said, "I saved this bunch to last because they are all from women alcoholics, and we have a woman alcoholic now. Sybil Maxwell, come on up. I am going to put you in charge of all the women."

Sybil's first thought was like a flash: *in charge* of all the women! Sybil's *in charge!* She loved that idea! Then she realized how shaky she was, with a nervous tic, so she looked up at the big leader and said, "I can't, sir."

"Why not?"

"You said I have to make all those calls by next Friday, or somebody might die. Well, I'll be drunk by next Friday unless you have some magic that will change everything so I can stay sober. I've never been able to, and that's why I'm here. I've just got to drink to live, to get the relief I need. Unless you can help me right now, tonight, I can't take on a job that is a matter of life and death."

"Well," he said, "I'll tell you something. It's not magic. And it's not coming from me. . . . It's coming from this Big Book here that tells how the founders of A.A. did it. And it says right in here that when all other measures fail, working with another alcoholic will save the day. That's what you will be doing, Sybil, working with other alcoholics.

"You just get in your car and take your mind off yourself. Think about someone sicker than you are. Go see her and hand her the letter she wrote, and say: 'I wrote one like this last week, and they answered mine and told me to come and see you. If you have a drinking problem like I have and if you want to get sober as bad as I do, you come with me and we'll find out together how to do it.'" Then he added, "Don't add another word to that, because you don't know anything yet. Just go get 'em."

And Sybil said, "I believe I could do that."

It worked and she never had another drink. Cliff W. became her sponsor, with Frank R. as a co-sponsor. When the first General Service Conference of AA was held in New York in 1951, Cliff attended as the delegate for California, later becoming the Pacific Regional Trustee. Through him, Sybil became aware of the Third Legacy of Service and what was happening in other parts of the country.

Sybil's brother, Tex, also an alcoholic, joined AA at her second meeting. A big, energetic, outgoing man, he immediately became involved and active in his own right, as well as being an immense help to his more timid and fearful sister. When he had been sober six weeks, he started another group, one in which everyone was invited to participate with three- to five-minute talks. The mother group immediately got a big resentment and excommunicated him. He returned to the original group the next Friday, along with Sybil, and was told, "We have taken further measures. One of our members is an attorney, and we have drawn up incorporation papers. We'll be incorporated as A.A. for California." Tex roared with laughter and said, "You may as well incorporate a sunset. You can't do it. A.A. is going to grow and nobody can stop it."

He appointed Sybil coffeemaker and greeter for the new group, so she would have to meet and shake hands with everyone. And he finally made his sister deliver her first shaky talk. He told her, "I've known you since you were born, Sis. You are so stubborn, you'll stay sober all right, but you'll be the most miserable person in the United States if you don't participate in A.A. and get active. Please, next week let me call on you, and you speak up. Let the other people get to know you, they are your friends."

When Bill and Lois W. made their first visit to Los Angeles in 1943, Sybil was one of the delegation of local AA's who met them at the Town House hotel, where they were staying. Later she met Marty M., her counterpart as the first woman to sober up in AA in the East.

Much later, when Sybil's beloved Tex died, she was devastated. She couldn't cry, couldn't cope, couldn't let anyone comfort her. Even her faith in her Higher Power was shaken. She finally wrote Bill W. a letter pouring out her overwhelming grief and crying out on the page, "What am I going to do, Bill? I don't crave a drink, but I think I'm going to die unless I get some answers." Bill replied with a letter that she said "saved my life then, and saved my life many times since." As she remembers Bill's letter, in paraphrase, it read:

> In God's house there are many mansions. And somehow or other, I see Tex sitting out on the porch in the sunlight of one of those mansions, talking to another drunk, and I believe that's okay. When my time comes, I wish to do the same. But, now let's get to you, my dear. Your letter has stirred me more than anything in recent years. But I will tell you, Syb, that life is nothing but a looong day in school, and some of our lessons are hard, and some of our lessons are easy. And it doesn't matter much what happens to us. It is what we do with our experience that counts. Keep on passing along what you have learned. Pass on what you have learned, for what more can one alcoholic ask of another?
> Affectionately,
> Bill

Soon after Sybil joined AA, the group relieved her of her job of being "in charge" of the women. But immediately and increasingly as AA spread rapidly in the Los Angeles area, she went to meetings, meetings, meetings, plunged into Twelfth Step work and sponsorship of her own, and consequently was seldom home. Dick Maxwell—the nonalcoholic "wonderful man" who had rescued her from the taxi-dance hall, who had driven her to her first AA meeting, and who had provided her with a beautiful home, a Packard car, a housekeeper, and, above all, with love—felt abandoned and lonely. He began to complain, "Honey, you've been sober awhile now. Do you have to keep on going out all the time? Can't we have any kind of home life?"

Sybil would reply, "Oh, darling, I promise I'll cut down on meetings—but I just don't see how I can." When she came home from meetings, he would greet her with his arms folded belligerently or seated in a rocker with his jaw jutted out, sulking. For her part, Sybil felt more and more guilty but reasoned that if she left AA, she would drink, and if she drank, she would die. Her husband couldn't understand this. He had grown to hate AA and refused to read the Big Book or discuss the Twelve Steps.

Finally he announced one night that he had a solution to their marriage problems, which was for her to go back to drinking and he would be responsible for taking care of her again. "I'll have you home more then that I do now," he concluded. After he retired that night, she went upstairs, packed a suitcase, crept quietly back down, and left. She caught a bus downtown to Adams and Figueroa, where she rented a housekeeping room with a gas hotplate and a bath down the hall for nine dollars a week. She went to work on the L.A. *Times* newspaper to support herself. "A.A. just had to come first with me," she says.

Sybil was perhaps best known as the first executive secretary of the Los Angeles Central Office of AA, a position she held for twelve years. These were probably the most turbulent years for AA in the City of Angels, a period of unbridled growth, of proliferation of meetings, of troubles with clubs and other "outside issues," and the kind of disunity and controversy within the groups that led to the Twelve Traditions. In fact, Sybil remembers that she was executive secretary when the Traditions came along. The groups regarded them either with opposition or indifference, and the Central Office couldn't sell many copies of the Traditions pamphlet. She credits Cliff W. with going around to all the groups and explaining their value, keeping it simple, so that the Traditions gradually became accepted. "Now they have caught on to the point that we read them at nearly all group meetings," she exclaimed. "Well, I tell you!"

While she was there she saw the number of groups and meetings in greater Los Angeles explode from a handful to thousands every week. Today, women not only constitute a healthy proportion of those attending every regular AA group, but there are countless women's groups and women's conferences. And when it is pointed out that the mighty tidal wave of women sober in AA all began with the tiny trickle of Twelfth Step calls made by Sybil Maxwell, then the only sober woman west of the Mississippi, Sybil just shakes her head.

Understandably, she took a dim view of the rigidity that has crept into the requirements to make Twelfth Step calls. Some central offices and intergroups have rules that six months or even a year of sobriety are necessary before calling on a newcomer. "When I was at the Central Office, we just used our judgment to match up the person calling for help with the member we assigned to call on him or her. It is important when you are new in A.A. to go out and talk to the sick drunk. Just take somebody with you and keep it simple. If you don't get prospects from the Central Office, look around the meeting room. There is always the forgotten man or woman, nervous and scared, who would love to have you come up and shake hands. Just feel what the new person is feeling. It kept me sober, it kept my brother Tex sober, and it will keep you sober when all other measures fail."

Sybil's fifth and enduring marriage is to Bob C., whom she met in Alcoholics Anonymous, a high-spirited, warm, and loving man fourteen years her junior in age and twenty-two years junior in sobriety. "Bob and I are very happy," she declared. "This has been the best years of my life." They have been enthusiastic meeting-goers and enjoy an incredibly wide circle of friends in the fellowship. Bob said, "I once asked my sponsor, 'How long do you have to go to A.A.?' He said, 'You *have* to go to A.A. until you *want* to go to A.A., and then you'll never *have* to go to A.A. again." To which, Sybil added her own exclamation point, "Ain't it the truth!"

During her tenure at the Central Office, Sybil became greatly in demand as a speaker. Gradually she lost her natural timidity and fear of speaking and enjoyed carrying her unique message to AA conferences, conventions, anniversaries, and gatherings all over the United States. Bob C. said, "I didn't join A.A. to be a public speaker," but he accompanied his wife and enjoyed the adulation she received.

Nowhere was this more evident than at Montreal, Canada, in 1985, when—most appropriately—she was honored at the Fiftieth Anniversary International Convention of Alcoholics Anonymous. With the death of Marty M. five years before, Sybil was, pure and simple, the longest-sober living woman in AA in all the world. And among the fifty thousand AA's and their families who packed the vast Olympic Stadium on the opening night of the convention, fifty-three countries were represented to help her celebrate. She shared the platform with such notables as Lois W., then ninety-three; Dr. Bob's two children, Bob Smith Jr. and Sue Smith Windows; Dr. Jack Norris, chairman of the General Service Board for twenty-seven years; the family of Dave B., the founder of AA in Canada, who had died only two weeks before; and many others, including Ruth Hock, Bill's and AA's first secretary, who had replied to Sybil's call for help.

When she was introduced, Sybil C., a tiny figure in that vast stadium, rose and recounted, in her talk, the colorful beginnings of AA in Los Angeles, in which she had played such a pivotal role. As she turned to resume her seat, the crowd of nearly fifty thousand rose as one to give her a standing ovation that seemed as if it would never stop.

Ester Elasardi

As unaccustomed as I am to public speaking, I don't think I can get started unless I introduce myself as we always do in AA in Texas. I am Ester, and I'm an alcoholic, and for following the program of AA to the best of my ability, I was dry twelve years yesterday.

But I know [that] the only way that I can maintain my sobriety is to remember always what I was like twelve years ago this weekend. I am shaking like a leaf all over, but at least I know where I am. If I continue today what I have done in these last twelve years, I will stay sober until I die.

I didn't know that when I came in. I knew that I wanted to try AA, but that it would work—well, I didn't think anything would work. I think that we have to do time in AA before we realize that it is going to work for us.

I wish I could tell you how and why AA works, but I don't know. I only know that it does, if you desire it with your whole heart and without reservations. I think that none of us comes to AA until we have tried everything we can think of. I thought that if only I had found AA years before I did that I would have saved myself much of the shame and degradation of the last few years.

But as I have grown in AA I realize that a person with as much self-will as I have and as hard a head and as diseased an ego had to try everything I could think of and bump my head against every stone wall before I was ready to come in. The only thing I have really and truly to offer you is my own story and tell you just what style of drunk I was. It is kind of hard standing up here sober and smiling, to think that I was ever in the horrible shape that I was.

I came from a family where alcohol was socially accepted. I lived in New Orleans, Louisiana. There were cocktail hours and barrooms. Alcohol was served openly. I am Episcopalian, and we bless our sacraments with wine. I can't remember a dinner at home that we didn't have white wine or claret on the table. When cocktails were served when I was growing up, the family used to drink sherry every now and then. And we always had cordials after dinner, and my sister and my brother and I loved crème de menthe, which was like a snowball—scraped ice with the green mint sucked through a straw. I would have claret maybe with my dinner, but with a lot of ice and about two tablespoons of claret, with a little water and some sugar. Drinking it with your meal, you didn't feel the effect of it.

The first time that I ever realized what alcohol could do for me was when I married. I never thought that I was maladjusted. I know now that I was, in spite of coming from a happy home—I had an indulgent father and everything. Yet I was extremely sensitive and so self-conscious that I just hurt all over all the time.

On the night that I married I had a big church wedding, but I couldn't enjoy anything. There were friends like this girl down from St. Louis for my wedding. I was scared to death that my dress wasn't going to be right, that the church wasn't going to be filled, that I would fall flat on my face walking up the aisle. God, I was frightened to death that I wasn't going to be a prima donna at the place where I should be a prima donna. In those days and time—I've been married twenty-nine years—you didn't carry a little bouquet. I carried these great big bouquets like a funeral spray, and you didn't have your picture taken until just before you went to the church.

They are kind to brides now. I think they have their pictures taken two or three days ahead of time.

With being as self-conscious as I was, I had to be dressed about two or three hours before going to church and pose for these pictures, holding this huge enormous thing. I would love for you all to see those pictures sometime. I look like somebody was sticking me in the back with a sword. About the time we were getting ready to go to the church, I really was in a terrific state. My father loved it, and he turned to the servants and said, "Miss Effie is about to faint. Get her something to drink." The servants returned with our old cook, and we had the waiters from the club there and all. Our old cook was one of the guests at the wedding, and she liked to drink. The poor lady ran into the kitchen, and she came back with a water glass half full of something, and I drank it down. The church is just three blocks from the house. It was February and it was cold. I got right into the car, and they drove me over. As soon as I hit the church, they started the band. And baby, when I hit that aisle, that whiskey went right through me. Never have I felt so good! I walked up that aisle just like Mae West in her prime! I don't think I was conscious of what happened to me.

That drink was wonderful for me. It was medicinal that night and on many occasions after that. I landed at ease in situations socially, and it helped just fine. But somewhere along the line it backfired. When I passed that line, something just went haywire. I got to depend on it, so I could do nothing without it.

It was in about 1931 that my drinking first caused comment, yet no one was perturbed about it, except my family, because I decided that after seven years of marriage, I would divorce my husband. So, the night that I married, I was very hardheaded and probably a problem at home. My father must have told my husband, "Thank goodness she's off my hands, but you sure have got your hands full!" The poor man really did. But anyhow, I decided to divorce him, and I did in July. It doesn't take you long to get a divorce in Dallas, where I lived at the time. I went on home. I really was free, white, and over twenty-one, and I had a time. I put my poor mother and father through the agony of the damned. Finally I couldn't stand living with them watching everything I did. My husband was coming down, and I had no feeling of security or anything else. It was a very asinine thing that I did, when I did get the divorce, but finally I went back to Dallas and remarried him.

We moved up to Tulsa, where all the boys and Ester got drunk. The wives didn't, and they would talk about it.

That went on for about three years, and then we moved back to Dallas. Then I started drinking heavily. And Frank would come home day after day and find me passed out. Or he'd leave on a trip, and every time he came home, I was passed out.

Finally he said to me one morning, "Ester, why do you do that?"

And I said, "Well, I don't know why. But I have been reading a lot about psychiatry and I thought well, maybe if I talked to a psychiatrist, he could find out some mental quirk and put me straight, and then I could drink like a lady."

So Frank said, "Would you like to talk to a doctor and find out who to go to here?" So Frank left with my problem, and he got the doctor. I was drunk when they came home.

They didn't want to take an alcoholic at first—they didn't call me that—because I was drinking too much. But Frank told the doctor that I wanted to talk to any doctor I could get. So I got drunker and drunker, and then I woke up in the booby hatch.

I had never been on the inside of an insane asylum. I had really thought that I was going to a private hospital. But I woke up in this bare room, with nothing around it but these bars. They wouldn't even let me smoke, and they treated me like, well, like I was nuts! Of course I was. Look how sick I was! Right away I got furious, and I would not even talk to the doctor in the place. I wanted to come home. They kept me there. I was supposed to stay a month, but they only kept me for seventeen days. I was terribly screwed up when I went in, but I came out much worse, because I could not identify myself with the people whom I was with. There was no understanding, and I couldn't stand confinement—it was all these things. I had hysterics on the seventeenth day, for the first and only time in my life.

So the doctor let me go home on one condition. He asked me if I would cooperate with him after I went home and if I would let a trained nurse stay with me for at least two weeks. So, to all those conditions, regardless of the cost or anything else, I said yes. I was so happy over getting home and all the changes overnight. I was crazy about Doctor Happy—his name was Dr. Witt, but I had been calling him "Dr. Happy."

I said for years after—this was in 1936 or 1937—that I cooperated with that man 100 percent, which is how dishonest I was with myself. I answered all his questions and told him what I wanted to believe about myself. The questions he asked me that I didn't answer honestly—well, I thought they were none of his damn business! I could see no reason for them, or that they had any relation to this problem of getting drunk every now and then. It drove me further into this psychosis that I had or whatever you want to call it.

And I hated, oh, deep down in my heart I resented that Frank had done this to me. I didn't know where I was going, and life was pretty miserable.

About this time it was Christmas, after I had been in Dr. Witt's place. After six months of being under his care, we decided that there wasn't anything more to do. Every time I got drunk he'd send me to a nursing home, and they sent me back to that hospital. I think I disrupted the hospital. But when we got back from Christmas, my husband had given me a carpetbag. Frank had to go to New York. Because I had a daughter, I just had a duplex, and I thought, "If only we had a house. A duplex or an apartment isn't any place to raise a daughter." So I went on this American treatment. He even had people come out there and tell me what kind of a room I was going to have, and that he could come see me and that my dog could come see me, and all the things that I couldn't have when I was in the booby hatch. So I chose this American treatment. I guess there are plenty other graduates of this American treatment. There are no easy ways to sober up, without a doubt, but that is the most excruciating. It's the ERC treatment. So I took that three times, and that didn't work.

Then our minister at the church tried to help me. There was a doctor in the congregation who was pretty interested in me.

He thought that it was a vitamin deficiency, so I went down to him for quite a few months, and he would stick me full of all this stuff, medicine experiments. After each session I'd go across the street to this little triangle drugstore, and I would take a glass of beer or two beers and stop at the liquor store and get myself a pint, and I got home. You know those vitamins just don't keep you sober. Too bad!

Finally, in 1940, we went down to Houston. My husband thought maybe a change of environment, a new town and everything else, would help me be all right. We moved down in 1940, and that year was my last. There was nothing else left to try. We had tried everything. So the only thing I could do was to call the doctor to help sober me up. I wouldn't go to hospitals because I wanted my dog there, and so I would have to have a trained nurse. When I had a hangover, I was so sick, and the dog would come, and he was the only one who would have anything to do with me. It was a tragic thing.

I have told you some of the funny things, but not much of the pain and degradation. I fell down and knocked out my front teeth. I dropped a two-quart hot water bottle on my big toe and I couldn't walk. I had it in a cast, and the doctor left the cast on three weeks longer than it should have been because he never found me sober so he could take it off. He was afraid that as soon as he took it off, I'd break it again. My dress caught fire on the bathroom heater, and I didn't sit down for three months. It was one thing after another.

So finally one afternoon, in April of 1941, I got as drunk as a skunk, and all of you who know me, know that I do not walk straight sober. You should see me when I'm drunk. And I was drunk as I could be. It was time for Nappy's afternoon walk. Out I went, weaving with the dog, and a patrol car passed me, and he must have been able to tell the condition I was in and decided to take me home. When he picked me up, I must have gotten kind of sassy and told him that they couldn't do that to Mrs. A.; they took my dog home and brought me to jail. As I said before, I don't like to be fenced in. Those bars. You don't get hotel service. Nothing. They told my husband they couldn't leave me at home, because there was no one there. I was in such terrible condition, they didn't know what I would do to myself. They realized that there was no place for me, but told Frank to wait a while before he got me, because when they called him to come over for me, I was knocking a tin cup up against the wall. I wanted some cigarettes and some service, which I didn't get.

I was in just a few hours, but somewhere during that time, I remember going back on that bunk and crying my eyes out. I think that that is when I hit bottom. I went completely haywire on the inside. Yet still I had this defensive front. Many people say, "He doesn't want to sober up," or "She doesn't want to sober up." Stop and think of your behavior. My husband couldn't tell that I wanted to do something about my drinking by looking at me. I was as defiant as anybody could be—because I was too scared. I didn't know which way to turn. Finally, I was walked down the stairs, and I looked out through these bars, and Frank had finally come for me. I looked at him and I said, "Don't you sign anything in this place." I was going to sue the city of Houston for what they did to me! But Frank turned around and looked at me, and he said, "Ester. Remember, you're in jail, not at home." My friends, I never want anybody to look at me like that again, with the contempt that was in his face and voice. Yet I had more contempt than he had. That was really bad, because just a week before, someone had sent him that *Saturday Evening Post* article on AA. There was some glimmer of hope in it for him, that there was something out there that maybe I could try. But he was frightened to death to give it to me because I resented everything that he said and did. So he waited another week or two. During that time I don't think I stayed sober.

He was out of town and had gotten home one night. I was drunk, and the next morning he came in my room, and he said, "Now Ester, I am not going to lecture you anymore, but I want you to read this article. If you want to try this thing, I'll go along with you. If you don't, you'll have to go home. I cannot sit by and watch you destroy yourself anymore." When he left I thought, "What is this crackpot thing?" I took two or three drinks so my eyes could focus, and I could see this small picture of this awful drunk. I don't know if any of you ever saw it. He couldn't get his hand around the glass, and he needed a shave. I shuddered when I looked at that. But from the very first paragraph on, something happened to me. I realized that other people in this world behaved and acted like I did, and that I was a sick person and suffering from an actual disease that had a name and symptoms, just like diabetes or TB. I realized I wasn't immoral, I wasn't mad, I wasn't vicious. Just for the feeling of relief, I wanted to know more about it. With that, for the first time I came to the realization that there was something horribly, horribly wrong with me. Up to that time I was so completely baffled by my behavior that I never stopped to think. As I said before, I don't know how or why AA works, but it was the first medium that ever reached me, and it reached me through this article. When Frank came home, I said, "I want to try this thing."

He said, "There's a post office box to write to in New York." I wrote on the Saturday. In fact, I was shaking so, I wanted my husband to write the letter. He said no; he had gotten enough out of it. This was something that I had to do all by myself. So I wrote this letter in my shaky handwriting, and in just one week, back came a letter with literature from New York. They sent me just the regular little letter they send to everybody, but along with it Ruth Hock wrote a little note in her hand, because she could read between the line that I really needed help. Her personal touch was something. That was on a Saturday. My husband was leaving town on Sunday night, and he said, "Let's wait until I get back, and I will go with you to see this man." I was sober that whole week, while I waited to hear about AA. I wanted to try it with my whole heart and soul because I had learned an awful lot about myself in that one article. Monday morning I was feeling like a million dollars, telling myself, "All you need is a half-pint of the White Swan." So I got a half-pint of White Swan, and at midnight I called the number of the man who had started the local group within the hospitals. They didn't know what to do. They were afraid to send me any of the men, so they made me stew in my own juice. Hell, I stayed drunk from Monday until Friday. And I call that my spell in AA. I am glad I had it then. In spite of knowing that my drunkenness was a symptom of the things that were wrong with me—that's what the article had told me, that I could never drink again—I couldn't yet feel right giving it up. But I was going to try, and I never want to forget that last drunk as long as I live. It was one of the worst I ever had. It was the first time in my life that I could not get a lift out of what I was drinking.

And so, on Friday night, May 16, at five minutes to six, I had half a water glass of White Swan gin, and that is when I asked God to help me.

I wish I could tell all of you what I think and feel about AA. But it is something I have experienced and could never put into words. I know that I only have a daily reprieve, that I must work at this as long as I live. I do know that it is only by working at it that I will stay sober and live a happy life. I think of the words of Dr. Bob and Bill. They are with me all the time. Dr. Bob said that love and service keep us dry. And Bill said always remember that our first duty is face-to-face help to the alcoholic who still suffers. Dr. Bob tells us our program is simple and not to louse it up. It is the last thing I ever heard him say.

I think there are some of us who at times try to read mysteries and complexities into the Steps, but they are not there. To me, AA is within the reach of every alcoholic. It can be achieved in any walk of life, because achievement is not ours, but God's. I would just like to leave you with a feeling—that there is no situation too difficult, none too desperate, no unhappiness too great to be overcome in this great lifesaving movement of Alcoholics Anonymous.

Sources:

AA convention tape, circa 1951.

Eve M.

EVEN TODAY, ALCOHOLICS ANONYMOUS OLD-TIMERS IN SOUTH AFRICA AND (THE FORMER) RHODESIA REMEMBER with love and gratitude the first American member of AA to visit their countries in July 1965. It was a woman named Eve M. on unpaid leave of absence from the staff at the General Service Office (GSO) in New York so that she might make this yearlong trip at her own expense, carrying the AA recovery message abroad with verve and enthusiasm.

Eve M.'s personal life rivals a romance novel: colorful, dramatic—and yes, miserable in the years of her worsening alcoholism. Balancing a busy family life, which included three marriages, children, and grandchildren, she put together fifty-three years of continuous sobriety in AA after she entered in 1944. She served as both a volunteer and a paid hand at two intergroups: New York in her early recovery and much later in Florida. She was a busy member of the GSO staff for eighteen years. Then, after her "retirement" at age sixty, she plunged into professional work in the alcoholism field as director of a local alcoholism council in Florida, an affiliate of the National Council on Alcoholism, the agency founded and headed by the legendary Marty Mann. There Eve engaged in programs beyond the scope and Traditions of AA.

Even before she became associated with the GSO staff, she was in demand as an exceptionally dynamic and effective speaker. As a staff member, she had a strong service message and was welcomed at area assemblies and state conferences, and was later a frequent keynoter at conventions, roundups, and every other kind of AA event. Even when she developed cancer in the late 1980s, her indomitable spirit prevailed, and from AA platforms she became as much an inspiration for her winning battle with cancer as for her recovery from alcoholism.

In her mid-eighties, Eve left Florida to enter a retirement home near her daughters, Ruth and Liz, in Rogers, Arkansas. But Eve found the home confining and moved out to live independently in a first-floor apartment where she could be more active. Her main frustration was that the limitations of age made traveling to AA conventions impractical; nor was she able to drive a car. Her daughter Ruth created a weekly meeting, and Sundays found Eve surrounded by the AA love which fed her soul. She died peacefully September 26, 1997.

Eve was born in New York City on March 5, 1908. She was the eldest of three daughters born to Alice and Arthur Goodrich. Her father, fascinated with theater, was a playwright and novelist of repute recognized in *Who's Who in America*. Her mother, also a noted artist, died when Eve was twelve. Her uncle Walter Hampden, one of the most celebrated actors of his day, lent a certain panache to the family. Eve always longed to equal her heritage.

Thus, from the beginning, Eve's life was a dichotomy. On the one hand, reared in a genteel household of books, theater, and good music and educated in private schools, she became an intellectual snob, scorning the people who were "in business." When Uncle Walter was opening in a Broadway production, the family would get a box, and the girls would invite several of their friends to attend and go backstage afterward to meet the cast. She also acquired a passion for the opera (which remained for life), listening to records of Puccini, Verdi, and others after school. And she gloried in the fact that Geraldine Farrar, *the* belle of the Metropolitan Opera at that time, was a friend of her father's.

On the other hand, Eve suffered feelings of inferiority, based on "lack": lack of wealth, lack of good looks, lack of charm. Everyone else, it seemed to her, had bigger homes, more servants, better clothes, and a car with chauffeur. The other girls seemed prettier, for Eve was tall and gangly (she stood five feet, eight and half inches tall at age fourteen) and developed "a high bridge to my nose, which was absolute anathema."

Her mother's death had a traumatic effect on Eve, on the threshold of her teens. "My memory of her is almost entirely gone," she muses. "It is as if I blocked my mother out of my life. I remember the funeral, but only as a drama that evoked everyone's sympathy for me. That evolved into terrible feelings of guilt as I grew older. 'What kind of monster am I,' I would think, 'to equate such a loss with my own ego?'"

Her father needed several months to face his loss, and her grandmothers took turns supervising the household. Finally, however, he engaged a housekeeper.

At twelve, Eve knew nothing about being a woman—nothing about the onset of her monthly menstrual periods, which she considered "unpleasant and dirty"; nothing about sex or birth; nothing, in fact, about boys. "I had a great yen for boys," she recalls, "but knew nothing about how to attract them or get along with them. My knowledge of social graces was zero." She already had theatrical ambitions, however, and got involved with the drama group at her school. She wasn't cast often, but when she was, she basked in the compliments and approval.

When it was time for college, her father took her by train up to Poughkeepsie to Vassar, where her mother had gone and where one of her mother's classmates was the current dean. Eve was excited at the prospect, confident that everything was going to be different, that she would "belong" and would be "big on campus." Once there, however, her innate feelings of inferiority surfaced. The other girls seemed better dressed, more sophisticated, and easy with one another. She knew she didn't belong after all and felt rejected and confused.

She tried to compensate by being aggressive and eager. She learned to play bridge, and over the bridge tables she was able to live vicariously her friends' weekends away from campus. "It seemed to me," she says, "they all had beaux and dates and knew how to handle any situation." Eve was occasionally asked on a blind date. This was the era of the rumble seat and the hip flask. She was frightened to drink for fear of losing control of herself, and she had never been kissed—so the dates were not a success.

Outwardly, she was living an active campus life: studying, attending classes, trying out for plays, playing bridge and field hockey. She had a wide circle of friends but was not a part of any group or clique. Inside, she was fearful, lonely, romantic, and incredibly naive. She fantasized that some magic outer force would somehow solve her problems.

Between her freshman and sophomore years, she made a trip to Europe arranged by her father. There were to be ten other young women in the tour group, accompanied by two chaperones and a male tour guide.

She envisioned that in Europe she would learn to drink like Europeans, graciously and properly, which would solve the problem of coping with rumble seats and hip flasks. So she dreamed of becoming the belle of the dance floor, bowing to the applause after a brilliant performance on an imaginary stage, wooed by myriad handsome lovers.

They sailed on the old SS *Caledonia*, and as the ship passed the twelve-mile limit—and hence became free from Prohibition in the States—the steward began to serve drinks. Eve ordered an orange blossom because she heard someone else say it. After the first few sips she recalls, "No longer did I need to seek answers in Europe, for I had found the magic I was seeking in that first drink. Suddenly, my shyness was gone. My height and my awkwardness disappeared. Somehow I became okay. I felt that I 'belonged' and my aching emptiness had been filled. The fear and guilt were gone, replaced miraculously by confidence and hope. With this magic I knew I would be able to cope from now on." Europe was almost an anticlimax.

Back at college, she was more at ease and content. Her father, a trustee of Wesleyan University, was also teaching a course in drama there. Trying hard to be helpful, as always, he arranged a weekend at Wesleyan for Eve, with a young man to be her date. Frightened and uncomfortable to be paired with a fellow who really had no choice, she ditched him and joined forces with two attractive young men who were dateless. It turned into a drinking weekend, topped off with a golf game at 6:30 A.M., played in evening clothes. More important, one of the boys, Chris, became her boyfriend.

Back at Vassar, she was now "one of the group" as they waited around the mailbox for letters from their "men." She began to party at other campuses and on occasional weekends in New York, with drinking always part of the picture. In her junior year, she was making plans for the junior prom with Chris as her date. She had even had a daring prom gown made in bright red crushed velvet for the affair. Then the bottom dropped out of her world as Chris wrote he couldn't make it. Angry and in despair, Eve wanted to drink. Remembering two freshman girls in her dorm who had frequented a speakeasy in Wappingers Falls, about ten miles from the campus, she looked them up, and the three of them found a ride to the speakeasy, returning undetected, as they believed.

A few days later, Chris called to say he could come to the prom after all, so the event turned out to be a triumph for Eve. Her glory was short-lived, however, because the trip to the speakeasy had been discovered and she was in deep trouble. Drinking was not only strictly forbidden while on campus, it was also illegal. Facing possible expulsion, she was relieved to be allowed to return the next fall, but on probation. Meanwhile, she was ordered off campus before sundown. "You can take this semester's exams in September," the authorities told her. "Your father is waiting outside."

Her father, despite being a New Englander with high personal standards of conduct, was surprisingly compassionate. Hiding his disappointment with his daughter, he said, "The past is past. Let's see what you want to do now."

What she wanted to do was to be on the stage. Always starstruck, she longed to be an actress, glamorous, famous, recognized for her great talent. Howard Lindsay, director of one of the oldest summer theaters, was a friend of her father's, so it was arranged for Eve to apprentice with his stock company in Maine. "That summer," she says, "was the happiest and most idyllic in my life." All thoughts of returning to college left her. She fell in love not only with the theater, but with the leading man, Jimmy, eighteen years her senior, a gentle, kind person.

On Maine summer days they would drive in his Studebaker to a picnic ground, or after performances in the evening to a secluded spot. Despite Eve's passionate willingness to make love, Jimmy would never take her that far. She was still a virgin, and he was her father's friend. After the stock company dissolved in the fall, their summer romance dwindled away. Jimmy departed to join the Cleveland Playhouse, and Eve joined the repertory company of her distinguished uncle, Walter Hampden. Ethyl Barrymore had been his costar the previous season. Eve, of course, was a neophyte, doomed to play flower girls or courtesans lest her uncle seem to favor his niece.

Her father had sent her two sisters to boarding school and had sold the family apartment in Brooklyn Heights. He had taken quarters in the National Arts Club, a magnificent mansion on Gramercy Park. Eve moved in with him, though they maintained largely separate schedules and lived separate lives.

In the theatrical company, no drinking before the performance was the rule, so her drinking was confined to occasional parties after the performance. She recalls she didn't drink often, but when she did, she was greedy. "I never drank just a little. The 'dis-ease' at the center of my being was healed only by 'just one more.' I was a mixed-up kid: fearful and loud, shy and hostile, a virgin but sexually aggressive."

The following season, a tall, young actor of Portuguese background joined Hampden's company. He had black, curly hair, deep blue eyes, and an easygoing disposition. His name was Francis Dears. He and Eve began to date and soon fell in love. Francis didn't have the inhibitions of Jimmy, and soon begged Eve to stay with him in his apartment. She did so on many nights, feeling close and loved. But in the morning she felt clandestine and afraid as she hastened to the National Arts Club to sneak into her rooms before her father awoke.

Francis was stricken with a serious illness, so his understudy took over and he was rushed to a hospital in Boston, to be near his parents. Hardly had he left when Eve discovered she was pregnant. Panicky but resourceful, she found a justice of the peace in Hoboken who would, for a fee, provide an undated wedding certificate. As soon as he was able, Francis returned to New York and they were married with a predated certificate, which his parents as well as her father accepted with some coolness. A beautiful baby boy, whom they named Donn, was born in August.

Marriage and motherhood, for a stagestruck girl of twenty-two, quickly turned sour. The next three years they spent living in drab apartments and worse hotels, depending on their families for meager handouts of money. Eve's father gave her the inheritance left by her mother: two thousand five hundred dollars. It seemed like a fortune at the time, but it was soon spent—part of it on gallon tins of bootleg gin at one dollar a fifth! Frank looked unsuccessfully for acting work, while Eve planned to move from a furnished apartment in New York to a house on Long Island, through the kind offices of her Uncle Walter.

Suddenly Frank's illness returned, so the couple had to move in with his family in Brockton, Massachusetts. When he recovered, Frank acted in a Broadway production scheduled to open in September. So they moved back to New York, to a drab old hotel on Forty-fourth Street, where Eve alternated between casting interviews and washing Donn's diapers in the bathroom basin at the hotel. Frank's new show was a quick failure and closed. As he went off to Maryland to try out for a stock production, Eve moved to another furnished apartment to enjoy their growing son—and to have the freedom to drink.

She recalls most vividly a Christmas dinner that year with her family at Uncle Charles's house in Brooklyn Heights. Uncle Charles was a doctor whose lovely home was staffed by four servants. A few days before Christmas, Eve was down to her last dollar. Her icebox contained an orange, a potato, and some milk—enough for Donn—so she spent the last dollar for a bottle of gin. At the party, she was with her younger sisters, whom she hadn't seen in some time. Eleanor, now a raving beauty, was doing well at Vassar; Ricky, the younger, with a naturally loving disposition, was still in boarding school. Eve shamelessly dramatized her starved condition and her plight in general (omitting mention of the gin, of course), which evoked some extra monetary gifts from her father and uncle, to tide her over.

All too soon Frank's season in Maryland was over, and they were broke again. He was offered a small part in a new play, *Tobacco Road*, which paid seventy-five dollars a week; he turned it down because he wanted a hundred dollars. To compound Eve's feelings of failure, her husband's lovemaking had become hurried and perfunctory.

Summoning nerve to talk to her father about leaving Frank, she called on him at his sumptuous quarters at the National Arts Club. After a long silence, he rose and paced the floor, his black eyebrows in a frown. Finally he said, "You know I was against this marriage in the first place. But now I want you to be sure, to be really *sure*, that you're not just tired of poverty and not your marriage. Give it a few more months."

With a little extra help from her father, Eve decided her little family should get away from their dreary walk-up apartment and spend the summer in Provincetown. There, Donn would be outdoors in the sun and everyone would be happy. Perhaps she would even be "in love" again. It turned out she was—but with another man!

His name was Eric, a tall, blond, handsomely tanned neighbor, who was a successful writer. He and his wife and son became summer friends of Eve and Francis. As Eric's marriage was also at the point of breaking up, it was easy for him and Eve to fall into a sexual flirtation that remained unfulfilled because of Eve's conscience regarding adultery.

Back in New York after summer's end, Uncle Walter offered

Frank several good, minor parts in his repertory company at a modest salary. He refused, saying, "That would be a dead end for me. I must stay here on Broadway." Eve reminded him he was turning down a full season's work at a steady income. He wasn't interested. That did it. Eve screamed, "Get out! I'm through with you. You're too damned lazy to work." Years later, in sobriety, she acknowledged that she was really using this instance as an excuse to get out of the responsibility of marriage, to prove herself—and to have an affair with Eric.

When Frank had gone, Eve called Uncle Walter and told him what had happened. He offered her the same kind of contract Frank had turned down. Donn was sent off to live with an aunt, and Eve plunged into several years of touring the country, fulfilling her ambition to be an actress. Her affair with Eric did not survive the long separations.

Now, free of responsibility, the tours were, for her, a time of wild drinking punctuated with periods of being "on the wagon." Drinking, she was the belle of the tour. "I was anybody's gal," she confesses. "I never knew whose berth I might end up in, on those long train jumps." On the wagon, she was reclusive, withdrawn, feeling sorry for herself. Between tours, she spent several weeks with Donn in Skowhegan, Maine. But still she drank, she partied, she played around, but felt ever more lonely.

By the end of the second year's tours, she was sleeping with the stagehands and hiding her occasional drunkenness and frequent trembling hangovers. Finally, Walter Hampden said he wouldn't have a place for her the following season. After pounding the streets, she landed a job on the road producing amateur theatricals for various local organizations such as the American Legion or the PTA. She had to cast the amateur actors, sell program advertising, promote ticket sales, and so on. She found it terribly degrading. She nearly lost her life when she passed out with a lighted cigarette that set her mattress on fire. She ended up ill and in a hospital in Springfield, Massachusetts, for surgery, feeling a hopeless failure, frightened, and alone.

She chose to recover back in New York at her father's quarters in the National Arts Club while he was writing a screenplay in Hollywood. One weekend her sister Ricky was also there getting ready to double-date with her college roommate. Her date—an "older man named Roger," in her words—arrived before she was quite dressed, so she asked Eve to entertain him. He was tall and broad shouldered, dark haired, with an infectious laugh. As the two had a drink together, Eve discovered he had been a network radio announcer, which enchanted her. He and Ricky went out to join the other couple—but the next day he called Eve for dinner. "That was the beginning," she says, "of the love of my life."

Roger was not only a lover and a poet, but a major drinking companion. They quickly moved in together, first at her father's apartment while he was in Hollywood, and then in a brownstone apartment that she rented with an allowance from her father. She had made a halfhearted, unsuccessful attempt to find a job, and Roger was casual about going to his own job, so they lived close to the poverty line.

Eve hadn't gotten a divorce from Frank, so now she contacted him and persuaded him not to contest divorce proceedings, which were arranged. During the required waiting period, Eve, who had left Donn with her aunt during her torrid weeks and months with Roger, now brought him back to live with her. Roger, who had his own apartment nearby, loved the boy and tried to play a "daddy" role.

Although it was a happy time for Eve, she says in retrospect, "In the light of today's knowledge, it is difficult to realize how we could rationalize the drinking. Obviously, alcoholism was our design for living. But we didn't know there was such a thing! For me, drinking was my way of coping with life. Fun, parties, sex, work, play, none of these could be successful without drinking. Sadly, there were those opposite times when fighting, brutality, and despair were the end results."

After one evening of fighting, Roger stormed out, yelling it was all over. Eve rushed to the window, threw her legs over the sill, and screamed into the night that she would jump. She says, "I simply rationalized it was not 'drinking' that caused these problems, but 'too much drinking' or 'his drinking.' Through it all was the sense of poverty and lack. We never had any money, so we 'deserved' to have a few drinks because we didn't go to the theater or opera or anywhere. Of course, it was really the other way around; we didn't do anything else because we drank. I just didn't recognize the poverty of spirit."

Finally, Eve and Roger were married. It was a small wedding held in her father's quarters with only the families present.

The years that followed were filled with ups and downs. Eve bore two daughters, Ruth and Elizabeth, who were two and a half years apart. Eve felt fulfilled and happy to have Roger's children. And he adored them. In 1941, her father died, leaving Eve and her sisters a modest inheritance. There were many moves, climaxing with the purchase of a country home, for summers, in the wandering, wooded area between Amenia, New York, and Sharon, Connecticut. Eve was content.

The downside was that she and Roger were sliding into the depths of their alcoholism. Punctuating happy times were anger and fights, screaming and brawling. Roger would go off for days at a time; when their second daughter was born, he didn't reach the hospital until three days later, so drunk the nurses threw him out. Eve would drink alone at home, seething with resentment, often ending in blackouts followed by shaking, sick hangovers that virtually immobilized her. They once gave a dinner party for old friends and neighbors to show them how well they were doing, but Eve got into the booze and the evening was an embarrassing disaster.

In 1941, she had read the famous Jack Alexander article on Alcoholics Anonymous in the *Saturday Evening Post,* but related it totally to Roger's drinking. "How wonderful," she thought, "if Roger joined this thing and stopped drinking, because it would solve *my* problem. Because he's such a bastard when he's drinking, the only way I can stand him is to drink too much."

By 1943, Eve's life was beginning to fall apart. Her marriage was disintegrating; she was sometimes too drunk to handle her responsibilities with the children; and her friends were asking her why, with so much to live for, did she have to drink so much. She couldn't tell them, because she didn't know why herself. She was sure she was having a nervous breakdown. She needed a rest.

She ended up going voluntarily to a private mental institution in Hartford, Connecticut. As she had been drinking before her entry interview, she inadvertently hinted she had been so desperate she had considered taking her own life. She was immediately consigned to the suicide ward, rigidly scheduled and tightly guarded with no access to a doctor or other authority. She and the other patients were literally imprisoned behind double-locked doors except for a half-hour daily outside in an exercise yard. Even trips to the bathroom were monitored. Her weeklong incarceration was a nightmare, until she was rescued by an aunt who lived nearby. Only then, for two weeks at her aunt's serene home, did she have the "rest" she had longed for.

Back in New York, things went from bad to worse: "The fights and black eyes came more frequently. The two- or three-week benders were almost constant. I was so sick so many days. I wore an old pink chenille wrapper to keep me warm through the shakes and to absorb the sudden sweats. 'Get me through this one, God, and I'll never drink again,' I would pray. Mornings, I would have the dry heaves, that interminable retching, sitting on the floor by the toilet, heaving up bitter, acrid green bile, fearing I would die, despairing that I wouldn't."

The final humiliation was when her son, Donn, a young teenager now, said, "I can't stand to stay around here and watch you get drunk."

"I know I cannot drink," she told him. "I promise you I'll never drink again."

"No, Mom, you've made that same promise to me before."

She says her self-loathing was absolute. She tried desperately but unsuccessfully to do it alone. The pain became too great, and on a Monday she made the call to AA, reaching the desk of the old Twenty-fourth Street Clubhouse. It was obvious she was drunk, so they suggested she come in the following day. By morning, she had totally forgotten her call, but *they* called *her*, not once but several times, urging her to come in. By late afternoon, fortified by a few drinks, she pulled herself together and set out to find 324 1/2 West Twenty-fourth Street. She recalls:

I opened the door, and before me lay a long dark hall. At the end was a brightly lit room where I could see a big fireplace and over it two portraits. I could hear voices. Old feelings of shyness and inferiority rose up, but there was warmth in the light of that room and it drew me on. . . . The room was large, with lots of chairs and a staircase to the left, leading to rooms above. By the staircase was a small desk with a girl to answer calls like mine. There were a couple of people talking at one table and a man sitting alone at another, all drinking coffee. When he saw me, the man came over and said, "Hi, my name is Dan. Can I get you a cup of coffee?" He had brown eyes and he was smiling.

I began to relax. He let me talk, so I told him I thought I drank a little too much—not wanting to let him know how awful I was. Then he told me about himself. He had gone from being president of his own company to panhandling. His wife and children were gone, and he now had a menial job. But he hadn't had a drink in ten months! Not only that, he seemed happy! I was illumined with such hope, I wanted to cry. The sense of belonging was overwhelming.

"There's a meeting Thursday night," he told me. "Can you get here?"

"I'll try," I told him, "but I've been hitting a quart a day, and I may be awful shaky."

When Roger came home that night, he was surprisingly accepting of her decision to quit drinking and go to AA. "Just leave me out of it," he said. Eve tried to taper off, but as she had feared, she was too shaky to make the meeting on Thursday. So she called Dan at the clubhouse and agreed to meet him at a large open meeting on Sunday at the Hotel Capitol at Fiftieth Street and Eighth Avenue.

Thus she attended her first AA meeting on Sunday, October 24, 1944. As she walked up the front steps of the hotel, a tall, white-haired gentleman spoke to her, asking, "Are you going where I'm going?" Together they went in, where she learned his name was Bill W., the cofounder of Alcoholics Anonymous. Two or three hundred people crowded the small auditorium. She identified with the speakers, joined in the unexpected laughter, and returned home on a pink cloud of hope.

The next few weeks of sobriety, as she continued to attend the Thursday and Sunday meetings, were, she recalls, "the beginnings of joy. I could take the children to the park and enjoy the crisp autumn days and cloudless blue skies. I tackled the accumulated piles of ironing, found time to play rummy with Donn, time to darn socks, time to read—including the AA literature. I began to enjoy eating. I loved it when a neighbor said, 'My, you're looking awfully well, dear.' My body was beginning to heal, but my emotions were still raw and close to the surface. I remember feeling rejected and got on a crying jag at a crowded AA meeting just because my friend Dan and others were paying attention to someone newer than me!"

On that occasion, Dan advised her, "The trouble is, you are too wrapped up in yourself. Start thinking about how someone else feels. Any of the women here would have liked to talk to you if you would let them instead of hiding behind a wall of self-pity. And remember that there is nothing more important in your life than not taking that first drink. Not your children or me or any situation. Nothing. Now let's go have a cup of coffee with the others."

When Eve had gone to AA, her husband, Roger, had also stopped drinking—possibly to show her he could do it *without* going to AA. That helped make those weeks happy ones. Christmas was only two weeks away. She made plans to do her shopping on a Thursday night when the stores were open late, so Roger could stay with their son. As she returned to their apartment building that night, her heart full of holiday excitement and family love, she heard the children screaming. "I raced down the long hallway," she recalls with horror. "I dropped my packages and hastened to open the big front door. Inside, Roger, dead drunk, was pummeling Donn. He looked like some animal as he tried to punch the child's head. Dead calm, I pried Roger away, grabbed Donn and got him to his room. Rage consumed me, and I handled it the only way I knew; I rushed to the kitchen and poured myself a tumbler of whiskey. 'I'll show him!' I thought, as I belted it down."

That set off a two-week relapse, ending when she was too drunk to manage her daughter's birthday party. A call to Dan put her in the hands of Dr. Ruth Fox, one of the first New York doctors to understand Alcoholics Anonymous. A few days later Eve ended her bender and returned to the clubhouse, where Dan reminded her that alcoholics simply cannot handle such luxuries as anger and resentment, and that she had to stay sober for herself, not her family. He also made her buy a Big Book and begin reading it.

She had one more slip, that Christmas Eve. She tried to control her drinking for two more weeks and then surrendered in earnest. This time she made AA the most important thing in her life. The clubhouse had now moved to a much larger new location on West Forty-first Street, with a large auditorium, smaller rooms for discussion meetings, and basement rooms for card games (not allowed during meeting times!). There was a kitchen, from which inexpensive meals were served. Eve acquired a sitter for the children every Thursday and spent the day at the clubhouse.

She heard cofounder Bill W. talk several times. One of the things he said, in particular, opened a door for her: "No longer do we have to drink against our will." She also recalls that Bill's tenth anniversary of sobriety was celebrated at a special theater party to see the play *Harvey*, singularly appropriate for AA members.

"I heard at that time that AA had reached the terrific total of ten thousand members," she says. "I knew I was not alone. I began to want to emulate the people who had a kind of contentment in their sobriety because they had put the Twelve Steps into their lives. I now truly accepted that not drinking was the most important thing in my life, and that AA had the tools that would help me maintain my sobriety. What I didn't realize was that these tools and Steps would *change* my life. I was to learn that sobriety is not just not drinking, but involves a whole new way of life."

Roger continued his drinking while Eve continued to try to sell him AA. Frequenting the new clubhouse, her AA acquaintance broadened. She began to put into her life the Serenity Prayer:

> *God grant me the Serenity to Accept the things*
> *I cannot change,*
> *The Courage to change the things I can,*
> *And the Wisdom to know the difference.*

Except that she had her own interpretation; to wit: "Okay, I'll 'accept' the fact that I'm always going to be shy and scared of people, and that I'm not pretty. I cannot change those things. 'Change the things I can?' I would change Roger, make him want to go to AA. I wanted him to be sorry for the hurt he had caused me." She became increasingly resentful that he continued drinking, oblivious of her efforts to change him.

One night when she had been sober about five months, she was talking with a friend named Doris, complaining on and on, as usual, about her problems with Roger. Doris asked, smiling, "My dear, have you ever thought of how dreadful it would be if Roger *did* come to AA?"

Stunned, Eve asked, "Whatever do you mean?"

Her friend delivered the punch line, "Then you would have nothing to complain about." Eve recoiled in anger, and Doris went on, "Don't you see, you cannot change him, you can only change yourself. 'Live and let live,'" she concluded.

Eve declares today, "It was a miracle of AA that anyone as sick and disturbed as I was could have stayed sober only through love and friendship, with only the most superficial grasp of the tools offered me." She began to see that she could stay sober only for herself and that her own sobriety was all she could deal with. She began to realize that events that happened to her were not as important as her *attitude* toward them. She moved on, with the help of Dan, to take the Third and Fourth Steps.

Not long afterward, she had "a miraculous awakening." She relates, "As I was traveling downtown on an old trolley, thinking about the Steps, an old man stepped in front of the tram. The motorman clanged his bell and screeched the brakes, but it was too late. The trolley ran over him. As soon as I could, I leapt out and headed over to the sidewalk, feeling shocked and nauseated. I had no desire to see the gory scene. As I walked on, I was suddenly hit with an overwhelming sense of freedom. 'My God,' I thought, 'if that had happened before AA, I would have headed for the nearest bar. I would have *had* to have a drink. And here I am walking down Broadway with no desire at all to have a drink.' I shouted inwardly to a God I did not understand, 'Thank you! Thank you!' I never had a desire to drink again."

As Eve's sobriety grew, Alcoholics Anonymous in New York was growing, from a scant handful of groups in 1944 to more than one hundred by 1947. The phone at the clubhouse could no longer handle the flood of calls from drunks seeking help, so an intergroup association had been formed, with its office on East Seventy-sixth Street. The coordinator of the office, a friend of Eve's, invited her to volunteer. "We need you," she said, and Eve instantly felt the elation of being needed.

Her initial tour of duty was to staff the phones on Thursdays. As she recalls:

> The intergroup was in a large storefront. In the waiting room there were two large desks where another volunteer and I were to answer the phones and visit with people as they came in. In the back, separated by a low railing, sat the two full-time, paid secretaries, who supervised the service and coordinated the activities of all the

metropolitan area groups. My job was to explain to the callers how AA works and where they could find the nearest meetings. If they wanted to talk to someone personally, I would invite them to come to the office, or would take their name, address, and phone number and would then try to reach one of the contacts from the Intergroup list to make a Twelfth Step call on the prospect. If the person was too drunk or too sick, one of the secretaries might refer him or her to Knickerbocker Hospital, which had an alcoholism recovery ward under the care of Dr. William Silkworth and the legendary red-headed nurse Teddy.

Eve's first day was happy and rewarding. She felt useful and fulfilled. "From then on, Thursday was the day I lived for," she says. Stimulated, she began to go to more meetings, more regularly. She found that a new group, the Lenox Hill group, had been formed at Ninetieth and Fifth Avenue, convenient to where she and her family were living. As she began to attend Lenox Hill regularly, she felt a part of it, making a new circle of AA friends with whom she socialized outside the meetings. As the group grew rapidly to two or three hundred attending the open meetings, it was feared that a new person would feel overwhelmed and lost. So Eve was asked to serve on a newly formed "hosting committee." She says, "No one will ever know the overwhelming sense of gratitude and joy at that experience." She even overcame her shyness to invite her new AA friends to her home regularly for Saturday night poker games or Sunday night suppers.

"I learned," she says, "that an 'attitude of gratitude' left no room for those old handmaidens of self-pity or envy."

Terrified of speaking though she was, she was persuaded to speak at a friend's anniversary at Lenox Hill. She wrote her talk out in longhand and memorized it. She even bought a new dress for her "debut." It was a success; she was applauded and congratulated and was invited to speak at several other groups. "Joyously I embarked on this new aspect of sharing in AA," she recalls. In those days, the groups traded teams of speakers at their meetings, usually two men and one woman, if possible, so Eve was often included. And with experience, together with more maturity in her sobriety, she abandoned the security of her "canned" talk to speak from the heart.

A watershed experience came some time later as she found her way to faith in a Higher Power. The first harbinger came when she was overcome with claustrophobic panic in a crowded subway car. Hanging on to a strap, she closed her eyes and repeated AA's Eleventh Step: "Sought through prayer and meditation to improve our conscious contact with God *as we understood Him,* praying only for knowledge of His will for us and the power to carry that out." Her fear subsided, replaced by a feeling of peace.

In her quest, which included some metaphysical and spiritual reading, she read, "God is love." Love was what she had found at AA meetings, as she had learned to turn her will and willfulness over to the group. "I got out of my own way," she says. The reality of the presence of God within her became a part of her.

After Eve had served about two years as a volunteer at Intergroup, the woman in charge left and Eve was selected to take her place. Concurrently, the office moved to larger quarters on Lexington Avenue at Twenty-eighth Street. Here were three desks for volunteers instead of two; and, separated by a railing, the office space where Eve and her full-time, paid assistant could do the paperwork, arrange hospitalizations, and oversee the handling of the visitors. One of the exciting functions of the office was to arrange for the annual "Bill's Birthday Banquet," where two thousand or more AA members and their spouses gathered to hear Bill W. talk.

"Now I truly felt as if I were giving back a little of what I had received," she says. "I loved sharing with newer people as they came in, and I loved working with the volunteers.

"I saw that AA never failed; but individual alcoholics might fail to utilize it. As for myself, I knew I had not *given up* anything when I stopped drinking; but I had *gotten rid* of the thing that stood in the way of my learning to live as I had always wanted to. I had needed a drink to cope with the problems of life. Now, the AA program had given me the tools to cope with living. As a result of working the Steps, my new life was happy and content.

"Also, working at the intergroup office where I coordinated the activities of over 350 New York area groups, I got a better understanding of the importance of AA unity—and the part that the Twelve Traditions played in maintaining that unity."

In the early 1950s, Eve began attending churches connected with the "new thought" movement. She explains, "I knew that 'God is love,' but the glimpses of peace of mind I had gained from the Third Step only increased my desire for more knowledge. . . . Now I began to realize that the source of my spiritual power was not outside but within. I came to believe that the AA program was not only the answer to my drinking problem and how to change my life, but it also opened the door to spiritual growth. In the Big Book, it says, 'We finally saw that faith in some kind of God was a part of our make-up. . . . Sometimes we had to search fearlessly, but He was there. He was as much a fact as we were. We found the Great Reality deep down within us. In the last analysis, it is only there that He may be found.'"

A measure of Eve's spiritual growth was found a couple of years later when she said, "There was no question in my mind that indeed 'my cup runneth over.' My needs were always met; perhaps not my wants, but my needs. It was amazing to find, sometimes, that what I wanted turned out to be not what I wanted at all. This business of 'turning my will and my life over to the care of my Higher Power' had become an experiment and an adventure. How many times had it been demonstrated that my will would not have been the right course, and that I had been divinely guided into the right action!"

Through her active participation in the Lenox Hill group and her frequent speaking at other New York groups, and especially her job as secretary (head) of the Intergroup office, Eve was well acquainted with the staff of the General Service Office of AA—from Bill W. on down—and they were well acquainted with her. So it was only natural that when an opening on the staff occurred in 1952, she was invited to join. Thus her viewpoint expanded from citywide to nationwide and worldwide. She was to remain on the GSO staff for eighteen years.

It was a seminal time for Alcoholics Anonymous, as annual General Service Conferences were being tried on an experimental basis, leading up to the "Coming of Age" convention in St. Louis in 1955, when all authority and responsibility for AA was turned over to the groups, acting through the newly formed service structure.

The policy at the AA office was for staff members to rotate biannually among the various assignments. Of Eve's talents, Herb M., general manager of the GSO during much of Eve's service there, once said, "Eve M. seemed to handle the duties at each new desk as if it was the most important job in the world. She was simply born for the work, bringing to it warmth, enthusiasm, and intelligence, plus an unmatched articulateness. The fellowship just loved her."

By the mid-1950s, Eve's life had blossomed. She lived in a large, well-furnished apartment; her children were attending private schools; food and clothing were adequate if not opulent; and, she was able to enjoy theater, opera, summers on Fire Island, and, above all, many friends. But when a friend showed her some pamphlets about overseas travel by freighter, she began to dream about visiting some of the faraway places with which she had corresponded at the GSO.

She approached the manager about the possibility of a leave of absence. He agreed that it might be possible if and when an additional staff member was needed. When such a person was hired, Eve could take a year's leave and rejoin when she returned, thus augmenting the staff by one.

Her opportunity came in 1965, and she departed on a year's leave of absence. It began with a three-week voyage via freighter to Capetown, South Africa. As she docked, a local AA member was waiting eagerly to take her under his wing and show her his country. The AA groups showered her with gratitude, partly because she represented the country where the lifesaving program of AA had begun and, additionally, because she was the first person they had ever met from the World Services Office in New York.

Eve's pioneering journey, made largely by freighter, took her on through Tanzania, Zanzibar, and Kenya to India, where she was "able to contact many AA's." She wrote later, "I found that within the AA groups the same principles of love applied regardless of differences in faith—Hindu and Christian side by side.

"I had the terrific advantage," she said, "that through correspondence [in her service at the GSO] I had come to know a great many people in AA in other parts of the world. I wrote many of them to let them know I was coming. I felt I had really come to know and love them, and yet I had never seen their faces. I was excited at that opportunity." And sure enough, those faces were waiting at the dock to greet her and make her feel at home. "It was a fantastic trip," she said.

Eve's voyage continued to embrace Australia and New Zealand as well as European countries. Returning to her position at the GSO at the end of her year's sabbatical, she found the nervous strain of working in New York at a nine-to-five job was getting to be too much. She set a goal of retiring when she reached sixty years old, in two years.

She was invited to revisit South Africa in 1970 to participate in their annual convention. "It was a joyous reunion," she recalls. She went on to Rhodesia (now Zimbabwe) before returning to the United States in time to attend the Thirty-fifth Anniversary International Convention of AA in Miami Beach, Florida. The Sunday morning closing ceremony at that gathering was the last public appearance of the ailing Bill W.—a moment of great poignancy and emotion for Eve and the ten thousand others in attendance.

While in Miami Beach, Eve learned that the small

Alcoholism Council for South Florida, located in nearby Fort Lauderdale, was looking for a new director. She applied for the job and was accepted.

Thus, in her sixties, she embarked on a whole new career. Beginning with almost no staff and a tiny budget, she was able to accomplish an astonishing amount over the next three years. With the help of a small grant from the state of Florida, she instituted a detox center and later a DWI (driving while intoxicated) school where offenders were sentenced to attend. The greatest problem in the field, she discovered—and consequently, her first priority—was to try to correct the misconceptions about alcoholism and the stigma associated with it in the eyes of the public, and even among doctors and other professionals. In other words: *education*. Her depth of personal experience as an alcoholic and a member of Alcoholics Anonymous was invaluable.

At the end of 1973, Eve M. retired as a professional in the field of alcoholism—but not from AA! For the next fifteen years and on into her eighties, she remained one of the most sought-after and well-known speakers at AA conventions, conferences, and special occasions. Undaunted and unstoppable even when battling the ravages of cancer, her voice was always strong and vital in timbre. Her talk was spunky, saucy, spiritual, and full of zest for life.

Perhaps her crowning moment came in July 1990 when, at the age of eighty-two, she spoke at the Sunday morning closing session of the Sixtieth Anniversary International Convention of AA in Seattle, Washington. As she sat down, an estimated sixty thousand people in the domed stadium rose in a standing ovation. As Frank M., AA's archivist, stood applauding with tears in his eyes, he said in admiration, "She's a piece of work, isn't she?"

And indeed she was.

Sources:

Eve M. Personal journal. 258 pp.
Personal reminiscences
Taped AA talks

Geraldine Owen D.

BACK IN THE 1960S OR 1970S THERE WAS A POPULAR AD FOR MINK. IT WAS IN THE DAYS WHEN MOST PEOPLE STILL CONSID- ered the costly fur a desirable luxury. To make the point, the ad used glossy, glamorous shots of the day's most admired women wrapped from head to toe in soft, sensuous mink coats. The caption read, "What Becomes a Legend Most?" We think they may have missed the point, but then . . . they never met her— Geraldine Owen D. "Gerry" to some; "Mrs. D." to others. And then there's "GOD," "Grambo," and probably a long list of names known only to a privileged few. But what about the woman, the alcoholic, the tireless worker, the devoted wife, the loving stepmother? What about the little girl who grew up to be a legend?

Geraldine was born of a wealthy, prominent, multitalented, community-icon father and an insecure, distant, socialite, closet-drinking mother. It didn't take long for her to figure out her role in the family. Rebel, troublemaker, outcast. She watched quietly as her mother lavished love and attention on her older brother, and a little girl's heart broke silently into hundreds of tiny pieces. So she got into trouble—at home, in school, with friends, and with anyone else who would pay attention. She stood in the corner at school and was locked in the closet at home. Even in the closet, she found the only way she knew to express her loneliness, frustration, and desperate longing for love. She spit all over her mother's beautiful, ankle-length satin and velvet skirts.

When she was still young, something happened that would begin forming the extraordinary woman Geraldine was to become. True to form, she struck up a friendship with a little girl named Vivian, from "the wrong side of the tracks." They would bike all over town, Gerry pedaling just as fast as she could and Vivian perched happily on her handlebars. And then one day, Gerry got mad and said she wasn't going to take Vivian riding. Vivian was so hurt, she never spoke to Gerry again. A childhood spat—nothing really. Grown-ups laughing softly at a silly little argument between two children. And suddenly a child is not a child anymore. Suddenly, the precursor of the woman emerges, a destiny is hatched, and nothing is ever quite the same. On that day, something touched the heart of Geraldine D., and she knew that she didn't want to hurt anyone anymore; she wanted to help people.

As Gerry grew from childhood into adolescence, her mother's alcoholism progressed. In those days, heroin was seen as a treatment for drunkenness, although any reference to alcohol would be merely whispered about in back rooms. And so the family doctor would arrive and give Mother a "little shot" to get her through the day. Alcohol, of course, took its toll. By the time she was seventeen, Geraldine's parents had divorced; and she, her mother, and her brother, Oscar, were living in an apartment building. More rebellious than ever and desperate to get out of her mother's house, Gerry eloped with their fifty-seven-year-old landlord.

A quickly arranged annulment ended her brief escape. But at the age of eighteen, her freedom finally became a reality. She went off to college, looking to all the world like the confident, self-assured young woman she wanted people to see. Her shining intelligence and gutsy determination masked the low self-esteem. Searching for a way to belong, she found an unexpected answer. On a trip into Canada, she strapped hot water bottles filled with Canadian whiskey to the inside of her legs and began an extracurricular smuggling career that made her the belle of the ball. Popular, fun-loving Gerry—and she hadn't even tasted her first sip of alcohol. Prohibition had yet to run its course when she had her first drink; and it wasn't long before she discovered over-the-counter magic pills—phenobarbital, Nembutal, and Seconal.

On a beautiful November afternoon in 1929, her father called and gave her the startling news that he had just lost every penny he owned in the stock market crash. She had long harbored a desire to go to medical school, but for Gerry, as for many, many others that November day, her dreams were to take her down a different path. With a determination and resilience rarely found in young people, especially young women of her day, she faced her circumstances and stepped into 1928. Within a few months, she had her first job.

Editing books for a group of professors at Northwestern University Medical School gave her a tremendous grounding in many aspects of medicine that would later serve her well. One of her doctor employers was writing a basic "how-to" book about babies. Since the primary target audience was other pediatricians, Gerry was fascinated with the simplicity of his approach and questioned him about it. He responded with, "Doctors are tired at night. I want them to *read* it," and how right he was. The book became the first medical best-seller ever written. His simple approach was a winner because it appealed to everybody—not just doctors, but parents, grandparents, and thousands of other ordinary people interested in children. And Gerry learned a powerful lesson long before she realized its significance: *Keep it simple!*

The pathway to destiny has a way of opening up in such small, insignificant, sometimes unnoticed little steps. One person leads to another who leads to another, and so on until suddenly a pattern begins to emerge. She met another group of doctors, moved to be near the Mayo Clinic in Rochester, Minnesota, and began working with a wonderful man by the name of Dr. Andy. Together, they founded the second national medical certifying board in the United States. While her career flourished, her downward spiral into alcohol and other drugs had begun. Ultimately, she would find herself in a chasm of such unthinkable blackness and despair that hope, as she had known it, would disintegrate into nothing more than puffs of smoke arising from the dying embers of her dreams.

At about this time, she fell in love and married a man with a four-year-old boy named Dick. The marriage lasted twelve years, but her love for that child lives on today. Although technically a stepmother, Gerry raised Dick as her own. She was a firm disciplinarian, but she loved him fiercely; and when she and his father divorced, Dick asked the judge to allow him to live with his "mother." His father had been a generous provider, giving the boy anything money could buy, so Dick's request was unexpected. When she asked him about it, he responded, "Mom, you loved me enough to make me behave, and you tell me the truth." Not surprisingly, she shunned offers of alimony and child support, telling the court she could support him herself. And when, on the terrible day some years later, she received the dreaded news that her boy had been killed in action, she knew that a light had gone out in her life that would never be rekindled.

So many times she went on binges, blacking out and waking up in one more institution. Incredible escapades and unremembered pranks became a way of life. From driving a tractor trailer alone through a field in Iowa to a near-fatal overdose in San Francisco that left her in a coma for eleven days, fear became her constant companion. While the evidence of her *successful* life accumulated, the lows were becoming lower. Her arrogance and ego had long been fueled by her extravagant salary, expense account, airplane trips around the country, the house, the maid, the car, and the driver. And now it seemed to be closing in around her.

By this time, her older brother, Oscar, had discovered a way successfully to stop his own journey into the bottomless pit of alcoholism through a new program by the name of Alcoholics Anonymous. In an ironic twist of fate, it had been Gerry herself who had set off a sequence of events that would boomerang back to her at the lowest moment of her life. She had long been disdainful of Oscar's drinking, often referring to him as "that moral leper brother of mine." When he could no longer go on with his self-destructive lifestyle, she called the only psychiatrist she knew on the East Coast. In her own words, she tells of her conversation: "I asked him what to do about my brother's drinking. At first, he said he didn't know. Then he said, 'The other night I was at a meeting, and a man by the name of Bill Wilson was talking about doing something peculiar with men who drink too much. He gave me his card. I'll call him up.' Bill Wilson came to see Oscar and remained friend and adviser with him ever after. My brother got sober that year, 1941."

Following the predictable curve of any chronic, progressive disease is an easy task for the knowing, but a formidable maze for the unknowing victim. By the time she had left her twenty-third psychiatric hospital, Gerry had clearly demonstrated her inability to continue functioning in a professional environment. Her physician colleagues, baffled at what steps to take, offered her a year's leave of absence with full benefits; and in true, arrogant, alcoholic fashion, she refused! They gave her a five-figure bonus, and she went on a countrywide binge.

One morning, after a particularly memorable evening of attempting to do a striptease while drinking with a group of doctors, she woke up in a psychiatric lockup ward on the west side of Chicago. Taking in the iron bed, the iron bars on the window, the door with no doorknobs, the peephole in the door, she knew what she had to do. There had been many times before, in other hospitals in other cities when they had called her brother, but he had never come. This time he came. When he asked if she wanted to do something about her drinking, she said yes; but in her own mind, she was saying, "My own way." He took her back East and suggested how she might begin. She refused. So he left her in the lobby of a hotel without any money. After forty-eight hours with no alcohol or other drugs, she thought she was dying. She went into the ladies' room, intending to fix herself up a little before going into the bar and asking some gallant gentleman to buy her a drink. What she saw in the mirror stopped her dead. She realized in that moment that absolutely no one would want to be within ten feet of her, let alone buy her a drink. So she went home with Oscar.

And the war began. They never left her alone. Day after day and night after night. Meetings, meetings, meetings. Always the same "holy rollers" and the same boring, interminable meetings. But little by little, her brain began to clear. She got smart, and she got cocky. And after eight months, she decided to go back to Chicago, join her friends, and drink like a lady.

What happened next can only be described in her own words:

> Bill Wilson, my brother's friend, had given me a signed copy of the original edition of the Big Book. I threw it out the window in a snowbank. It reappeared on the night table. I threw it in the dirty clothes. It came back on the night table. I threw it into the garbage. Back it came, a little greasy and stained, but on the table. That was the night I packed my bags. We went to a meeting in East Orange that night. I don't know what was said, and when we came home, there was the book that had legs on the night table. You know, for eight months I looked at the book, but for some reason on this particular night, I picked it up. It fell open to page 57 in the old edition, "How It Works," and I started to read. That word *honest* in the first paragraph was about two inches high. Then I read down through the Twelve Steps. I didn't realize it at the time, but I read them in the first person, just like Bill had originally written them. Then I read one more paragraph, closed the book, and went to sleep. It was the first good night's sleep I'd had in eight months. And in the morning, I realized that the desire to leave and the desire to drink had left me. It was that morning that I first admitted I was an alcoholic, and I have never again wanted to run away, to drink or take drugs. This experience was probably the most important thing that has ever happened to me.

There weren't many women in AA in those early days. Most women alcoholics just went to bed and died. Gerry made friends with the few women who were there, but it was mostly the Al-Anon women (although Al-Anon had yet to be formed) who took her under their wings. Oscar's longtime friendship with Bill and Lois Wilson gave Gerry the benefit of their great encouragement, support, and wisdom. And she needed all the friends she could get! Stubborn, despite her spiritual experience, she struggled against rules, discipline, and enforced belief in God; it was only when a wise friend suggested she view God as *Good Orderly Direction* that she could begin to believe. So, little by little, the miracle of recovery took root in the fertile soil of her mind and spirit, and she became a willing participant in a way of life that would take her on the most fantastic journey of all—her own life.

Why is it that at the moment one least expects it, destiny once again inserts itself in the most unexpected ways? Tom Delaney was a good-looking, smooth-talking Irishman, a sober member of Alcoholics Anonymous, and Gerry fell hard. She smiles now as she remembers their marriage. They both had such high expectations. They were deeply in love; and in the way of those who love passionately, they thought it would be so easy. She talks about those happy, difficult, wonderful years: " I loved him and I married him. Was my life serene now? No! It is awfully difficult to marry another alcoholic. I didn't know it then; but in order to live together, each needs to use the very best of what is in the person."

By the end of her first year of sobriety, Gerry was back at work doing what she loved most—helping others. Because of her twenty years of experience in the field of pediatrics, she had met some influential doctors in New Jersey, who helped her get started. She formed a service to provide homemaker and home health-care services for long-term, chronically ill patients, teaching homemakers the skills they needed to care for bedridden patients. The service, later named Chr-ill, provided housewives with much-needed additional income and filled an enormous void in the field of home health care. It eventually became the first service of its kind in New Jersey and a model for others throughout the United States. She also founded what would eventually become the second branch of the National Council on Alcoholism.

Geraldine D. was born a leader and trailblazer, and the friends, colleagues, and supporters she gained throughout the years were themselves the pioneers of a movement that would transform history. Bill and Lois Wilson, Dr. Ruth Fox, and Marty Mann—just a few who would touch and be touched by this woman.

After about three years in AA, Gerry had another one of those unforgettable, eye-opening experiences: "I wanted to get well faster than I was getting well and I went to see Dr. Ruth Fox, the great psychiatrist who brought Antabuse to this country. I said, 'Ruth, I'm just not progressing as fast as I should.' She said, 'How long have you been sober'? 'Three years,' I answered. She looked at me a few minutes and said, 'Gerry, it takes two years to get your brains out of hock and three more to get them unscrambled. Then you begin to grow.'" For well over forty-five years, Gerry has been sharing those words with others, and they are just as important to newcomers today as they were to her so many years ago.

It was at about this time that she met a fascinating German immigrant by the name of Alina Rudolph Trivas. Growing up in Nazi Germany, young Ina had worked tirelessly smuggling Jews out of the country. She would ferry them across the border, drinking all the way. By the time she returned, she would be drunk, flirt with the guards, and walk merrily back home. She came to this country as the bride of an American artist, Newmar Trivas, who became curator of the Huntington Pasadena Art Museum in California. They moved to California and in short order returned to the East Coast. Back in New York, she awoke one morning from a late-night binge to find that her husband had died during the night from a heart attack. Shocked, bereaved, and still drunk, she went to High Watch

Farm in Kent, Connecticut, which in those days was a religious retreat. All that winter, Ina lived up there on the mountain with no running water or indoor plumbing and only a stove for heat. When she left, she was sober.

Gerry and Ina met in the early years of their sobriety and became friends. Ina loved sobriety and other alcoholics, and she wanted to help. She became involved with several unsuccessful attempts to build homes for the rehabilitation of alcoholics before it finally happened. In Gerry's own words:

> She found this tract of land—a hundred acres on the Paulinskill River in Blairstown, New Jersey. It was an old apple farm with a stone house, a carriage house with a little wood schoolhouse attached, and lots of apple trees. It was said to have been built during the presidency of George Washington, and it was believed to have been part of the Underground Railroad for slave movement during the 1800s. She was determined to buy it. One day she called me at my office in Essex County and said she couldn't get her mortgage for two weeks and she was going to lose the land. Could I loan her the money? I said, "Ina, I don't have that kind of money." Her reply was, "Yes, but you have credit because you've got a job and you've got a husband." Finally, I gave in to her wishes, and she bought the farm with money I had borrowed and given to her on unsecured notes for two weeks.
>
> Her mortgage didn't come through in two weeks or four weeks. Six weeks later, Ina dropped dead of a heart attack, and I was suddenly the unwilling owner of an apple farm with a very cloudy title. I had known very little about Ina's family other than she had two brothers somewhere in Germany—one a doctor and one a lawyer. After she died these brothers surfaced, and they wanted money. I didn't have it to give them.
>
> I believe fate played a great part here. I had a Jewish

lawyer who had just sold the most U.J.A. [United Jewish Appeal] bonds and won a trip to Europe. The destination of his choice coincidentally happened to be the little town in Germany where his grandfather had been born. It was also the home of Ina's two brothers. While there, he visited the brothers and settled the dispute.

So we started this little lodge—against *my* will. I did *not* want to work in the field of alcohol rehabilitation, and I did not want to leave my job in Essex County, which I loved. So I kept my job, thinking I could set this place up in a few months. That was over forty years ago, and I'm still here.

Ina died just before Christmastime. She *loved* Christmas, and we tried to go on with all the things she loved—decorations everywhere, the little German figures, and the carol singing. We hadn't had time to organize the caroling, but we heard the voices drifting across the snow, up from the carriage house—just a few voices—singing Christmas carols. Even now, Christmastime here is *very special*. We do a lot of decorating, have our own traditions, candles, and much singing. We remember Ina.

And so Little Hill Alina Lodge was born: out of coincidence, serendipity, or some strange quirk of fate. There are those who will tell you the hand of God touched this place and this woman and transformed a *reluctant* founder into one of the greatest leaders of the recovery movement this country has ever known. And that little apple orchard with the stone cottage, which began its life giving hope and freedom to those in bondage, continues its work today transforming the lives of those reluctant to recover.

The work at first was painfully slow and never easy. Gerry found herself filling the roles of housemother, mentor, cleaning woman, cook, chief executive officer, and all-around all-things-to-all-people kind of girl. And Tom was at her side, helping, supporting, and giving to the lodge. Side by side they worked, bringing to reality the dream that had begun with Ina so many years before. But the disease of addiction once again bloomed to remind all with the eyes to see that this disease is cunning, baffling, powerful . . . and patient.

Throughout Tom's years as a building contractor, he had lived with recurring bouts of back pain. On one of Gerry's trips out of town, a friend of his gave him a muscle relaxant to help his pain. And then the friend gave Tom a nonalcoholic cough preparation for his cough, but it contained triple bromide. Two days later he was drinking. He was hospitalized fourteen times in seventeen months and was sober only three weeks when he died. He would have had twenty-two years in this program he loved so much. If only . . . Gerry vowed the day he died that she would never stop talking about drugs. And to those who say that drug addicts don't belong in Alcoholics Anonymous, she'll say, "I pray that you'll see the day when somebody just like you turns someone you love away from the doors of Alcoholics Anonymous, and that you fall on your knees and beg the God of your understanding to forgive you."

For fifty years, this phenomenal woman has carried the message of hope to people around the world. She has put herself second so that her "students" can come first. She has devoted her life, her energy, her resources, and her love to a place "where hope becomes a reality." She has traveled around the country telling her story to community leaders, civic clubs, conferences, and anybody who will listen. She has been the physician's physician, the priest's spiritual adviser, and the politician's conscience.

"What becomes a legend most?" We don't know about other legends, but for this woman: grit, determination, hard work, perception, honor, a gentle heart, dignity, courage, steadfastness in the face of defeat, humor, grace, insight. We don't know about those other legends, but for Geraldine Owen D. . . . it fits her like a glove.

Geraldine Owen D. passed away July 9, 1998.

Sources:

Dick B. *Hope! The Story of Geraldine D., Alina Lodge and Recovery.* San Rafael, Calif.: Paradise Research Publications, 1998.

Further References:

Little Hill-Alina Lodge. Web site: http://www.alinalodge.org

Nancy O'D.

One of the first women to sober up in Alcoholics Anonymous in the New York area was Nancy O'D. Joining in 1944, she was the second female member in Westchester County—the first being her sponsor, Lois K., a founder of the *AA Grapevine*, whose sponsor, in turn, was Marty M., the first woman *anywhere* in AA. Together with Lois K., Nancy Twelfth Stepped many other female alcoholics, and the first women's meeting in Westchester was held in her house.

She knew Bill and Lois Wilson and recalls that Bill sent the early, long-form Traditions, one by one, to Nancy's Yonkers group for its "group conscience" reactions and vote. In 1982, Nancy moved to Lafayette, California, to live with her daughter and family, where she remained as active in AA as ever, attending meetings, always ready to help the newcomer.

Above all, Nancy O'D., throughout her eighty-five years of life and her fifty-three years of continuous sobriety in Alcoholics Anonymous (as this book is written), has been the quintessential AA old-timer: full of love and laughter, humble and serene, "happy, joyous and free."

She was born on New Year's Eve 1912, one of four girls. She grew up in Yonkers, New York, the borderline town separating suburban Westchester County from the city. She had her first drink of alcohol with high school friends at fourteen. At sixteen, she sat on the floor with her buddies and drank a whole bottle of wine. She felt so sick the following day that she ended up in the hospital, where they removed her appendix. "I wonder to this day," she said, "whether it really was appendicitis or just a hangover."

For the next two years she drank on occasion—parties and holidays—but thereafter she was a steady, daily drinker. At twenty she was married to Jim O'D., also a heavy drinker and an avid golfer. "He belonged to three golf clubs; I belonged to three bars," she quipped, with a chuckle. "He never let his drinking interfere with his golf; and I never let his golf interfere with my drinking."

The O'D.s had two children, a son named after Jim's father and a daughter named for Nancy's mother. In her twenties, Nancy worked as an interior decorator, which, she thought, required her to maintain a prosperous image. She spent a lot of money on clothes, beauty shops, facials, and massages. "It was a hard job keeping up appearances," she said. When she had awful hangovers, she took care of them with the "hair of the dog that bit her." She kept a stash of booze in the kitchen and always ensured she had a backup.

To keep up her image and her boozing, she took to forging her husband's name on checks. Although Jim was usually careless about balancing his checkbook, he sat down at the desk once and saw the number of checks for liquor. "I think I'm drinking too much," he told Nancy, and *he* quit. But not Nancy, who was convinced now that she couldn't stop. "I loved to drink," she declared. "I felt normal only when I had booze in me." She would awaken in the middle of the night and imbibe a few drinks to get back to sleep. Then she couldn't get out of bed in the morning. "I realized that drinking in bed is *not* social drinking," she admitted.

Her sister Katherine tried everything to get her sober. One time Katherine was hospitalized with a severe asthmatic attack, which the doctor feared would go into pneumonia. When Nancy visited her, Katherine confided that if she died, she wanted Nancy to raise her eight children. "There's only one thing," she said, "you're going to have to stop drinking."

"Katie, dear," Nancy replied, "you'll just have to stay alive because I will never stop drinking. Furthermore, if I had never taken a drink in my life and was confronted with raising eight kids—I'd start!" Her sister began to laugh, and laughed so hard she coughed up the congestion in her bronchial tubes and lungs. She became so clear that she was released from the hospital. All the nuns (it was a Catholic hospital) were saying, "It's a miracle."

"No," said Nancy, "it was me."

Somewhat later, Katherine showed up at Nancy's house bearing a chocolate cake, because her doctor had told her that what alcoholics really want subconsciously is sugar, not booze. She found Nancy still in bed about halfway through a bottle and none too happy to see her. Despairing, Katherine said, "If you'll just eat a piece of this cake, I'll leave you to your drinking."

"I can't eat the cake," Nancy said, slurring her words, "but hand me that Manhattan telephone directory. There's an outfit in New York called Alcoholics Anonymous that has a bead on this drinking problem. I'll call them and see what they do."

"You won't need to call," Katherine said. "My husband's best friend is an A.A. member. Would you like to see him?" Nancy agreed, primarily so her sister would leave. Surprisingly, however, she didn't finish the bottle, but somehow got up, dressed, and waited for "Mister A.A."

He didn't show up then, nor the following day. On the third day, Nancy called Katherine and demanded, "Where is this genius who's going to stop my drinking?"

Katherine replied, "He and his fellow members are discussing whether or not you qualify for A.A." The reason was that they had never had a woman alcoholic and didn't know what to do. Nancy was hurt and incensed that they would doubt she was eligible, but later that day the man's ten-year-old son appeared at her door with a brown paper bag in hand. He shoved it over to her and ran. In the bag was a copy of the Big Book, *Alcoholics Anonymous*.

Nancy read the book from cover to cover. "I couldn't put it down," she recalled. "I saw myself on every page. In the stories, I could see that the way they drank was the way I drank. I could see that it had gone bad on them and I knew it had gone bad on me, too. But I didn't want to join them. When I looked at the Twelve Steps, I didn't think a spiritual way of life was for me. Besides, I wanted to drink." It was summertime, so she hid the book behind the logs in the fireplace and continued to drink on into the fall of the year.

Then one morning she was having a bad time of it. She had a terrible hangover and felt that her life was falling apart. She picked up the phone and called her brother-in-law's friend, the AA member. "You know," she told him, "I read that entire book. I know all there is to know about alcoholism. I'm very well informed. So how come I'm still drinking?"

He didn't answer her question. He said simply, "Would you like to go to a meeting tonight?"

"I don't know. What's it like?" she asked.

He replied, "Everyone there will be just like you—an alcoholic. You'll feel very comfortable."

"What do they look like?"

"They look just like you do."

"Well," she said, "they must be gorgeous!" She went with him to the meeting.

There weren't any other women. There were six men in the group: three lawyers, a butcher, a cop, and a man who worked in a malt factory. (He claimed that he couldn't stay sober because the malt went into his pores. So the group found him another job.)

Nancy loved the attention from the men. "They were wonderful fellows, too wonderful to have to stay sober, in my sick mind," she recalled. She reasoned that since they had all crossed over this invisible line they talked about, if she could find that line, they could all cross back again. To accomplish this, she proposed to do research by interviewing other AA members. "Give me three months," she told them, "and I'll get us all out of this."

As she looks back now, she shakes her head in wonderment that no one tried to deter her. "They knew I was an alcoholic, so they just let me go about my business," she says. Her research idea involved considerable travel, as the meetings in those days were few and far between. She covered a radius of about a hundred miles, which included Manhattan, Long Island, Westchester County, and as far away as parts of New Jersey and Connecticut. She went to the meetings, listened to the stories, picked the best one, and interviewed that person. She recalled, "I actually worked at it. I was plenty thirsty, but I didn't drink. How nutty can you be?"

Of course, it was one of the best things Nancy could have done, because she got a solid grounding in AA. At the end of the three months, she had come to these conclusions:

1. The first drink activated the obsession. If you took that first drink, you were a goner.
2. Alcoholism is progressive. Once an alcoholic, always an alcoholic.

She discussed her remarkable findings with her home group. She told them yes, she knew she would have to quit drinking—but not yet. After all, she was only thirty-one. She would wait until her forties. Again no one told her no. One member told her to be sure and put her car up on blocks and not drive or she would get in a lot of trouble. Another fellow who happened to be a guard at a women's jail told her that if she landed there, he knew someone who could help get her out. In her own head, she heard her right mind asking her nutty one, "What are you waiting for? What are you waiting for?"

Suddenly her attitude changed as if someone had turned a key. She decided it would be a good idea if she became a member of AA. She even wrote a proper acceptance note, as if for a wedding: "Nancy O'D. accepts with pleasure the kind invitation of Alcoholics Anonymous to become a member."

"Nobody ever gave me a hard time," she said. "Nobody tried to reform me. How smart they were! They knew what was going on in my head because they had been there themselves. They just loved me, and in time—sober now—I felt this tug in my heart for them, the love of one alcoholic for another."

In the early days, the groups had at least one speaker meeting a week, and it was customary to exchange speakers. At three months, Nancy had to speak—at a group over in New Jersey. She was scared to death—so much so, she was throwing up. She called her sponsor, Lois K., who told her, "The reason you are so nervous is that you are thinking only of yourself. We all have that same problem. You are thinking only about what kind of impression you will make tonight. That's not the purpose. The purpose is to help one other person out there in the room if you can." Nancy said she always remembered that and never had a problem with nervousness afterward.

In her first talk, she told the New Jersey group what her sponsor had said. After the meeting, a blind woman came up and asked, "May I feel your face?" She touched Nancy's face and said, "I knew you must look like that. I'll remember you for the rest of my life." Nancy cried for an hour and a half on her return home, to think she could help someone who was blind and an alcoholic mess. "For the first time, I felt I had done something worthwhile."

As Nancy was one of the few women around, she was in demand to go out on speaker exchanges and on Twelfth Step calls where the alcoholic was a female. Her family was having fits because she was doing this. They said, "No one has ever disgraced our family this way." Nancy retorted, "No, we all died, and I want to live." When one of them said, "It's like wearing a sign on your back, Nancy," she was prompted to go out and buy a fire-engine-red dress. When she spoke, she would say, "The reason I'm wearing this red dress is because if there is a woman alcoholic around, I don't want her to miss me in the crowd. I just want her to know I'm here, I'm with her, and I'm for her."

Lois K. had been sober four years when she became Nancy's sponsor. Lois lived in White Plains, Nancy in Yonkers, and they were in touch every day. They did a lot of Twelfth Step work with other women alcoholics in Westchester County, frequently in jails, hospitals, and mental institutions.

One day she went to see a woman in a hospital. On the way

out, the patient's psychiatrist stopped Nancy and said, "My parents spent thousands of dollars on my education, yet the woman you have been talking with for an hour won't say two words to me. Can you tell me why you are succeeding with her while I'm failing?" Nancy told him that he had the education, but she was a recovered alcoholic with a story the woman identified with and understood. Nancy talked again to the woman, suggesting that she should cooperate with the doctor and that she would probably be helped by him.

The outcome was that Nancy and the doctor did Twelfth Step work together for five years, with a lot of good results. "I said to him once," she related, "'Don't ask them why they drink. They don't know, and you don't know either—nobody does. So don't ask them.'"

Another woman—whom Nancy was trying to help—set fire to her apartment and ended up in jail, labeled a pyromaniac. Nancy told the jailers, "She may be a pyromaniac, but first of all she's an alcoholic. I took a bushel basket full of bottles from under her mattress." When Nancy went to see her in jail, the girl said, "Saint Paul was in jail, you know." "Yeah," replied Nancy, "but not for burning up his tent!" Nancy took the woman to a number of meetings with her. She was a quiet person, but when she went back home to another city, she started an AA group of her own.

The second woman Nancy ever sponsored was a prostitute, who went in and out of jail like a revolving door. One time, when Nancy called the jail to say she would pick the woman up, her sponsee said, "Wait 'til this afternoon. I'm playing cards with the warden and I have him on the hook for a few dollars." After the prostitute sobered up in AA and embarked on a spiritual path, her life changed completely. She got a job, moved to a new place where no one knew her, and eventually she, too, started an AA group. "I didn't care that she was a prostitute," explained Nancy, "but I did care that she was an alcoholic."

When she was about seven years sober, Nancy started doing Twelfth Step work with relapsed alcoholics exclusively, a work she continued for the next seven years with notable success. She explained, "The first question I would ask was, 'Are you on the twenty-four-hour program?' I never got a yes. Same answer when I asked, 'Are you still going to meetings?'

"You work differently with relapsers; they've been around A.A., they know open meetings and closed meetings, they know people. I used to take the relapsers into Manhattan to one of the big meetings and tell them, 'Now, we're going to sit in the back. Never mind the speaker. Just look around the room and tell yourself, 'All these people are getting sober. And if I practice the A.A. program, I'll get sober too.'"

After forty-three years of marriage, Jim O'D. died in 1976. Six years later, at the urging of her children, Nancy O'D. moved to Lafayette, California, in the Bay Area, where all her family lived. To her continued joy, the family now includes four generations!

Reminiscing, Nancy told what it was like in AA before the Traditions: "At that time, we called A.A. a 'loosely knit organization.' It was so loosely knit I was afraid we were all going to fall through! It wasn't organized because nobody could organize us. We wouldn't accept outside contributions because we didn't want anyone telling us what to do. There were no leaders, so we had to figure everything out for ourselves. I called my first sponsor, Lois K., one time and wailed, 'I don't know what I'm doing!' and she replied, 'None of us do.' We used to pull alcoholics off of bar stools and bring them to meetings drunk. And the members, full of ego, would brag in the press about how they saved this one or that.

"It was out of our mistakes that Bill W. put together the Twelve Traditions—without help! I consider the Twelve Traditions to be the foundation of Alcoholics Anonymous."

She says there's nothing more important than having a home group:

> I couldn't have sobered up without a home group back east. It makes everything kind of automatic: You know that's where you're going every week, that's where

people care for you and where you reach out to the newcomers. I have been going to the same home group ever since I moved to California fifteen years ago.

When I first encountered A.A. we felt like the old covered-wagon train; we circled our wagons at night, and though we were a small band of pioneers, we all knew one another and were close despite our differences. Now it's like a Concorde jet. It's fast. People come in and either get sober or go out again. They get busy with life, they move away, they go to other groups. When I came in, membership in A.A. was estimated at five thousand. Today we are members of a fellowship numbering over two million! Just think of it! When we go to sleep tonight, there will be alcoholics meeting and working with each other all around the world! It never stops!

Well, that's a long way from 1944, when I came in. One thing has never changed, though: I need you just as much as you need me. We need each other—and above all, we need our Higher Power. That's where the strength is.

Marcelene W.

"I HAVE JOY AND GRATITUDE IN MY HEART FOR THE PRIVILEGE THAT GOD HAS GIVEN ME TO BE WITH YOU TODAY. IT IS ONE of the wonderful things about this program—that life begins to be an adventure and you never know where you will be led next. Life begins to be filled with wonderful things if we just 'let God loose.'"

Marce started one of her talks like that and that is the way she will be remembered—as a woman with gratitude and enthusiasm for her life. She likes to talk about "letting go and letting God" and the way that God changes her life or her attitude so she "doesn't care about the issue anymore." Either way, she has ultimate faith in her Higher Power as a God of love and laughter and enthusiasm.

Marcelene W. had a father and a husband who were alcoholic, so she says she was doubly blessed to be able to find this way of life.

As a teenager, she realized that her father was an alcoholic, but since she didn't know anything about alcoholism, she just got mad at him and tried to shut him out of her life. For sure, she vowed, she would never date, marry, or have anything to do with anyone who drank.

She now knows that her husband, Bob, didn't pull the wool over her eyes on purpose. She didn't see him drink before marriage and, of course, now she knows that it is a progressive disease. By the time they had three children fifteen years later, however, it was confirmed that her husband had just as bad a problem as her father did. What was she to do? She had three daughters—an older daughter and twin daughters four years younger.

She began resisting and fighting Bob and life, and what life and Bob seemed to be doing to her. She had hurt feelings and hurt pride and self-pity. She went through every cycle and tried everything that she ever heard of to try to control Bob and his drinking. She tried drinking with him. She tried not drinking with him. She tried pouring it out. She tried fussing. She tried not saying anything. She tried trying to understand. She tried saying she didn't give a damn and that she didn't even want to understand. She says today that she knows just about everything she did was the wrong thing to do, but she was mixed up and so confused, she hardly knew what to think or do. She told her girls that Daddy was sick and thought she was lying. She told her friends that he was sorry and no good and thought she was telling the truth. She thought that he was ornery and no good and that if he loved the girls and her, he wouldn't be acting like he was.

She frequently told him those very words, "If you love me you wouldn't do this. Why do you have to act like this? Why don't you act like other people? Why don't you drink like other people? Why? Why?"

Then finally she hit bottom—a bottom of deep despair. She got to where it seemed as if she really didn't care anymore, about anything. She built a wall between herself and other people. She shut herself off from her husband, from her family, from her friends. She vowed that she wouldn't be hurt again. She wouldn't care. She shut God out too—that was a miserable existence. She shut God out as one of the first things because she thought God had let her down—that he had turned his back on her. She had no idea what the real problems were; she only knew that she was miserable. She was in a squirrel cage and was frustrated, and the outward manifestations of alcoholism heaped on the fire made it total despair and misery.

One day the sheriff called and said that their "stolen" car had been found. She hadn't known it had been gone for a week. She and Bob weren't talking much at that time. What had really happened was that Bob didn't remember where he'd left it.

One time Bob went "to work" and came home ten days later having detoured to Mexico and having learned to pierce ears and in the process got himself a pierced ear with a gold earring for it. He was a little insulted that she didn't appreciate his handiwork.

Those shenanigans kept her in a state of confusion, not to mention despair. She wondered, begged, and whined, "Why do you keep doing these things?" Finally she lost all hope and all faith that anything could be all right between Bob and her and gave up on him.

Bob had been gone two or three months, supposedly working out of state. She found out that was not the case and finally decided to take the girls and get out of the marriage. It was an important decision. She was fed up with taking care of her four children. She decided to kick one of the kids out of the nest—he was barely there anyway.

She had always tried to protect the family's good name, particularly with the rest of the family. She had told both their families as little as she could get by with. As they did not live in the vicinity, it was possible to let on very little.

She sat down and wrote her in-laws a letter as to what was really happening, that she was sick and tired of tending to Bob—she didn't mince any words. She said the time had come that she was going to go to work and try to support herself and the girls and that Bob didn't fit anyplace in her picture. She said that they could have him back, that they could keep him from smoking in bed and keep him from burning down their house, that she was through staying up all night with him if he was home and worrying about his falling in the street or getting in a fight if he wasn't home, that they could have him. "You can take him and do as you please. Good luck and God bless."

She told the girls that Daddy was sick and was going to a hospital near their grandparents. She was just trying to smooth things over for them. However, when she heard back from Bob's parents, they reported that he was being put in a mental hospital and it looked like a long stay. So she was glad that she hadn't actually lied to the girls. But she was still mad as a hornet. What she now says is that she was "sick and tired of being sick and tired."

Marce and the three girls went home to Mother and Marce's alcoholic dad. She looked so tense, tired, thin, and ill that her mother said, "I have never seen anybody in as big a mess. I've never seen such a bundle of nerves. I've never seen you so thin and so drawn and so shaky. Why don't you wait about a month before going to work and let me stuff you full of vitamins and food, and see if you can't get to looking better." Marce kind of liked someone feeling sorry for her and tending to her, so she agreed.

Meanwhile, Bob contacted her. She had been away from him for about three months by this time and didn't want to see him. She wanted to get her life together. It had taken a lot of gumption for her to take the stand she had, and she didn't want to back down so soon.

Bob, however, was always a good salesman and was always able to talk her into just about anything if he set his mind to it. So he talked her into letting him come to see her and the girls. He was in Mississippi. Marce was in Midland, Texas. Are we surprised?

When he came over, he told her he had joined AA and had been sober about a month. Since they had been separated for some time, she could see the miracle God had worked in his life. He did seem different. He was talking in a different way as well. Before this conversation, their communications had spiraled downward to fussing and fighting—not real conversation. This time he wasn't trying to make her go back to him. He told her that if she would let him, he would spend the rest of his life trying to make it up to her and the girls. He told her he had been wrong to have treated them the way he had. He told her about some of the things he was hearing and learning at AA. He told her he didn't blame her if she wanted to get a divorce and that if she did, he would help her any way he could. He told her he had a job (when he had been telling her for years that there were none to be found in his field).

Money had been a big problem and they had fought about it for years. Bob told her that he was making six hundred dollars a month (this was August 1954) and that she and the girls could have five hundred of it and he would live on one hundred of it. She accepted his offer, and she and the girls moved into an apartment. Bob said he would stay where he was—in a small room in a boardinghouse.

Bob kept his word. And something else happened. The wives of the men in Bob's AA group started calling her and trying to make friends with her. They told her how fine Bob was and how well he was doing. They wanted her to come to the meetings they had at the AA club. They wanted to come visit her and talk things over with her. She was reluctant. She tried to be nice about it, but she didn't trust any of it. She had been through too much to trust Bob or his friends or his friends' wives yet.

So her life went on. Bob kept sending her the money and keeping his commitments. The wives, also, kept their word; they kept being friendly to her and the girls. They kept calling and inviting her to meetings. She kept thanking them politely but refusing their friendship.

Finally, Bob's sponsor's wife called her again, as she had on numerous occasions. Marce was beginning to feel a little guilty that she kept on refusing invitations from these people who had, at the least, helped Bob so greatly. So when Anna called her this time with an invitation to her house for dinner, Marce accepted. She had run out of excuses and her conscience was beginning to bother her. As soon as she accepted, Anna said, "By the way, Bob is coming too. Would you like for Henry to come pick you up or would it be all right if Bob picked you up?" Marce said, "Well, we are speaking now, so I guess it will be all right if Bob picks me up."

At the dinner were the three men who had gone to Mississippi and brought Bob back to Midland, thereby helping save his life. Their wives were also there. The table was set with beautiful silver, china, and linen, and it was obvious that "these were real nice folks." She began to relax a little. She could be at ease. She knew that they knew just about everything about Bob and her and so there was no point to the pretenses that had been her defense in the past. She started being herself. What a relief. That was just about the time someone said, "Oh by the way, there is a meeting tonight down at the club and we are all going. Wouldn't you like to go?" She says that she thought to herself, "No, I wouldn't like to go. But what can I do? Here I am. I've enjoyed their company. I've enjoyed a lovely dinner, and what can I do but go?" And that, she tells, is how she got to her first Al-Anon meeting (though the group was not yet named). She was tricked into it.

Once she got there, however, she began to "have a real good feeling down deep inside. I liked what I saw and I liked what I heard." She read the Twelve Steps and thought, "Yes, these are fine." The turmoil in her ceased just a little bit from that first meeting.

She couldn't let on that she was "giving in" that easily, however, so she made comments such as, "Well, no one is going to pull the wool over my eyes so fast. No one [meaning Bob] is going to wrap me around his finger again too easily." So she went home that night on that note.

Life moved on and Marce went back to her Al-Anon meetings—just not always with Bob. They were both making progress in their separate programs, but she didn't want to move too fast. She did let Bob come over sometimes to see the children. He had appealed to her sympathy. She knew that it wasn't easy for him to give them the five hundred dollars and for him to live on the one hundred, and it was worrying her. But one night he came up the stairs carrying a whole armload of his clothes. She said, "Whoa, what are you doing?" He, it is reported, innocently replied, "Well, I just didn't know what to do with all this stuff. I had it in the back of the car and I don't have anyplace to put it, and you've got a whole big closet here that you aren't using. . . . I thought maybe I could store them in that closet. Wouldn't that be okay?" Marce replied, "No! You can do no such thing! You get that stuff out of here right now, and get it out of my sight, and I don't want to see it anymore."

She says she believes that was the turning point. She didn't like herself afterward. She didn't feel good about her words or actions. She knew he had been trying to make things right for all of them. It hurt her to think that she could act that ugly—that she could be that mean to anyone, much less her husband who really had been doing his best to set things right. So she called him back. They had some talks over two or three visits, and Bob moved back in with his family.

Over these visits, the two of them sat down calmly without all the fussing and crying that used to go along with their "fireside chats." Bob went first and told her all the things that he knew he had done that he was sorry for. And then he asked Marce to tell him the things that he had done that had bothered her. She said that she unloaded on him with both barrels. They shared with each other how it had been and what had happened in their lives. They got it all out on the table—all the dirty mess, all the wreckage of the past. Then it was Bob's turn to tell Marce about the things she had done that had hurt and upset him. When Marce had unloaded, Bob hadn't done anything but sit there and let her talk. She couldn't do less when it was his turn, so that's what she did. He had set the example. There was no chance for their marriage before this happening. She later learned that Bob was ready to take the Ninth Step before she was. He had had more time in the program and had learned some things that would help their lives and their marriage to work.

She began to feel more and more gratitude for their finding the program and for all the people who had helped them. She said she had not previously looked at her character defects of pride and self-righteousness. She then had a moment of truth. In her married life she had said, "If only Bob wouldn't drink." Well now, Bob was not drinking, but Marce was still messed up. She realized that she wasn't happy inside herself. When she looked over at Bob, he seemed happier than he had ever been. He seemed to be growing spiritually as well as other ways. She realized that she had a way to go to become the person she wanted to be. The program of Al-Anon and the Twelve Steps were the way for her to move along and grow toward this ideal. It was a breakthrough, and she was glad.

The wives' meetings that she was attending were precursors to Al-Anon, but they were following the AA program the best they could and were trying to work the Twelve Steps from their perspective. The *One Day at a Time in Al-Anon* book was not yet written and Al-Anon had not yet gotten fully organized. The original family groups were linked together for the first time in 1950, but many AA groups had wives' meetings before then. Al-Anon's first book, *Al-Anon Family Groups,* came out in 1955.

Now Marce says, "You never can possess this program. You just have to keep pursuing it." She has spoken about the many levels of the program. Her experience has been that we use just enough of the program to keep us out of the pain of living. She believes in the saying "We absolutely insist on enjoying life." If we want the diamonds of life, we need to keep digging deep into the soil of the Steps.

So her adventure of taking the Steps and working the program began. She said that if she had been alcoholic, she would have had many slips because she got off the track of the program many times. She remembers that one night, they had company. One word led to another and another until in the middle of this she went all to pieces and fled the room, crying. She said, "All of my Al-Anon training and everything that I had been trying to do just flew right out the window and I went all to pieces. I reverted right back to what I used to be like." She shut the door and left Bob to the company, but she did remember where help was. And she knew that there was a Power that understood her and could help her. "I had learned enough by this time to get on my knees, and I talked to God like I have never talked to Him before. I said, 'God, you know how I feel. And maybe nobody else understands, but you know and I know that I am powerless over this situation. There is nothing I can do about it. But I know you can, so I am turning it over to you.

I am turning everything about the situation over to you.' And then I started seeing the way it had been. I saw the way I had been. I had still been trying to manage Bob. I had said that I had taken the Third Step, that I had turned my life, and my will over to the care of God as I understood Him. But all of a sudden I realized that I had never turned Bob over to God."

That was a turning point. She no longer "suggested" that he read chapter such-and-such in the Big Book, or that he make the phone call to so-and-so whose wife had asked Marce to ask Bob to call him, or that Bob sure could use that meeting tonight, or that he was really getting off the beam of his attitudes.

It was apparent to her that God could and would take it from there and she made a deeper decision to let go and let God with Bob, her children, and everything about her life. She has since been heard to say that God did a much better job with Bob than she had up to then, that she's glad she let God do the job. She was tired and even exhausted and so ready to relax from all the efforts at managing where she lacked the power. She started realizing that God was doing for her what she couldn't, that wonderful things were starting to come to pass.

That was a real awareness in one of the truths of life for her, of things in life "coming to pass." Of nothing staying the same. When she prayed about a situation, she found that God always did one of two things. He changed either her attitude or the circumstances. Whatever was going on in her life at the time was destined to change. "It would either go or it would cease to bother me anymore" was the way she put it. Another way she puts this wonderful spiritual law is, "When I really let it go to Him, God either changes me or it and either way I am okay with it."

She began to put much more emphasis on her spiritual growth. She kept having "loads lifted" as she kept working the Steps and using the program in more and more areas of her life.

One night Bob asked her, "Marcelene, have you ever thought what would have happened to you if I had stayed sober and continued in this program and you hadn't come on in to it?" She had not thought about it. But a day or so later as she was mulling over the question, a picture flashed across her mind. She said that it was just like watching a television screen. She even saw it in color. This is what she saw:

> She hadn't gone back together with Bob. She had just left her work with the three little girls trailing along. She had been to the grocery store and was carrying heavy grocery sacks, trudging along the sidewalk. She looked so tired, actually miserable and feeling sorry for herself. She could see herself feeling like a martyr, feeling as if life had passed her by. She could almost feel the self-pity and the resentments still all stored up inside. Just hating Bob.
>
> All of a sudden he came onto the scene. He was in a red convertible. He was laughing and smiling and happy looking. Sitting next to him was a peroxide blonde wearing a mink stole, also laughing and smiling and happy looking.

Finally, she says that she "got the message": "Grow or go." Either grow up and grow spiritually or go backward into the misery of the ways of thinking and feeling that were off the beam of the program. It was probably at that time that she truly "abandoned herself to God in all her affairs."

As part of her growing through Step Eleven—"Sought through prayer and meditation to improve our conscious contact with God *as we understood Him*, praying only for knowledge of His will for us and the power to carry that out"—she got an idea that she was supposed to start a meditation and prayer chapel where people could come and learn things that would help them to grow spiritually. She shared her idea with like-minded people. The Chapel of Light in Lake Whitney, Texas, was built in 1975. Bob and Marce's oldest daughter, Sandy, died of cancer about that time, and the first service held in the chapel was her memorial service. The chapel has helped many people with Step Eleven and in many ways since that time.

As Marce continued to grow in the program, she found other pockets of resentment and despair. She knew that it was time to forgive her alcoholic father. By now she knew that her father didn't want to act and be the way he was. By now she also knew that she could help out in that area.

She had some guilt because in the past, not understanding the disease of alcoholism, she had tried to get her mother to leave her dad. She had not known that he was a sick person. She just thought he was a bad husband and a poor father. So now that she knew better, she wanted to do better. She began by praying for her dad. She would pray "God bless Daddy" if she couldn't do anything else at the time. Pretty soon she was able to give her mother encouragement about the situation. She started loving her daddy and showing both her parents that she loved them just the way they were. She started helping her mother to see that her dad didn't want to act the way he did sometimes, that he was sick and needed help, that he needed their love. She began to show her dad that she did understand more about him and loved him through trying times. She started hoping that her mom and dad could be happy, that things could turn out all right for them. In her mind's eye, she started seeing the family having happy times. She started seeing her father well, happy, and laughing even, with pleasantry all around.

What happened next was that God used her to help her dad. The night that she "saw" them all happy and having a good time, she felt a nudge to go over to her parents' house, so she did. When she got there, her father put his arms around her and told her how sorry he was about the way he had been. He started crying, and Marce said, "That's all right, Daddy. I understand. I love you. You are sick and you need help. I know you don't want to be this way." He let them call for help that night and he started his own road to recovery. Marcelene received a blessing that night and she passed it on.

Marce and Bob both will be long remembered for passing many blessings on to others on this happy road. Before Bob's death in 1984, they both made significant contributions to the programs they were so dedicated to. They both spoke nationally and internationally for many years. They were responsible, along with some other close friends, for at least five new conferences being started—probably more, as they didn't tell about everything they did. But so many people have started life over and jump-started their programs by being introduced to conferences such as Ceta-Glen, Brownwood, Brazos Riverside, Woman to Woman for AA, and Al-Anon Women at Brownwood, Young People's AA conference, or Crested Butte conference. From these, several other significant conferences have developed. Marce was the third national Al-Anon delegate from Texas to World Services in New York. When Alice B. was asked to get a meditation book together, Marce was on the literature committee with her. In that way, she helped give us the beloved *One Day at a Time in Al-Anon* meditation book. While she was a delegate, Marce also helped start the first U.S. Alateen State conference. Before that time Alateen wasn't even in existence in much of the country, much less throughout the world.

Marce has a unique theory about the programs' blessings. She says that if we were a "blessed child" receiving the blessing from our parents, then we were fortunate. If we weren't, however, it wasn't because our parents didn't want to give them to us—it was because they couldn't give them to us. We can receive the blessing from God through the Twelve Steps of AA and Al-Anon. When we receive that blessing, then we can bless others with it: our parents, our husbands, our wives, our friends. Marce believes that we cannot be "hateful and grateful" at the same time. When we are grateful, we can spread God's blessings. She always ends her talks with "God bless you and I love you."

Arbutus O'N.

My name is Arbutus O'N. and it is by the grace of God that I belong to the Al-Anon Family Groups.

I'm powerless over people, over places, and over things. My life continues to be unmanageable when I fail to practice the principles that were given to us by a bunch of ex-drunks who found sobriety in Alcoholics Anonymous.

Because of the program, I can say this without feeling guilty.

I'd like to believe that the early members of the Al-Anon Family Groups were convinced by the miracle of sobriety that this program would work for everyone. It was out of this conviction that Al-Anon Family Groups grew to reach all over the world and have shown astounding results. We subscribe to the concept that alcoholism is a family illness, and then we get so carried away telling people how sick we got that we forget to say that we have a program for family recovery. Ours is a program that shares. But please, let us share our recovery, not our sickness. That's what we're about here this weekend.

I'm sure that people are here this morning whom you haven't seen since your last roundup. It's difficult to see growth within ourselves, but we can see it in other people. Regrettably, we can also see regression.

I'm just delighted with AA people. They're always so pleased to see each other. They charge across a room and beat each other on the back. As Chuck Chamberlin used to say, "Everybody's talking, nobody's listening," especially at these big gatherings out in San Diego and other places that we've been. They're just pounding each other, and then somebody comes in the door, and they stop right in the middle of a sentence and they say, "Oh, look. There's old George and he's still sober." They don't even expect each other to stay sober! Love without expectancy I think it's called.

I'm delighted to be here. Our pretty little girl asked me this morning how long it has been since I've been to the Gopher State Roundup, and I said I've never been here before. Many of you know that my husband, Bill, has probably the oldest tape library in the world. Not the largest, but the oldest. He used to tape with the gentleman that you all mentioned last night, Don B. They had a kind of thing going. Bill would tape down in the hot country, and Don would tape up here in the cold country, and then they'd swap tapes.

But I have never been to this particular roundup before. I can't wait to go home and tell my home group how many people were here. I've seen larger crowds, but not often.

Bill sends you greetings. He doesn't travel with me anymore. Bill's health has stabilized to a large degree, but he's almost totally blind. It's tragic, because he can't read the labels on his tapes and he can't drive his automobile. It's a handicap for Texas people not to have wheels. But he sends you his warmest regards. People say to me often, "Does Bill mind you wandering around the country by yourself?" He doesn't, because he knows you will take care of me. He expects it. And I'll come home and briefly tell him that you took wonderful care of me this weekend.

As I told you, I'm called a longtimer. Not an old-timer, a longtimer. I'll tell you how you get to be a longtimer. You just keep coming to meetings and stay alive, and you'll make it. There are two categories for longtimers, I believe—those who are dropouts and those who are pushouts.

I wonder what you do with your longtimers. Once upon a time I didn't feel charitable toward dropouts, but now that I'm getting older I'm beginning to understand a few things that I once didn't know. Now those of us who stay around a long time, our hair gets white, but most of us hear pretty well. We hear what you say. You say, "The newcomer is the most important person in this group." And that may be true, unless I'm there. It's been my privilege to talk to a lot of people in a lot of places. I've learned about people, and people are all alike.

Every one of you who is here this morning is here for exactly the same reason that I'm here. We were driven here under the cruel lash of alcoholism because we had nowhere else to go. Nowhere else.

I once thought that alcoholism was the product of my generation, but that isn't true. Alcoholism is as old as time. Alcoholism is a progressive, insidious, fatal illness. It prompts the unthinking to make jokes about drunks, but it can leave a family homeless and penniless. Alcoholism is a public cancer. It can turn men or women against themselves. Alcoholism is a blight on the history of mankind. The Bible warns against it. Shakespeare diagnosed it. Tennessee Williams built a prizewinning play around it.

But no one, as far as I've ever been able to learn, seemed to do anything about alcoholism until the advent of AA. Priests and ministers were baffled at their inability to cope with this insidious habit, this dreadful malady if you please. They preached to alcoholics. Prayed over you. Had you sign pledges. And when these things failed, they damned your soul to hell. Scientists wanted to find a cure for alcoholism. They wanted to find a pill or a vaccine that would stop compulsive drinking. Failing to do this, they said to the medical students and other generations, "Don't waste your time on these people. They're hopeless."

Preaching failed and there was no cure, so there was only one other thing they knew to do with alcoholics—they must be punished. So we locked you up in jails. The more you drank, the longer we kept you in jail. The longer we kept you in jail, the more you drank when you were released. It became a vicious cycle. We tried to change the body chemistry of sick people with punishment. And society allowed this to happen. Nay, we insisted on it, to our everlasting shame. We'll never know how many sick alcoholics died in jails around our country at the hands of sadistic jailers.

But there was one group of people who never gave up on the alcoholic. These were the families of alcoholics—the people who loved you.

We took jobs to feed the children whom you were too sick to be responsible for. We doctored your hangovers. Some of us bought your liquor. We picked up your hot checks. We bailed you out of jails. We pleaded with judges. We said, "John's a good man when he's sober." And to complete this ridiculous paradox, we gave you hell every time you got drunk.

Society was puzzled at the behavior of the families of alcoholics. Did you know that? We were a far greater puzzlement to society than the drunks were. They could understand when the drunk wrecked his car, and left his job in midafternoon, and partied all night, and wore lampshades on his head, and all those ridiculous things. But they couldn't understand us families. They could not understand why we continued to love and care for the alcoholic.

Some people thought we were endowed with some special goodness that made us better than other people. They were the ones who gave us halos to wear. One of my AA friends told me that if my halo slipped six inches, it'd choke me to death.

But we accepted these halos, and quite willingly. I put mine on every morning when I put on my lipstick. My halo had a name—it was called *self-righteousness.* Did you ever notice that word? Does it taste good? It doesn't.

We don't wear those halos anymore. You can find them discarded in any Al-Anon meeting that you want to attend. We don't need them anymore. I'd like you to know that we did not find them comfortable.

Then of course there were other people who thought we were just plain fools to live under such circumstances. My mother came in this group. Mother used to say, "God looks after fools and drunks, and that takes care of Arbutus and Bill." Mother was right. God did look after us, when we didn't have sense enough to look after ourselves.

Then a little time went by, and the professionals got interested in us. I never want to leave out the professionals. These were the dear people who did research on us.

I remember one particular research project that was going on in the early sixties. A lovely lady who shall remain nameless was doing a survey to determine what kind of women married alcoholics. Marty Mann was still at her peak at that time, when I was in and out of the National Council Office when I went to New York to the World Service Conferences. Marty asked me to go across the hall and be interviewed by this lady as part of the survey. Marty kept shaking her head. Of course the survey was absolutely and totally worthless—a waste of good government money, because women do not marry alcoholics. They marry men because they love them, and some of the men have alcoholism. But this woman kept asking me questions, and I answered them. She kept saying, "But you're not like other people." I didn't want to tell her that I had made a career of that all my life. But it was an exercise in futility. I got a little ticked off at these people doing all their research without giving us equal time. So I decided that I'd do some research myself.

I learned that Alexander the Great was an alcoholic. He'd conquered the whole known civilized world when he was only thirty-three years old, and he wept because there were no more worlds to conquer. But he could not conquer his desire to drink. He died prematurely in an alcoholic convulsion.

I learned that Stephen Foster was an alcoholic. Stephen Foster gave the world his most beautiful folk music, but he was a compulsive drinker. It seemed to come on him like a sickness, his wife once said. And so it does. They found Stephen Foster sick unto death on the New York Bowery. When he was dead, they found in his pockets thirty-eight cents. One penny for each year of a misspent life, and the lyrics to another song. Stephen Foster loved his wife—his "Jeannie with the light-brown hair." But the love of his wife couldn't stop his drinking, and he died drunk.

Robert Louis Stevenson was an alcoholic. He could weave the magic of children's stories. Yet he all but destroyed himself with the magic that he found in the bottle. It could have been a fifth of gin or a quart of bourbon. He describes the personality change of an alcoholic in the story *Dr. Jekyll and Mr. Hyde.*

I watched this sort of changing personality right in my own living room, just like a lot of you did. You watched the man you love turn into a babbling idiot, a degenerate animal—into a Dr. Jekyll and Mr. Hyde.

Now, history said little about the families of these men and others like them. But I believe that I know the fear and the loneliness that Jeannie knew when she waited for her restless, talented husband to come home from a spree. I believe that I know the homesickness that Fannie Stevenson knew when she left her home in California to go to a South Seas island with her husband, in hopes that he might regain his health. Robert Louis Stevenson had a dual problem. He also had tuberculosis. I believe that I know the joy they knew when he did regain his health. I believe that I know the serenity to some degree that they both knew when he found sobriety.

Venoah hasn't been in Texas for the last several years, and so I haven't been the brunt of her criticism. I don't recall that she ever said in so many words, "Arbutus, why do you think it's necessary every time you get in front of a microphone to give us a history lesson?" Well, I'll tell you why I do it. I can't tell jokes. I always forget the punch lines.

No that isn't it at all. I want to point out something that I think is significant. These selfsame people who were so totally baffled about their inability to do anything about alcoholism in other generations are doing a great deal about it right now. Priests and ministers now feel that alcoholics are God's children too. They send them to treatment, and they send their families to us so they can get well too.

It's now possible to get a man in a hospital for a simple diagnosis of alcoholism. This wasn't true when alcoholism was a critical point in mine and Bill's life. You couldn't get an alcoholic in a hospital. Not unless the doctor was willing to jeopardize his license and give a false diagnosis. I don't know how many alcoholics must have died of "the flu." But you couldn't call them alcoholics and get them in a hospital. County judges and law enforcement people send alcoholics to treatment now instead of sending them to jail.

Every time you turn around there's something new being done about alcoholism. Now you see that newspapers have articles about it. I was absolutely amazed a couple of years ago to find an article on alcoholism in the *Atlantic Monthly*. That's a prestigious publication, and they just don't publish junk. There it was, big as life, and twice as natural. It's almost impossible anymore not to hear about treatment for alcoholism.

I said to you last night, "If you don't have an alcoholic in your family, please get one. Don't marry them, just borrow one. They're the handiest things you can have. They're as handy as a pocket on a shirt. You can blame everything that goes wrong in your life on the alcoholic." I'd have been happy to share with you a few years back. I was overstocked. It's good now to laugh about these things that we used to cry about.

But I'd like to make clear to you that despite the failure and lack of understanding prior to this generation, or the one before, these people are doing marvelous things about the treatment of alcoholism. Please don't misunderstand me, Bill Wilson said we should be "friendly with our friends." I would not put down professionals. I have tremendous respect for their willingness to help and for their training. But they just don't know all there is to know about alcoholism, and they're not getting the job done.

But this morning I'm looking at a whole roomful of experts. You're the people who know about alcoholism. You know about alcoholism because you've lived with it. You know the symptoms of alcoholism. You know the progression. You know about slips and AA. You know about the alibi system. Some of you, bless your heart, know about alcoholic convulsions. Some of you have lived through the terrors of D.T.'s. There isn't much that you do not know about alcoholism, because you have lived with it.

So, in my opinion, this is a job for you to do—a job for you and for me. I learned this a long, long time ago. You see, I came into this outfit before we had an outfit. I came here when we had fifty Al-Anon groups in the world. I think the latest delegates report that I heard gave us over thirty thousand Al-Anon groups in the world. Our literature has been translated into many languages. Anywhere in the world you can go and hear the same preamble that you heard read this morning.

It has been my privilege to watch this society evolve for the last forty-six years, and it has been fascinating. I wouldn't take a million dollars to give up my experiences. By the same token, I wouldn't take another million dollars to do it again. When I came here, we didn't have any literature. We didn't have a program. All we had in those early days were the growing awareness of the need for help and the dubious permission of some people who were new in AA to come to their meeting places while they had a meeting. That's what we did.

We met in dirty little hallways and kitchens, anywhere we could put a few chairs. We sat together and we talked. I'm not going to have to tell you what we talked about. It was kind of a morbid competition to determine which one of us lived with the sorriest man. I wasn't comfortable in those meetings because I did not live with a sorry man. I lived with a fine young man who drank too much.

But these dear people who put the life-changing program of Alcoholics Anonymous together were visionaries. These dear people knew that in time Al-Anon, the families of alcoholics, would become aware of their great need for help. Al-Anon is a kissing cousin to invention. They were both born of necessity. And these dear people knew that in time we would become aware of this necessity.

So they made provisions for us when they wrote the book *Alcoholics Anonymous*. They included in that book two chapters for the families. One of the chapters they entitled "To Wives." That is not intended to be a put-down for you fine young men who are members of the Al-Anon group. The truth is that when that book was written, no women were in AA, so they addressed that chapter to wives. The early groups in Canada called their groups the "Wives Groups."

The other chapter is of course entitled, "The Family Afterward." And down in our part of the country, we took a paragraph out of this chapter and used it for a preamble to open our meetings. I keep hoping one of those things will surface. Some of the things that I gathered together went away in a tornado back in 1979, along with that first preamble that we used. But this is what the paragraph in the chapter says:

> The past is the principle asset of the alcoholic's family, and frequently it is almost the only one. This painful past can be of infinite value to families still struggling with their problem. We feel that each family who has been relieved owes something to those who have not. And when the occasion requires, each member of it should be only too willing to bring former mistakes, no matter how grievous, out of their hiding places. Showing others how we were given help is the only thing that makes our life worthwhile. Cling to the thought that in God's hands your dark past is the greatest possession you have, the key to life and happiness for others. With it you can avert death or misery for them.

My dear friends that's heavy stuff. The past several years there's been a little controversy in some parts of the country that says that we should not have anything to do with AA literature. I don't know where the idea started, but it's the silliest thing I've ever heard. You heard these beautiful young ladies stand at the podium today and talk about the Al-Anon program. Al-Anon doesn't have a program. Al-Anon never *did* have a program. And Al-Anon never *will* have a program. We use the AA program.

I don't listen when they say these are the Twelve Steps adapted from AA. I just don't listen, because these are the Steps of AA. AA has given us permission to use them along with their Traditions and their Concepts. But that's another soapbox.

I've also been misquoted a number of times as saying that I expected every Al-Anon member in the world to own and study the book *Alcoholics Anonymous*. That is not true. I simply say that I require the people whom I sponsor to study the first 164 pages of the book *Alcoholics Anonymous* or get themselves another sponsor. If you want to stay sick, I don't have time to waste with you.

I was privileged to be exposed to the spiritual giants of this program when I came here. I was seventeen hundred miles from my own family, and my own mother wouldn't speak to me. My father never did find sobriety. I'll talk about him some more in a few minutes. He was most unhappy when I left to come to Texas with our four children. I brought four children across the continent on the strength of an alcoholic's promise that he'd never take another drink. So I didn't have any trouble with Step Two.

I came to Texas expecting to find a support group and Bill's family, only to learn that they were quite aware why Bill had a problem with drinking: He married a girl up in the Carolinas where they make all the good bourbon and all the cigarettes the people are killing themselves with. So I didn't have a support group.

But I was privileged to know people like Al Badger and Horace Spore, and all of the spiritual giants. I was scared to death. I was alone and defeated and didn't know how to quit. That's a spiritual poverty, to be whipped down to your knees, and you can't quit fighting. That was my state of mind and being.

I went to these people and said, "I don't understand Bill. I just don't understand him. Bill hates a liar worse than anything on earth, and he can't tell the truth. He's irresponsible. I can't depend on him. I don't understand it." And they said, "Read this book, Arbutus. It will describe the illness that Bill has." My God, that's what I wanted.

You printed it in a book, and I believed it. I grew up with books. I believe books. And the book *Alcoholics Anonymous* explains the illness. It goes on to say it will teach you the philosophy that you need to get well, and it does.

Now, I don't care what I have to learn. I want the top authority. Don't you? I want the expert. I want the people who know what they're talking about. And it's recognized worldwide that the book *Alcoholics Anonymous* is the top authority on alcoholism. If you don't read that book, you're cheating yourself, and I feel sorry for you. I best get off my soapbox.

I think you want to know what happened to me. I attended my first AA meeting in Amarillo, Texas, in 1948. I didn't want to go to that meeting. I put myself under obligation to a lovely lady who was married to a member of Alcoholics Anonymous. When she invited me to go to the meeting, I didn't quite know how to refuse. If you haven't picked up on the accent yet, I'm a hillbilly, and hillbillies don't like to be obliged. Hillbillies don't like to lose either. We get an equalizer every once in a while, but we don't lose.

So I went to this meeting reluctantly, and for that I shall always be grateful. It was an open meeting. There was about 150 people there. You probably notice, I drink a lot of coffee. I'd been to the coffee bar a number of times, so when the meeting started, a lovely lady who I later learned was a member of Alcoholics Anonymous leaned across my friend, Marguerite, and whispered to me. What she said was, "How long has it been since you had a drink, honey?" I wasn't embarrassed by the lady's question. I'm not a teetotaler. I once said I didn't trust teetotalers, though I don't say that anymore. I have a friend down in Wichita Falls, Texas, who never even tasted liquor. She's really a teetotaler. I trust her with my life, so I don't say that anymore. But Marguerite was terribly embarrassed and answered the lady's question for me. She said, "Mrs. O'N. is not an alcoholic, but she knows about alcoholism."

I grew up in a house with two men, both of whom was my father. My father was a two-fisted construction man who worked hard. He played hard. And he drank hard. Dad was a gray-eyed Irishman who taught me to love poetry, who taught me to sing Irish folksongs, who had the patience to teach me to work my geometry problems with his framing square.

But on Saturday night my dad turned into a devil. My dad was a hallucinating drunk who saw creeping, crawling things. He was totally insane when he drank. And my dad's alcoholism destroyed both my father and my mother. My father's alcoholism turned my lovely mother into an old, ugly, hateful woman. She hated him as long as she lived. She hated him long after he was dead and in his grave. In the last years of her life, which she spent in total darkness, she hated anybody who had ever loved John Martin, and that included me.

My dad was a craftsman, the likes of which we don't have anymore. He loved to build things for my mother. In the cold, long, winter nights, the days in Carolina when we had snow up to the windowsills, he'd build mother a china closet perhaps, or a table.

He loved wood. I've watch Dad caress a piece a wood, much the same as a lady caresses a piece of velvet or a piece of satin. He would say of the wood as he caressed it, "This wood has a beautiful fault." I didn't know what he was talking about until I got into this program.

He would carefully select the wood that he used. He would put it together with great precision as only a craftsman can do. He would sand it and polish it, and make of it truly a thing of beauty.

Then later he would smash it in a drunken fury.

Alcoholism destroyed my father and my mother. My father was one of those who never found this program. He used to come to Texas, and he'd go to meetings with us. He'd come home from the meetings and ask Bill a question. He would say, "How do you get the 'want-to' Bill?" Dad couldn't find the want-to, and he couldn't stay sober.

For years after I gained the courage in this program to ask the God of my understanding for special favors, I closed my eyes every day of my life with a prayer: "God, don't let my dad die drunk." I cannot tell you why this is such a terror to those of us who love alcoholics. I can only tell you that it is. My father died in 1965. He had throat cancer. He did not die drunk. I had pneumonia the first eight years that I lived in Texas. I think I was trying to escape. I had just come home from the hospital, and my brother Mike called to tell me that Dad was not going to be with us long. He said, "We have to pray extra hard for Dad, Arbutus. He's not going to make it." And I said, "No. No."

I didn't want that filthy stuff to destroy that baritone voice. I didn't want that filthy stuff to make it impossible for my dad even to have a drink of water. But I prayed, "God, don't let my dad die drunk."

I do not tell you these things about my dad or about my mother that you may weep for them. My dad's all right. My dad doesn't have to drink anymore. And Mother doesn't hate him any longer. I tell you these things that you may know that I have always loved an alcoholic.

And because I love alcoholics, I want to restore their families. I know a lot about alcoholics. I believe with all my heart that of all the things an alcoholic loves, he loves his family most. Even when they tear us down over and over again, they love their families most. Of this I am convinced.

When I married that tall Texan who became the father of our children, I was not concerned with his drinking. Not the slightest bit. I drank with Bill.

He worked for a company that sent us all over the United States, and we got drunk everywhere we went. We've been terribly drunk in Minneapolis. We've been terribly drunk in San Francisco, Chicago, St. Louis, San Antonio, anywhere we went.

It was important in my generation to have fun. One of my AA lady friends said that she had so much fun it'd like to kill her. That's just about what happened to Bill and me.

But then in 1940 two things happened that should have made Bill and me grow up. We became parents, and the world became involved in a war.

I quit drinking. I was too concerned about casualty lists. I was following the troop movements in Europe and later in the South Pacific. We had relatives in the military and things were too serious.

We had our second child the next year, but Bill was not there when Nancy was born. Nancy came on Wednesday, but she didn't meet her dad until Sunday. When Bill finally came to the hospital—it was in Cincinnati, Ohio—he caused a great deal of confusion in the maternity ward. He wanted to teach the Catholic nun who was in charge of the maternity ward the Texas stomp, and the good sister didn't want to dance.

When he left the hospital with the help of two big, burly orderlies, he sat down on the streetcar track in full view of my window, forced the motorman to stop so he could tell him about our new baby girl. See, Bill was still having fun with his drinking.

Our only son came the next year. Now this goes on and on, and I better explain it to you.

My brothers were in the military, and my sisters and my mother were in the defense plants, and I stayed home and kept up production. We had our little boy. I couldn't talk about this for a long time because we had two little girls, and Bill wanted a little boy. I guess all men want a son. So I manipulated that pregnancy and I gave Bill a son—a son the doctor said would never walk.

I was totally and utterly overwhelmed with guilt, and I spent the next several months and years going from one crippled children's hospital to the other to find a doctor who would make my boy walk. I didn't have anything to pray to. But I expected a medical miracle, and I dragged this little fellow from one children's hospital to the next.

Of course, Bill's drinking was progressing, and he changed jobs pretty often. One of these jobs took us down to Knoxville, Tennessee, at just about the time that they brought that atomic energy plant into town. It turned that sleepy little southern town into a madhouse. Thousands and thousands of people came into Knoxville, Tennessee.

Bill had a good job with Holland Furnace Company. He was

sales manager. He got a good salary and commission on sales. Bill wasn't a bit reluctant to take a little money under the table if you needed a furnace real bad. We were evicted from a rental house in Knoxville, Tennessee, for nonpayment of rent. This was not the last of the eviction notices that I was to see.

Because of the town's overpopulation, I couldn't find a place in Knoxville, so I had to leave the doctor who was attending me and my fourth pregnancy. I had to go up into Kentucky seventy miles away to find a garage apartment.

When I checked with the hospital there, I learned that I was not eligible to go there to be delivered of my child there, because this hospital was for the exclusive use of the coal miners in that area.

About the time I got that wonderful news, they carried Bill home. They'd carried him home before, of course, but this time his leg was broken. He'd had an argument with his boss.

Bill is never one to start a fight. He must have felt ten feet tall when he was drinking, though, because he'd pick on the biggest character in the bar and get the bejabbers beat out of himself. He was usually defending the reputation of some lady in the bar when the men used obscenities in her presence. I don't think the dear ladies even knew he was there.

But they carried him home, and they did agree to put a cast on Bill's leg at the emergency room at the hospital.

Then I was faced with the necessity of going home to Mother, who lived in Cincinnati. Mother didn't even know I had been pregnant.

We got a Greyhound bus—those buses played a role all my life in Illinois. We got a Greyhound bus and went into Cincinnati. I don't know who was the most relieved when we arrived, me or the bus driver. We went out to Mother's apartment in this exclusive neighborhood that doesn't allow children. There was no elevator in the building, so I went up the stairs carrying Luther in my arms. Luther could not walk. My stomach looked like a watermelon. I knocked on Mother's apartment door, and she'd like to died.

My mother was only eighteen years older and Lord, she hated my Bill with a purple passion. She just despised that boy. But after he got sober in AA, she thought she hatched him.

I knocked on her door and literally, she almost passed out. I said, "Mother, will you go down in the lobby and help Bill please?"

And she said, "What is the matter with him? Is he drunk?"

And I said, "No ma'am, his leg's broken." So she helped him up the stairs and set us down on the living room couch.

She looked at me, and she said, "Of all my children, Arbutus, I have always known that you are the most brilliant child I have, but it takes a damn genius to get in a shape like this."

And soon after, Theresa, our third little girl, was born in a charity ward of a Salvation Army hospital. I don't like to tell this part of the story, but Bill says I should because it's real good for you high-bottom drunks.

This didn't take ten thousand years, it only felt like that. This was fast. Bill was a boy who was at the top of the heap, and he hit the skids and went down fast. For that I'm grateful, although I wasn't then. It was the end of the world for me then.

Fortunately for her, Theresa was one of those healthy little people who thrived on loving neglect, because that's all she got as I continued to haunt the halls of children's hospitals.

The day that our little boy took his first step, I will never forget as long as I live. Dad had gone shopping for me that afternoon. He bought Luther some red corduroy overalls, the kind whose straps have to be adjusted. You move the buttons to fit the particular little body. I put those red corduroy overalls on Luther, and Dad was sitting across from us. I stood him up, and Dad said, "Walk to me, son." And he took nine steps. Dad and I cried. But he did learn to walk.

When I came to Texas over fifty years ago, I had never heard the term *alcoholism*. Not one time had I ever heard the term *alcoholism*. Mrs. O'N. indeed is not an alcoholic, but I know about alcoholism. I'd never heard this term. I watched Bill lose everything he had that he wanted to keep. My Bill lost his left eye in a drunken accident. He terminated his naval career, and he couldn't quit drinking. My Bill lost his left arm in a drunken accident, and he could not stop drinking. I watched him lose the respect of the people he worked for. I watched him lose the affection of his family. I watched him lose his own self-respect, and that was the darkest day of all.

When he looked up at me, physically and spiritually sickened to death, he said, "Why don't you leave, honey? I'm no damn good." I watched him lose everything that he wanted to keep, and I could not help him. I wanted to, just like you want to help the people you love.

I'm going to say something to the alcoholics at this point. Please understand me. I would never want to say anything from this podium or any other place that would hurt you. You've been hurt enough, God knows. I've heard you stand in places like I'm standing right now and say, "A nonalcoholic doesn't know what they're talking about."

I want you to know that I know what I'm talking about. I've held alcoholic women in my arms. Walked them up and down and fed them black coffee, grateful with the knowledge that but for the grace of God they might be feeding me black coffee. I would gratefully go home the next morning, send my own children to school, and know in my heart: but for the grace of God.

I've held an alcoholic in my arms through the long nights when he was in convulsions, not knowing whether he'd live until morning and scared to death that if he did live, he wouldn't have any sanity left. I couldn't tell which of his arms was artificial.

I know what I'm talking about. There are people in this room who wouldn't be here today if it wasn't for somebody like me. I want you to remember when you criticize a member of the Al-Anon Family Groups that we wanted to help you, but you wouldn't let us. We are not callous and insensitive people. We know the mental anguish you endure. We know the physical torture. It seemed to me that you put us on the other side of a thick glass wall. We could see you and we could hear you. But we couldn't get through to you because you wouldn't let us.

You parents know the feeling I'm trying to describe. It's a feeling you have when you want to help a sick baby. The baby's burning up with fever, and it cries, and you want to help the baby. Oh, you want to help that baby. But you can't, because the baby can't tell you where it hurts.

You alcoholics couldn't tell us where you hurt, and we couldn't help you. But God, we wanted to! We did so want to. I wish you'd remember that when you criticize a member of the Al-Anon Family Groups. We don't make jokes about drunks at Al-Anon meetings. Please remember that.

But this thing of seeing someone recover from alcoholism is a shaky, frightening, and, finally, glorious thing to watch.

I was privileged to see this take place in our lives also, because you see, I met some more people. These were weirdos who called themselves AA members. They tried the best they could to help me, but they couldn't help me. They didn't push me over the precipice, but they let me dangle, because they didn't understand me any more than I understood them.

I never will forget the first AA member I ever met. I'd learned that there were some AA people in our community from Raleigh, Texas. I called the minister, and he put me in touch with a nice man who was a member of Alcoholics Anonymous. He came out to the house in the middle of the afternoon and described to me what I referred to then as this "rehabilitation program for the alcoholic." I didn't know anything else to call it.

After about two and a half hours I asked him a question, "What do you have in this rehabilitation program of yours for the wives and children of alcoholics?" Nobody had ever asked him that question before, and he couldn't answer it.

He said, "We don't have anything for the wives and children, Mrs. O'N. *You* do not have a problem."

At that time I couldn't wear sleeves on my arms because of a rash that the doctor said was caused by nerves. I was so nervous I couldn't stand in my own shoes. And that dear man said, "You do not have a problem." I thought he was wrong then and still think he was wrong.

On that selfsame cold November afternoon when I stood in the living room of a mean little rental house in Brownwood, Texas, I made up my mind that someday, somehow, I would find a way to help the families of alcoholics. By the grace of God, that opportunity came to me when I found some more people.

Now if I thought those AA folks were weird, these other folks were doozies. Their eyes were dead. Do you know what I'm talking about? They were busy as all get out. They like "eating meetings" in Texas: They bake cakes and cookies and all that good stuff. I'm the sorriest cook in the world. I only cook because people have to eat. They scared me to death.

When I got here, I was totally and utterly destitute in all areas of life. I was whipped and didn't know it. Gradually I came to understand that my life depended on these people.

I'd been reading articles, of course, in ladies' magazines about something they called group therapy in the field of mental health, and I thought that's what these family group meetings were. They weren't Al-Anon then.

I went out to one of those meetings. I was twenty-nine years old at the time. There was a lady in the meeting who was twice my age, and I was worried about her. She was so old I thought she'd drop dead at the podium. They put my nose in those Twelve Steps, and I had the distinct feeling that if I didn't work those Steps, they'd not let me come up for air. I got busy in that department and I was going to slap the paper in front of the gray-eyed sponsor of mine. I was going to get an A+ up in the corner, of course. And I took those blasted Steps and they didn't work, but they did. And no one was more amazed than I was.

When I got here, I wanted to regain the affection and respect of my own husband. But most of all, I didn't want my children to be afraid of me anymore.

Now don't misunderstand me. I am not a child abuser, but our children were scared to death of my disapproval, with good reason. I would not tolerate a C on a report card. I repeatedly told them that anybody could be average; I expected more and I got it.

I punished them unmercifully if they spilled a glass of milk on a white tablecloth, and I insisted on white tablecloths. I've never been able to understand that. I've always been afraid to ask a psychologist, but it didn't make sense to me that you would try to convince your own children that you're an aristocrat. But I did.

That tornado took care of my white tablecloth. I made the mistake of saying that over in Arkansas one time. I got enough white tablecloths to cover Minnesota.

But I wanted my life to change, and that's what they promised me. They said, "If you practice these principles, your life will change." That's what I wanted.

The first thing I noticed was the children were no longer afraid of me. They got so brave, they even sassed me. That took a lot of nerve.

Then I became aware a little later that once again Bill was proud of me. This is important to those of us who love alcoholics. We truly have a sick need for approval. And the approval that we want most of all is from the alcoholics that we love.

We don't need much. It's quite all right if you'll just occasionally tell us that we look nice or that we smell good. But this is a truly sick need for approval, and I was grateful when I realized once again that Bill was proud of me.

I made friends first right in my own little group that I came into in Abilene, Texas—there were seven there, and I made number eight. I watched that group grow, and I made friends first in that little group. Then I was privileged to serve as a panelist and delegate for the state of Texas. Not west Texas, not east Texas, but Texas!

I've never driven an automobile. I'm dyslexic, and they wouldn't give people like me a driver's license, and I don't like people who drive without a driver's license. I learned about a tour that was available to teachers or retired teachers that would enable them to travel ninety-nine days for ninety-nine dollars. So that's what I did.

I covered the whole state of Texas on a Greyhound bus. I was on a Greyhound bus every day and in a meeting every night from October 16 to November 19. I lost ten pounds, but the people in Texas knew about the World Service Conference when I got through with them.

When they asked me about the qualifications for a delegate, I remembered what Marty M. said about the people who worked in the NCA offices—she said all you need is a willingness to learn and a compassionate heart.

When I was ten years in the program, I served as a delegate. When I was twenty years in the program, I was privileged to serve on the board of trustees. Now that I'm forty-six years in the program, I've had the opportunity to meet and speak at the same convention with Marty Mann.

I hope I'm never guilty of saying I was a close personal friend of Lois Wilson, because I was not. There was no way in the world that we would have ever known each other except that both of us married a drunk named Bill.

That created a problem for us when we were talking together, so we got in the habit of saying "my Bill" and "your Bill." But it was a tremendous learning experience for me.

I've tried to share the things that you taught me on that level with the people who followed me. I believe that we have a good strong structure because of the format that Bill Wilson set up for the Al-Anon conference, just the same as he set up the structure for the AA conference. You AA people only served two years.

I guess he's tried repeatedly to get you to change that, because he has the Al-Anon delegate serve three years. In the first year you go up there, you're just a junior senator, and by the time you learn what to do, you rotate. But by the third year you get a great deal of work done. That's what we do in Al-Anon.

I never know when to hush. But I must because Venoah is going to talk a little later, and I get to chop her down. But I'll say to you the same thing I say to every group that I ever talk to. The principles of this program carry a message that the whole world needs to know. You are the most qualified people on earth to carry that message.

Very likely today, within a stone's throw of this building, there are drunken men and women who will die in total ignorance, never knowing they're alcoholic—as did Stephen Foster—if you fail to carry this message.

And there are people likely within a stone's throw of this building, or down in my little sleepy town called Brownwood, Texas, or yes, out in California, who will not have the courage to face life one more day with an alcoholic, and they'll break up their home—if you fail to carry this message.

And there are kids all over the world who have never heard of Alateen. These kids will grow up with deformed personalities. These kids will grow up afraid for their dad to come home tonight. This is Saturday, the worst night of all. These kids will be afraid for their dad to come home, or their mother—if you fail to carry this message.

If you fail to carry this message, my God, have mercy on these people! And my God, have mercy on us!

SOURCES:

Arbutus O'N. Speech. Gopher State Roundup XXIV. 23 May
1997.

Barbara D.

THIS IS THE FIRST TIME I'VE TALKED. I'VE TALKED TO SOME GROUPS, BUT I MEAN THIS IS THE FIRST TIME I'VE TALKED OUT in public since Charlie died. And to say I miss him is an understatement of the world, of course. But today I was out at Restland with a lady who left us, one of our longtime friends and one of the real cuties. That Charlie loved the pretty women. She was pretty and she was sweet and he loved her. And she loved him. I couldn't help but wonder and believe that maybe Charlie was up there and was welcoming her into her new home. I just hope it's so. We don't know. We'll know someday, but we don't know today. But I'm glad to be here. My name is Barbara and I'm an Al-Anon.

I'm a real Al-Anon. Do you ever hear someone say, "Is he a *real* alcoholic?" I'm using *real Al-Anon* now because I needed Al-Anon. My husband was an alcoholic, and I was losing it. Lost it lots of times. And I really needed you people.

I've been in Al-Anon for forty years. I celebrated my fortieth Al-Anon birthday last November (1995) and they couldn't find a chip for forty years, so they took two twenties and taped them together. That kind of made me think of Charlie—he was always threatening to turn me in and trade me off for a couple of twenties.

I'm a real Al-Anon because I go to meetings regularly. I read my Al-Anon literature. I read something every day. I try the best I can most of the time to work the program. I'm willing to talk to new people or people who want Al-Anon or people who I think need Al-Anon. So I can consider myself to be a real Al-Anon. And if you're here today and you've been all those miles that I've enjoyed, you're just lucky. Because they've been wonderful miles that we've traveled. So it's good to see everybody here, all of our old-time friends—it's just wonderful. But that's not what you came to hear me say.

What brought you to Al-Anon? Now you alcoholics, some of you don't ever go to Al-Anon meetings, but you might try one once in a while and find out what we do in there. We don't talk about our alcoholic. I remember one time I came out of an Al-Anon meeting and met this little fellow at the door. He said, "Well, I guess you know all about me."

I said, "What?"

He said, "I bet you know all about me. I'm so-and-so. My wife went in there. I guess she told you all about me."

I said, "Well I'm sorry, she didn't mention your name." And we don't. We're too busy taking care of ourselves, trying to get well.

But what brought me to Al-Anon was I needed help. I needed help because my husband was an alcoholic. I needed help because I had done all the wrong things for the right reasons, I'm sure. But I did all the wrong things. As I talk tonight, think about what brought you here, and the first thing you thought about when you came here, and what you felt like you needed when you got here. See if Al-Anon has helped you. If you know what brought you here, maybe you can tell somebody else. The world is full of people out there who do not know that there's any help for them. They may hear Al-Anon mentioned, but they might think that's not what they need. They need something big, something instant. Al-Anon is not instantaneous, but it works.

Charlie and I were married fifty-eight years. It would have been fifty-eight years. He died fifty-seven and a half years after we were married. I'm figuring that took us back to 1937. If you're right quick with the mathematics, that was two years after Bill and Dr. Bob got together. So you see, we went way back there.

Before we married, I'm sure Charlie was an alcoholic, but I didn't know it. Charlie and I had more fun than just about anybody. If you knew Charlie, he was always in for a party and fun and the good life, and he loved it. I did too. We dated a long time, and we would get together and cook.

During the depression you didn't have the money to go out and eat. So Charlie would go by the store and get a steak. We'd go to the park, make a little fire, and sit out there in the moonlight and roast our steak over the fire. We'd sit there and talk and catch the streetcar and go back home.

That was a big date for us back during the depression. Most of you weren't alive then, so you don't remember that. You hear about depressions now, but they don't even know what a depression is. Hope we never find out.

Anyway, we had all this fun but Charlie liked to drink. He made home brew. I could tell you some wild stories about the making of home brew, but we'll leave that for another time.

I want to tell you about what I did. I made gin. People are always surprised about that. I don't know why they're surprised. It seems the logical thing for me to do. I worked in a doctor's office as a laboratory technician. If you worked in the doctor's office, he could write a nice little prescription. That was during Prohibition. Anybody here old enough to remember Prohibition? It was during Prohibition, and you couldn't buy the stuff without going to a bootlegger. So I'd get the doctor I worked for to write me a prescription for alcohol.

Now, it wasn't the kind you rub on; it was the kind you drink.

I'd go down to the drugstore and get my pint of alcohol, or whatever it was that he gave me the prescription for. I'd come back upstairs, where we had these beakers. I'd put in a pint of distilled water and my pint of alcohol and some gin drops. I'd mix all that up, and then we had two pints of gin. I made gin. So if you ever said you didn't know anybody who made gin, you do now.

That was just one of the things we did.

They voted to legalize beer in Louisiana. It was a long way to Shreveport from Dallas in those days. We didn't have I-20. We had a little two-lane road going through.

Charlie was over at my house, and he says, "Let's drive over to Shreveport and go find a saloon and put our feet up on the bar and have a real beer." So we hopped in the car and drove to Shreveport. I wasn't always as sedate and proper as I am now.

We drove to Shreveport and finally found the saloon, which was open. We went in. There were three winos with their heads down. It wasn't attractive, but we had our beer and drove back to Dallas. We got there before daylight. Nobody was the wiser that we'd even been gone.

Charlie probably liked his drinks pretty well in those days, and I drank some of them too, as you noticed. But I wasn't an alcoholic. It didn't do for me what it did for Charlie.

We married and moved to Mt. Pleasant, which was undoubtedly the drinking capital of the world. Anybody from Mt. Pleasant, Texas? Usually two or three people are from Mt. Pleasant. Well they won't admit it now, I guess.

We moved over there, and Charlie made friends with all the bankers and the drugstore owners and everybody. He loved to golf, so he'd play golf with his buddies. He also knew all the drinking people, so he had his friends.

Remember, I was a little worried about his drinking when we married, but I knew when we married that he would quit drinking. He didn't know that, but I did. In fact until we were married, he didn't know that I expected him to quit drinking. I just knew that I would be such a wonderful wife, and he loved me so, and everything was going to be so wonderful, he wouldn't even want to drink.

Well, that was a mistake. He didn't agree with that. So he kept up his drinking. I quit drinking and became very sanctimonious about it.

When we moved back to Dallas, he really drank a lot. I was really going downhill.

We had three children, and Charlie was crazy about the children and was good with them. They were crazy about him. But his drinking got worse, and I became very vocal about what I thought about it. I'm sure I caused lots of problems. I was in a spiral downward. Things got so bad that I decided that I had to do something about it, but I didn't know what.

In the meantime the Lord had sent a friend to us, Hub J., who was a member of the Suburban Club. Hub had about five or six years' sobriety at that time. He and Charlie were more or less in business together. Charlie was an electrician, and Hub had a light company. They worked together making lamps, and they became friends. Hub and Charlie were very fond of each other.

Hub would talk to Charlie about his drinking. Of course, Charlie would say, "Yup, if I ever get bad enough, I'll quit." But he wasn't bad enough. God himself sent Hub into our lives, because he was just what I needed.

One night I had decided I had to leave him, that I had all that I could handle. I don't know why I called Hub. I didn't call any of my family. I didn't call a lawyer, but I called Hub. I said, "Hub, I think I'm going to leave him because I can't stand this anymore."

And he said, "Oh, don't do that. Everybody's got to be crazy to live with one of us for twenty years. Go to AA."

I said, "Well, Hub, I'm not an alcoholic." I didn't drink by this time. If there was a beer ad on the television, I'd turn it off. You can see I was a little rabid.

Hub said, "Go to AA."

I said, "They don't want me."

He said, "Oh, yes we do." This was over forty years ago. They didn't know much about nonalcoholics in AA then. But they were so good to me.

I did one of the things that changed my life. I don't know how you feel about the first time you went to AA or Al-Anon—whichever one it was. But I know that was one of the greatest things I ever did for me and my children and my husband and anybody else who loved me.

I remember going over to the old Suburban Club—it was on Dixon and Sale—maybe some of you are old enough to remember the old Suburban Club. It was in a nice house over there, but kind of had a lightbulb hanging down from the middle. It wasn't exactly an uptown group.

I went over there and met Hub and his wife. I went to the door, and they introduced themselves as Molly and so forth.

I said, "I'm here to be with Hub J."

She says, "Well he's not here yet. But he'll be here. He always comes to the meetings."

Later he and his wife came in. I sat down, and three men told their stories that night. When they did, I knew that if they could do it, maybe Charlie could if he wanted to. I didn't know I needed any help. I just knew that if Charlie sobered up, all would be well. Everything would be perfect.

I kept going to my AA meetings. I'd love to tell you that I went home that night and told Charlie about it, and he said he wanted to go, and the next night we went to the meeting. It didn't work that way. I went home and told Charlie all right, but he was not too crazy about the idea. But I went and I never lied to him about it. Some do lie to their husbands about it, and that's their business. I told him that I was going. I always asked him to go, and one night he went, but that's later.

I went to my meetings regularly at the Suburban Group. I got a lot out of them. They were so good to me, they'd even let me go out and have coffee after the meetings. It was so wonderful. Of course I'd tell Charlie everything I heard. He didn't care what I'd heard. That was the way it was.

One day I was reading a lovelorn column in the *Times*—"Dear Abby." Down at the bottom it said, if you had an alcoholic problem in your home, to write to box so-and-so in New York. That was the New York Al-Anon office. I sat down and wrote them. I'm sure it was the most pitiful letter they ever got, because I was pretty pitiful, I'll tell you. A short time later a lady called me and said, "Would you like to go to an Al-Anon meeting?" I said yes.

She said, "I'll be there to pick you up tomorrow night."

I said I could drive. In those days we drove all over Dallas, as we were not afraid at night like some of us are now.

She said, "No. I'm going to be having dinner in your neighborhood, and I'll come pick you up." The next night she came and honked, and I went out to the car. In the car sat my neighbor. You can imagine how I felt. I looked at her and I thought, "Now everybody in town will know that Charlie's an alcoholic." I'm sure everybody in town already knew that Charlie was an alcoholic, but I didn't know that. Anyway, that was Neal H.'s wife, Mildred. A couple of you here might remember Neal H. Mildred and I were going to an Al-Anon meeting.

We went over to Town North. Nancy is here tonight, and she was at that first Al-Anon meeting.

There were six or ten at that meeting. I went in, sat down in a chair, and started crying. I went to Al-Anon once a week for x number of months, and that's all I did. I sat down in that same chair and cried and got up and went home. But you know something? I got better. Why, I don't know. But it was good for me.

You say, "What did it do for you?" This week I was thinking about being out here, and I asked several of my Al-Anon friends, "How were you helped when you first came to Al-Anon?" I thought there would be some people here tonight who are just beginning in Al-Anon and some who need to go but hadn't yet. Maybe they'll get an idea.

I called different people. One person said she got hope—hope that maybe there was something that they could do to make their lives better.

Another one said she found out she should keep her opinions to herself instead of telling her alcoholic what she was thinking all the time.

Another one told me she learned how to be a married woman, because she had just married before she came to Al-Anon. Her husband was an alcoholic. She said Al-Anon really taught her how to be a married woman.

I was talking to somebody else who had come under different circumstances. This person was carrying a gun to kill her daughter's husband, who had walked out on her. You can imagine she needed some help. She said she learned how to have positive thoughts instead of negative.

I was talking to my daughter, who celebrated over thirty years in Al-Anon the other night. Some of you know Barbara Ann. She said that she found out she didn't have to be a victim anymore.

So those are just some of the things that people got when they first came to Al-Anon.

What did I get? Al-Anon gave me back a life. When I first came here, Charlie and I weren't doing too well in this world. In Al-Anon I found out that I could have some sort of a life, even though Charlie was still drinking. I had thought that the only way I could live was for him to stop drinking. I found out that wasn't necessarily so.

I could have a life—maybe not the one I really wanted, but I could have a life if I wanted it. I found out that I can become a part of a group and fit in.

I found out that I could take this simple program—one Step at a time. But I'd have to go through it all. But if I failed, if I slipped, they wouldn't kick me out. They would let me start all over again and try to do the Steps. I didn't have to be perfect. They would help me become what I wanted to be if I would let them help me. They gave me back my family; I could talk to my children and could talk to my husband. They told me that I was not responsible for the other person's actions. That was very important to me.

One thing they told me was that I should not try to straighten everything out for Charlie. Charlie was so nice, so sweet and calm and peaceful, and all.

He wasn't always that way. He had a few bad habits. If he ran out of liquor, he'd just go by the liquor store, kick the door open, and go in and get a bottle of whatever he wanted. Then he'd close the door. He'd go back the next day or so. The guy had missed the whiskey, I'm sure, and Charlie would pay for it. People say they can't imagine him kicking a door. Well, I said, you don't have to imagine it. He just did it. I saw him do it too.

Charlie was a heavy drinker, a daily drinker. And things went from bad to worse. Al-Anon told me that I didn't have to pick up his bad checks that he wrote. When Charlie needed a little money, he would go by the nearby grocery store and write a check for five or ten, some astronomical amount. Of course, five dollars then was like fifty now.

He would write this little check, and in the due course of time it would come back marked NSF. You know what that means? Nonsufficient funds.

We had an account there, but it was pretty well depleted. Mr. Hill, the Safeway manager, would call up and say, "Miss D.?" And I would say yes.

He'd say, "This is Mr. Hill down at Safeway. Mr. D. was in and gave me a check, and it's been returned." Of course, being the good little wife that I was, I would say, "Oh Mr. Hill, I'm so sorry. I'll be right down and pick it up." I would go to the Bible or Shakespeare, wherever I was hiding money at that time, and I would get that five- or ten-dollar bill, and I would go. Embarrassed? I was dying.

I'd find Mr. Hill, and he'd go in the little office and get the check. I'd give him the money, and he'd give me the check, and I would go home.

Charlie would come in later. I would wave that check under his nose and say, "Look what you did. I was embarrassed."

He would say, "Oh, I'm so sorry. I won't do that anymore." But he always forgot and did it again.

I was pretty smart. I never told him he wrote a hot check. I had too much pride for anything like that. In those days we didn't tell everything like we do now. I said they mean I don't have to pick up those checks.

So what happened then—Mr. D. went down and wrote his little check. Mr. Hill called me, so I made a different statement. I said, "Mr. D. will be down and pick it up." Mr. D. would come home. I would meet him and say, "You get down there to that Safeway store. You get some money and get that check. I've got to go down there tomorrow and buy groceries, and I do not want to be embarrassed." He would go down and get his check.

You know something? He quit writing the darn things.

Barbara D. ~ *221*

One time—it was a little later than this probably, in the afternoon—the phone rang. Has anybody ever called you from the jail? You know that's where they are. There's a background noise; I don't know what it is.

The phone rang, and Charlie said, "Honey, I'm in jail. Joe got me drunk. They picked me up."

I said, "Oh?"

He said, "Yes."

He said that I said, "No. I've been going to Al-Anon, and they told me to leave you there." This does not sound like me at all. I don't know what I said, but he got the message.

I asked Barbara Ann the other night if she remembered that. She didn't remember that particular occasion. He was in jail several times.

I said, "No. I'm not coming after you." In those days they gave you one call from the jail. Today I think they'll let you call as often as you like, if someone will take your collect calls.

I've received a lot of calls. They used to call all the time to collect Charlie from the jail.

He had this one call, and he wasted it on me, which I'm sure did not make him any too happy. He had a few resentments after that about this business. But he didn't say much.

I went into the children's bedroom. They were all there, and I said, "Kids, your dad's in jail. He's safe and he's not going to hurt anybody, and nobody's going to hurt him. We're all here, and we're going to go to bed and get a good night's rest." And that's what we did.

Charlie got out. He got a hold of a friend of his, who couldn't stand for Charlie to be suffering in jail. So he went down and got him out.

That was the last time Charlie ever got in jail. I won't tell you that he'll never get in jail again. But he did say it impressed him. He had lost his enabler. I was no longer enabling him to get out of jail.

Have you ever watched jailers? They never smile. Anyplace else, you go in, hand them some money, and they say thank you.

Jailers don't do that. They just look at you. And that's one thing I learned in Al-Anon, and I'm passing it on to you—you don't have to do it for them.

I'm not going to tell you any more wild tales. Between Thanksgiving 1957 and New Year 1958 Charlie was very bad off. He was in the back alley over in Lakewood, which was his hangout.

One night he was drunk in his car behind the restaurant. The police came, and the policeman talked to him and didn't take him to jail. He brought Charlie home. Charlie was very ill. He had D.T.'s. Have any of you ever dealt with D.T.'s? I hope you never have to.

I didn't know to be scared. I'd call Hub, who would tell me to get him some orange juice with honey, and all this stuff, and I would do it.

Charlie was having hallucinations. We had wallpaper in the bedroom. If he wanted one channel, he'd push "that button" and he'd hear "that kind of music." If he didn't like that, he'd push "this button" for some other kind. He had people walking under the bed. One time I asked him about the little people walking under his bed. He said, "Little, hell! They are six feet tall."

I said, "I thought they were little people."

He said, "No, they are big people."

He was sick for ten days. I didn't have any money to put him in the Texas clinic in those days.

Thank God I didn't, because on January 10 of 1958, Charlie went to Ten North Club and, as he says, "turned himself in." He lived for thirty-seven and a half more years and never had another drink of whiskey. Now that's victory. I could get all emotional about that if I tried right hard.

That's what happened. It wasn't always easy. Charlie wasn't working, but I was. Things weren't good, but they got better.

He used to go over where I was reading Lois's story. She would be talking about Bill and Ebby, who brought the message to Bill at first. Charlie told about his sobriety and took me back.

So things went on, and we went to meetings. Charlie had this old station wagon. He used it to move every woman there was to move in Dallas who was in AA. All of them moved every thirty days in those days. He would load 'em and move to wherever they wanted to go. He didn't drink. He carried the people to meetings, and we went to meetings every day. They didn't have them in the daytime then, just at night. But then he went over to the other club, sat there with the other drunks, and talked and played dominoes, and life got better.

We put on some fabulous feeds for them. We'd go out and buy chickens, then go home and fry them and take them down to the club. We'd charge everybody a dollar to eat. That's the way the club made some money.

The Al-Anons worked themselves half to death, and they sure let us work in those days. They didn't care, and we all worked and loved each other. We were all so happy. And we made friends.

What have I got from Al-Anon? I got meetings. The meetings were and are still wonderful.

I don't know why, but I can be all antsy on the inside, but I can go to an Al-Anon meeting and get home and feel so much better.

I don't know what it is about meetings. I have a theory that God's in the meeting place. You may not agree with me, but I have my theories, and you can bet I'm going to keep them. I'm kind of stubborn.

Anyway, I think God's in the meeting place. He knows what we need. If we're there, he just kind of puts his arm around us, and we can feel His presence.

The other night, our older daughter told about a wild time she once had with her dad. We were talking, and I asked if my going to Al-Anon before her daddy found AA helped.

She said, "Oh yes. Oh yes, it helped a lot. But if Dad hadn't ever sobered up, I don't know what would have happened to me. All my life I'd been able to say, Anything wrong with me, it's Dad's fault because he is a drunk. After he sobered up, I realized that I could no longer blame him for all my troubles." She had never told me that before. If you're a father of some children tonight, know that those kids are looking to you and will straighten their lives out and do better when they realize their dad is no longer drinking.

That's one thing we've got—our children.

Our oldest, Barbara Ann, is celebrating thirty years plus in Al-Anon. She doesn't know when she first came.

Then we have a son who's here and another daughter who lives in West Virginia.

We're going to have a wedding next Saturday night. All of my children, and their spouses, and my grandchildren, and their spouses, and seven great-grandchildren are going to be here for the wedding. It's going to be wonderful.

And how I miss Charlie, nobody knows, but he'll be there. He loved that family.

Al-Anon has paid off for me. Charlie and I had some wonderful times. We had friends you wouldn't believe. We've gone all over: to Europe, to Hawaii, to hither and yon with all these friends.

One Christmas Eve I had the flu. I was lying on the couch, and the phone rang. Some lady said, "Miss D.?" I said yes.

"Barbara D.?" I said yes. "Mrs. Charles D.?" Yes. She said, "This is so-and-so at the Prestonwood Travel Agency." I thought it was one of those come-ons. She said, "Would you like to go to Hawaii?" I knew what she was going to say. She would send me on a trip if I sent her a hundred dollars.

And I said, "Oh, yeah. I sure would."

She said, "Somebody wants you and Charlie to be in Hawaii for his AA birthday."

I said, "A lot of people do that I'm sure."

She said, "Somebody has been here, but I can't tell you who it was." By now, I was lying down gasping for breath. She finally convinced me that it was on the up-and-up. So I got hold of everybody in the neighborhood and all my friends and family and everybody, and I was wild with joy. I don't know to this good day who that was. Somebody no doubt in AA that he'd helped some way down the road.

We had a deluxe trip I tell you. It wasn't any little namby-pamby thing. It was just great. We called his brother who likes to travel, and he and his wife went with us. We were there for ten days.

We came back, and I tried my best to find out who the heck it was. All of a sudden, after about a year of trying to find out who it was and not succeeding, I decided I didn't want to know. Because you know what? I have to be nice to every one of you. It could've been anybody.

That doesn't happen to every AA, but it happened to mine.

Today, eleven trees have been planted in Israel in memory of my husband. Eleven trees. Now you say, "What does that mean?" When Jews want to remember somebody, they have a tree planted in Israel in the person's name. So there in Israel tonight are eleven trees with the name Charlie D. Maybe it doesn't touch you, but it sure touches me.

Charlie loved his church. When people came in AA, he said it says in the Big Book that most of us go back to our church. He believed in going back to your church. He went, and he loved the Lord, and he loved AA. And he loved all of you. Many of you he knew and loved personally. And the rest of you—if he was here, he would be loving you too.

I'm living in a retirement center. They cook me three meals a day, and I've gained five pounds and I'm trying to lose it. But I have it pretty good now. I don't have all the responsibilities I had, and Charlie's safe. He's where he belongs. I think maybe he's up there in the sky with a big meeting tonight. Maybe he and a lot of others who've gone on are sitting up there watching what's going on down here at Louisville's eighth anniversary and rejoicing at how wonderful it is to be here.

I want to read you a poem that I like. I was kind of down in the mouth one day, and Charlie and I were sitting at the table. We read our books together. I picked up a pamphlet I got at a church the week before. I hadn't read it before. And this is what I read:

> *I do not know the future*
> *But I know the God who knows*
> *And in his perfect wisdom*
> *Unknowing I repose.*
> *What good would come of knowing?*
> *How little I could do*
> *To meet the joys and sorrows*
> *That I'm coming to.*
>
> *I do not know the future*
> *But I know the God who knows.*
> *I make His love my study*
> *And follow where He goes.*
> *The path—its joys and sorrows*
> *I do not care to trace.*
> *Content to know His goodness*
> *His mercy and His grace.*

So what I wish for all of you tonight is the best AA and Al-Anon that can be had this side of heaven, and to feel secure in your love for the program and all it means to all of us and all AA's and Al-Anons everywhere. And thank you for asking me to speak. I love all of you.

SOURCES:

Barbara D. Al-Anon talk. Texas, 1996.

Dorothy Riggs M.

It's funny how the pieces of the quilt fit together. In those days during the depression, the South had a sort of natural way of taking care of its own. There was so much hardship, but the fields gave their food, neighbors watched out for each other, and families were the glue that held everybody together.

Little Dorothy always knew that she was different. Proud that she was "Daddy's girl," and far too much like her mother for these two to get along well, she naturally gravitated to men. Independent, capable Dot! They all knew she could take charge of and run the house just as well as her restless, liberated mother.

Mother—such a sad and lonely life she'd had. Deserted by her father at thirteen, she and her mother had to survive on their own, and it wasn't easy. Hard work and drive were sometimes all they had to sustain them. And out of tragedy and hardship, a pattern for life was born. Beliefs rooted in survival became the principles that would shape her life and the lives of her children. The day would come when those principles would become the deadliest enemies of those she loved the most. But in the beginning, they didn't know that. At that time, all that mattered was survival.

By her midteens, Dot was ready to take flight. Popular with boys and girls alike, she became the class party girl. Her mother, deprived of normal teen fun in her own life, became Dot's greatest ally. Any excuse at all was sufficient to move back the furniture, roll up the rugs, and dance long into the night to the sounds of the new Victrola. Laughter and gaiety filled the house during those years and provided the kind of nostalgic, innocent coming-of-age that Dot's old friends still reminisce about today.

One balmy summer evening, Dot drove to the home of some cousins in South Carolina for a week's vacation. Sometime during that week at a party hosted by her young relatives, Dot had her first magical experience with alcohol. Memory is such a strange, selective process. Somehow, the churning stomach and pounding headache she experienced the next day never seemed important. What mattered was the feeling! Oh, the thrill of flying through the great, blue Carolina skies. The contentment that accompanies total self-acceptance. The freedom that springs from the knowledge that you are loved, important, admired, and respected. Alcohol always promises more and smiles up at you with laughing eyes. It was a lie, of course. Alcohol always lies. The truth is, it deceives, destroys, and ultimately takes souls. Dot was no exception.

After graduation, she quickly became bored. Thinking she had a vocation for nursing, she entered nursing school in Savannah and completed about half of her training. One afternoon, her mother drove down to see her. Without a second thought, homesick Dot packed her bags and came home. But nursing was in her blood. It was wartime, and there was a shortage of nurses, so she was gratefully accepted to the nursing staff of the local hospital. She often reflected back on those busy, happy days and realized that she probably learned more about nursing in that hospital than she could ever have learned in Savannah.

By this time, many of the young boys had already gone to fight, but everybody wanted to help the war effort. Statesboro, Georgia, became one of the hundreds of little town all over the country to open its doors to the soldiers. They filled the club on West Main Street with boys in uniform, and Dot met them all. Working the long, hard hours at the hospital only whetted her appetite for fun! At twenty-one, or twenty-two, or twenty-three the body is an amazing machine; Dot's recuperative powers were enormous. But it couldn't go on indefinitely. She was drinking and partying every night, and the frenzied pace began to take its toll. The hangovers got worse, and she began having difficulty functioning at top form. Alcohol's promises were dimming, and change was afoot.

One day at the hospital, after Dot had had a heavy night of drinking with little sleep, a fellow nurse joined her at the always-present coffeepot. After a little small talk and commiserating over long, hard hours of work, her friend asked her if she had heard about the new diet pills, *amphetamines,* that everyone was talking about. Following up on the lead, Dot talked to one of the doctors and got a prescription for the pills. Now suddenly, she could do it all again! What a marvelous invention. But the descent had begun, and it wasn't long before new, more powerful drugs became necessary to do the job. She faked a bout of appendicitis to have surgery and get a rest. And then there were the narcotics and wonderful, blessed relief.

Life has a way of building bridges when the time is right to enter a new phase of life. Children are born, people die, and cycles begin anew. For Dot, it was her landlady's daughter, who was completing college, getting married, and moving home. Suddenly Dot needed a place to live. She had met a couple not long before—a doctor called Dr. John and his wife, Sally. When Dot, in a conversation with Sally, casually mentioned that she was looking for a place to live, Sally quickly offered their upstairs room, which had become vacant after their tenant—a college professor—retired. It couldn't have been more perfect. It was a few blocks from the hospital, so she could walk. Since she didn't have transportation, a close location had been one of her top requirements. Fate? Coincidence? Perhaps.

After Dot moved in, she was busy with her work and social life, and Dr. John and Sally were rarely home, so contact between them was practically nonexistent. One day upon returning from work, she was surprised when Dr. John knocked on her door. He calmly and unemotionally told her that Sally was gone and that they would be divorcing. In those days, it would not have been considered acceptable for a young woman to rent a room from a bachelor; but after some thought and some phone calls, Dot's sister decided to move in with her. And so began a romance, a love affair, a coming together of two souls meant for one another. A passion, a commitment, a bond so strong that they themselves couldn't sever it even when they wanted to.

At first, it was just a casual drink together on returning home. Getting to know each other and feeling their way. The divorce proceeded at a snail's pace; but when it was finally complete, Dot knew she had to leave. After Dot found another room not far away, Dr. John began courting. And what a courtship it was! Explosive, exciting, and fun! Dot was abusing alcohol and other drugs; Dr. John was the master! He wanted her love, total devotion, and complete attention; and she wanted to give it to him. He wanted to party; she wanted what he wanted. Her love for the fast life was a bonus, but she'd have given him what he wanted regardless of her own wants. Dr. John was used to being in control and getting his way. When her work began interfering with their social lives, she quit work. She left the career she loved and the life she had carved for herself without a second thought. She willingly turned her will, her love, and her life over to the man she loved; and by the time they married in 1947, no one had the courage to give voice to the almost unanimous fears and the objections of those who loved them.

In relationships, as in many other mysteries of life, two plus two never equals four. And so it was that a drinking, sometimes drugging woman and a drinking, always drugging man became husband and wife. And neither love, commitment, nor three beautiful children could save them from the roller-coaster descent into despair, degradation, and inhumanity that always accompanies the disease of addiction.

By 1950, Dr. John was going from hospital to hospital, getting detoxified, coming home, and quickly returning to alcohol and other drugs. Meanwhile, Dot was going from psychiatrist to psychiatrist, all the while keeping the dirty little secret of alcohol and drugs hidden deep inside. And then the depression came. Dot became so suicidal that a desperate psychiatrist finally prescribed hospitalization and shock treatments. And in the way of treatment, she found a new drug—sodium Pentothal. And with it came relief, at least for a while. So over and over, she came back for shock treatments. How many? Nobody knows. With the brief respites from pain came the destruction of the very thing that makes every human a unique and precious being—the brain.

As Dot continued to descend into her nightmare, Dr. John was rapidly spiraling downward in his own parallel pathway to destruction. The fabric of his life was quickly unraveling as his friends, colleagues, and the law gradually tightened the noose. He voluntarily entered a federal institution for the treatment of addiction but remained only a few days. Three weeks later, the sheriff escorted him back to Lexington, Kentucky, where he reentered the facility under court order. In the way of coincidences—or miracles—he was introduced to a man who would be instrumental in changing his life.

Houston Sewell was a well-liked, prominent citizen in his community; but more important, he was a member of Alcoholics Anonymous. Of course, Dr. John had heard about AA, but his awareness of his own addiction was limited to his dependence on narcotics. He was in complete denial about his alcoholism. Little by little, he began learning about this deadly disease. He was allowed to attend outside AA meetings in the company of his new sponsor; and by the time he arrived home, he had changed at some deep, mystical level. He was committed to getting well. He joined Alcoholics Anonymous and began going to meetings, but Dot was miserable. Their well-learned, familiar dance of souls had changed. He heard new music, and she couldn't follow until she learned the tune. So she, too, joined Alcoholics Anonymous.

Alcohol was gone and drugs were gone; and in the going, they left a gaping space filled with confusion, outdated old ideas, fear, rage, and uncertainty. Misery, despair, and devastation were at least a known, familiar quantity. The unknown loomed darkly on the horizon as their new day began.

The beginning of sobriety had an oddly touching quality to it. The year was 1960, a new, young, vigorous president was moving into the White House, and the country seemed to catch the sense of rebirth.

There was little knowledge about addiction, and treatment was practically nonexistent. It wasn't really surprising that people began hearing about the drunk doctor and his nice wife who were helping alcoholics. Dr. John went to a meeting of International Doctors in Alcoholics Anonymous that year and started bringing home young, struggling doctors. Most of them had never heard another doctor talk about taking narcotics, and they latched on to Dr. John like drowning men to a life preserver—which indeed they were. Suddenly their home began filling up with a constant stream of drunks looking for help.

And the sick began healing the sick. They would arrive, shaking and terrified, knowing they had to change and paralyzed with fear about the future. Not one of them ever believed he could learn even to live without alcohol and drugs, let alone be happy without them. So they'd struggle into their clothes, and off they'd go to a different AA meeting every night. Augusta, Atlanta, Savannah, Dublin, Waycross. Sometimes they'd drive for two hours to find a meeting. Soon they became a familiar sight—Dr. John, Dot, and a handful of shaking drunks. Whoever happened to be sleeping at the house went to a meeting every night—whether they wanted to or not. Those were exciting days, although nobody knew it at the time. They'd have a "meeting" on the way to the meeting, then have the meeting, then have a "meeting" coming home from the meeting. Most of the meetings were speaker meetings, so the drive to and from became the discussion meetings.

After a few years, a worried accountant told Dot and Dr. John that they couldn't afford to keep bringing people into their home without charging them anything. And so a plan was developed, and Willingway Hospital was born. It was an idea whose time had come, and no person, place, or thing could stop this train in motion. The need was present, and as the momentum built, it seemed to take on a life of its own.

The passing years brought a full range of life's experiences—the highs, the lows, and the in-betweens. But always at the core was the program of Alcoholics Anonymous and the promises it always delivers. Unlike the liar alcohol, recovery brought truth; and with truth came healing, contentment, peace of mind.

A friend called from Spartanburg, South Carolina, one night; and somehow they all ended up traveling to New York for a visit with Bill and Lois Wilson. They talked for hours on end, went out to dinner, came back, and talked some more. What began there became a friendship that would last until Bill's death. Dot remembered later how they talked about drugs, especially narcotics. If you ask her today, she'll tell you that Bill was as savvy about drugs as any other drug addict. For a long time, she talked primarily about the drugs because that was the hardest part for her. She smiles as she remembers, and if anybody tries to stop her from talking about drugs, she'll just say, "If Bill let me talk about drugs, you will too."

The disease of addiction is progressive, and so is recovery. In the early years, Dot struggled mightily to overcome the ravages of her disease. Sometimes the progress was so slow, it seemed as if it would never happen. After ten years of sobriety, twenty-two years of marriage, and four beautiful children, a day came that she would never forget. A day that was so crystal clear it would forever change her life and the lives of those she loved. While Dr. John had grown up in a loving, intimate, expressive family, Dot grew up fearing intimacy and affection. There was a huge lump of fear living in her heart that continually told her, "If you tell them how much you love them, they'll leave."

It's funny how fear can be transformed into a friend at the right time. That day, in a moment of desperation, she became willing to change. With that willingness came the ability finally to let go. Pride and ego that had previously seemed as essential as oxygen suddenly became a burden too heavy to carry any longer. For the very first time, she was able to tell her beloved husband how much she loved him and needed him. A small thing really, but the smallest drops of suspicion and lack of trust, left alone day after day, will eventually wear away the strongest of foundations. For ten years, each day had been a struggle. Freedom from bondage to fear and mistrust opened the doors wide for joy to enter, and a marriage begun under the storm clouds of addiction suddenly came alive with renewed love. And so it is that whenever she has a chance, Dot will tell anyone who will listen: "The miracles always come when you least expect them, so don't ever give up. They *will* come!"

One of the great tragedies of the disease of addiction is that it never stops trying. When thwarted in one direction, it will burrow down and pop up in another direction. Dr. John was no exception, and nicotine became the last, lost battle. For years, he had tried to quit smoking, but it was only when there was not enough breath for him to carry a sack of groceries from the car to the house that he finally succeeded. Then it was too late. By that time, he was already dying.

The last years were hard—harder than Dot ever thought she could have survived. But the program of Alcoholics Anonymous once again delivered—friendship, courage, strength—a pattern for living and a pattern for dying. Through the hospitals, the oxygen tanks, the monitors, the drugs. It showed the way. When the time came, death brought with it a grace, dignity, and beauty that lives on in the hearts of Dot, her children, and their friends. Her words tell an eloquent story:

> I was so tired. I had brought nurses in from time to time to stay with him so I could get some sleep. He didn't sleep much because of the pain in his back. But this day was different. I knew the time was close, but I was so tired. That night I said, "Honey, I feel like I need to get a nurse to stay with you tonight so I can get some rest." And he said, "No, I want you to get in this bed and sleep with me just like you've always done."

Always before, we'd go to sleep; and at about 4:00 in the morning, he would get restless and his body would jerk. So I'd wake him up and tell him to turn over, and he'd go back to sleep. And so that night, he started to toss around at 4:00. I remember looking at the clock, and I reached over and touched him and said: "Honey, why don't you turn over so you can rest?" And he said, "That's funny, they just called me. They told me that I'd finished what I had to do and that I'd done a good job. Now you wake me up and tell me to turn over and rest, so I think that's what I'm going to do." And he turned over and went to sleep. At 6:00, I missed his breathing and I knew what had happened. He hadn't moved. His hand was under his cheek just like he was asleep. When the doctor came, he told me he had been dead about two hours. So he died at 4:00, right after he turned over.

What I had dreaded was him having to watch us watch him die. I didn't think he could do that, and he didn't have to. It was—it was just spiritual. His funeral was spiritual. Everybody laughed out loud. There were people coming in and out. We had a meeting right there that night. We laughed and cried, and it was all spiritual.

She smiles now as she remembers:

He loved me. He had always loved me; but as long as I lived in the shadow of fear and suspicion, I couldn't believe it. But I waited for my miracle, and it didn't let me down. Alcoholics Anonymous is the greatest thing that's ever happened to us. We are privileged to have this program to live by—and die by.

Today there's a peace in her face that speaks louder even than the words she says. She talks about living alone, about her children and her grandchildren. Three of her four children are alcoholic, and all three are sober in Alcoholics Anonymous. The fourth is an active member of Al-Anon. She talks about AA, the changes, the past and the future. Fire burns in her eyes when she talks about those who would keep AA to themselves. She talks about being inclusive, not exclusive. Dr. John lives on through his family and Willingway Hospital. His children carry his message to the next generation of hopeless alcoholics. And when you ask Dot about the future of treatment, she'll tell you that Willingway has always been a place for people to get off drugs and alcohol and it always will be. She'll tell you, "I pray every day for God's will; and if it's God's will for us to treat alcoholics, we'll do it; and if it's not, we won't be there."

FURTHER REFERENCES:

Willingway Hospital, 311 Jones Mill Road, Statesboro, GA 30458. www.willingway.com

Dr. Joan K. Jackson

IN EARLIER YEARS WHEN ALCOHOLISM WAS IGNORED OR EVEN
SHUNNED BY MOST PROFESSIONALS, A FEW BRILLIANT PIONEERS
involved themselves deeply in the field and gave valuable help to
Alcoholics Anonymous; namely, Dr. Harry Tiebout, Dr. John
("Dr. Jack") Norris, and Dr. Milton Maxwell.

In this distinguished group, one nonalcoholic woman professional was a true pioneer: sociologist Dr. Joan K. Jackson. In
1951 she began studies of "The Skid Road Alcoholic," which led
to a paper on the subject in 1953. This was followed by research
into "The Tuberculous Alcoholic" and resulting papers. Even
before the advent of the Al-Anon Family Groups in Seattle,
Dr. Jackson's research there with the wives of alcoholics was the
basis for her seminal work, "Alcoholism and the Family," published in 1954. These three papers, particularly the last one, are
regarded to this day as the classic, authoritative sources in their
respective areas.

In 1983, Joan brought her depth of experience in alcoholism
and AA to the General Service Board of Alcoholics
Anonymous, serving as the first woman Class A (nonalcoholic)
Trustee for nine years. "I had a model to follow," she claims, "in
sociologist Dr. Milton Maxwell," whom she had known since
the 1940s and who served AA as a Class A Trustee from 1972
until 1982—the last four years a chair of the General Service
Board. In fact, Joan had worked with Milton Maxwell during
the writing of his important book *The A.A. Experience,* which
he hoped would improve other professionals' knowledge of AA.
"Milton laid down giant footsteps," she says.

Joan was born in Canada in 1922. (She became a U.S. citizen

in 1958.) Volunteer work at a settlement house in Montreal and an inspiring teacher, Forrest LaViolette, an American, instilled in her an enthusiasm for social science that led her to choose sociology as a career.

At age eighteen, she broke her back in a skiing accident. Once recovered, she took evening classes at Sir George Williams College for two years. Completing her undergraduate education at McGill University, she majored in sociology and anthropology, receiving her B.A. degree and graduating high in her class.

In 1946 she married Stanley W. Jackson, a returning World War II veteran studying for his M.D. degree at McGill University and planning to become a psychiatrist. Joan earned her M.A. at McGill in 1947, staying on as a departmental assistant and doing research projects until her husband graduated. Then, in 1951, they moved to Seattle, Washington. Four years later, Joan was the first woman to be granted a Ph.D. in sociology from the University of Washington, graduating magna cum laude.

"I knew absolutely nothing about alcoholism at that time," Joan confesses. She was interested in studying the "social aspects of mental illness," and alcoholism fell under the umbrella of mental illness. She says, "The state of Washington offered grants for research into alcoholism, and I was given one to work on a research project being carried on in the department of psychiatry."

This project involved studying alcoholics hospitalized at a local veterans' hospital and the county hospital. As the research progressed, she felt the need to broaden her knowledge of alcoholics and turned to the local group of Alcoholics Anonymous for help. Introduced by a fellow sociologist, Ralph Connor, the members put her in touch with recovering skid road alcoholics. Soon she became aware of patterns of behavior and attitudes that skid road alcoholics shared and that contributed to the persistence of their alcoholism and made recovery difficult. She expanded her knowledge by attending open meetings of

Alcoholics Anonymous with Ralph Connor—and going for coffee with the members afterward. The outcome was the paper "The Skid Road Alcoholic."

Having joined the staff of the department of psychiatry at the University of Washington as a sociologist, she began teaching medical students about alcoholism—and AA. The state of Washington was one of the more enlightened in its policies toward alcoholics. A so-called police farm was maintained on the outskirts of Seattle, to which alcoholics who were repeatedly arrested for public drunkenness were sent to "dry out" and be rehabilitated; those more ill were sent to the wards of the county hospital. At the police farm, a skid road alcoholic, Ron F., began his recovery as the farm's cook, going on to become the chief of the state program and later to establish a new, enlarged police farm facility. Joan, with the aid of Ron F., arranged for the medical students to receive an elective credit for spending time at both the police farm and the county hospital, each student having an AA member to consult about the alcoholic patients he treated. Joan consulted with them and engaged them in informal talks, so they could enter their profession with the knowledge that alcoholics *could* recover.

Another faculty member who presented opportunities for the medical students to learn more about alcoholism was Professor Thomas Holmes, an expert in tuberculosis. In Seattle, all incoming inmates of the jail were X-rayed. If TB was detected, they were sent to Firland Sanitarium. Because many of these patients were skid road alcoholics, Joan was appointed a consultant to the clinic, where she worked with the staff to help manage these patients. She also saw to it that her medical students recognized the link between alcoholism and tuberculosis. In 1956 she published the first paper on this subject, followed by others later.

Things were really changing in the field of alcoholism in that period, Joan recalls: "The recognition of the problem . . . the city, state, and national services to solve it . . . government agencies, professional committees and boards . . . more research funds . . .

everything was astir! Members of Alcoholics Anonymous were involved in every aspect, as was I." She continued to rely on her AA friend Ron F., who had completed his college education and who was crucial in teaching the medical students as well as in developing community facilities. Joan and Ron were part of a group that established the first alcoholism information service in Seattle and the Seattle Health Department's alcoholism clinic.

In the midst of this frantically busy time, social scientist Joan became fascinated with the effects of alcoholism on the family. What were the family's attitudes? How did they adjust? What happened to the marriages? to the children? So she started interviewing the wives of the alcoholics she knew. She focused on a group of four who met regularly and called themselves the "AA Auxiliary" (later becoming the founders of the Seattle Al-Anon Family Groups). Joan asked questions, listened, and took notes. As had happened with her research with the alcoholics, she quickly identified common patterns. The eventual product of this research was her now-famous paper "Alcoholism and the Family," which was eventually reprinted and adapted so many times that she has not been able to keep track.

"When I began, there were only these four women," she recalls, "and when I left Seattle thirteen years later, there were at least eight Al-Anon groups, each with about thirty members! By then, a regular alcoholism research *industry* had developed out of my original work. I was still working with medical students. I was doing my own research. I was supervising alcoholism research by others. And it seemed to me I ended up on every board of every organization! I was given the Matrix Award for Outstanding Women by the press of Seattle. But I was also near a breakdown."

In 1964, Dr. Stanley Jackson decided to accept a fellowship at Yale University and study the history of medicine. So he and Joan came East—and stayed. "I came back to New Haven with Stan, and as far as sociology or alcoholism was concerned, I quit! Just *quit!*" she exclaims. "I was no longer *Doctor* Jackson, social scientist and researcher. I had lost my identity, and it felt weird.

"Eventually Stan and I bought this lovely home in Bethany, certainly one of the most beautiful parts of beautiful Connecticut, 'midst rolling hills and woods. I tried all kinds of hobbies—first, painting, but I didn't have the eye for it; photography, but lacked the patience; piano playing, but I had no talent." Finally, two new and unexpected interests saved her. The first was raising beagles. She has owned seven of these affectionate, appealing dogs over the years and presently enjoys two of them. Her second absorbing hobby is bookbinding. She feels a sense of real accomplishment when she has found a valuable antique volume in dilapidated condition and is able to restore it to mint condition. Her hobby is put to good use right at home, for the Jackson ménage includes six thousand books!

In the early fall of 1982, Joan received a phone call from her friend and professional associate Milton Maxwell, then chair of the General Service Board of Trustees of Alcoholics Anonymous. He asked her if she would consider being a candidate for Class A Trustee. "Initially I was stunned," she said. "I was totally removed from the alcoholism field by then, and I didn't even know what the AA 'board' was!"

However, she was swayed by her long association with Milton and her respect and affection for him. They had met in Washington State when they were both working on their Ph.D.'s in sociology. His own research had led him to attend AA meetings, as she had. They had served together on the Governor's Advisory Board on Alcoholism. Over the years they corresponded voluminously, especially on the book he was writing, *The A.A. Experience*. Later, in the East, they had both taught in summer school at Yale and appeared on the same programs of their professional societies.

In addition, Joan points out, "There was never a time I wasn't involved with AA and Al-Anon. My mind went back to my first AA meeting in 1951. When I walked into that cavernous, smoky, dingy hall, I was very nervous. Perhaps a hundred people were gathered in one corner: all men, all over fifty-five, none prosperous looking, all with signs of life's batterings on their faces. I wasn't sure how they would receive me. Would they understand why I was there and be willing to help? They did and they would. A speaker rose and said, 'My name is Roy G. and I am an alcoholic' and spoke of skid road despair and how he came to find the beginnings of hope. My education in alcoholism and recovery began right then.

"It continued rapidly and dramatically," she relates. She remembers Les V. (Vaughn), who ran the alcoholism program for the Great Northern Railroad. She knew Eric B. (Bergman) from the time he came into AA; he later became a Class B. (alcoholic) Trustee for the fourteen-state Pacific region of AA. She tells of the lesson learned from Roy G.: "He was one of those people who helped so many others but was unable to stay sober himself. He disappeared one time. His sponsors and sponsees literally quit their jobs to find him and bring him back. This demonstration of selflessness had a dramatic impact on the medical students—and on me too!"

So, in response to Milton Maxwell's telephone invitation, Joan agreed to go down to New York City for the weekend to meet the other members of the twenty-one-person board and to be interviewed on Saturday by the trustees' nominating committee. "In that interview," she recalls, "my main fear was of becoming overinvolved. But they were warm, friendly, and welcoming. They assured me that the position involved only three weekends per year plus the week of the General Service Conference in April. That turned out to be a considerable understatement," she says wryly, "and I certainly did become involved. But I don't regret a minute of the board service in the years that followed." The weekend of Joan's visit happened to coincide with "Bill's birthday dinner," an annual banquet and dance benefiting the New York Intergroup, attended by more than two thousand enthusiastic AA's dressed to the nines. The General Service Board members were guests for the event, adding a festive bonus to Joan's trip.

"I was totally flabbergasted when the conference accepted my nomination to the board at their meeting the next April," Joan remembers. "And there began the best nine years of my life, bar none!"

Asked what makes service on the AA board different from the many other boards in her experience, she replies:

The effort is always worth it no matter how uncomfortable or trying it may become. For instance, I remember one conference during an unseasonable hot spell. The hotel was sweltering, and I was obliged to wait in the corridor outside a committee meeting room for hours, on call. I was furious with the chairwoman, whom I didn't like anyway. Yet in retrospect, the decisions the committee made with my help were worth all the discomfort and the effort. Incidentally, that chairwoman and I became good friends.

The ability of AA's to disagree violently without becoming disagreeable is astonishing. I have seen delegates have heated arguments, almost coming to blows, it seemed to me. Yet when their shouting match was over and the conference had expressed its group conscience on one side or the other, the two delegates would apologize and hug each other.

In the AA board meetings, there is no pursuit of power by anyone. There are no extraneous issues, no hidden personal agendas. Instead, they are always focused on the good of the fellowship. You can be absolutely straightforward and frank without worrying about what people will think of you. Although you are a nonalcoholic, you are so totally accepted by the alcoholics. They never say, "You're not an alcoholic, so you can't understand." They are grateful that you are there.

Let me give you an example of their caring. In 1991, I fell and broke my hip. The emergency room at Yale New Haven Hospital lost me: They just left me waiting. A member of Alcoholics Anonymous named Walter, who ran the AA program at the hospital, had found out I was there and came to talk with me. From then on, miraculously, AA took care of me. The orderly who pushed my gurney to X ray leaned down and said, "I'm a friend of Bill W." So did the orderlies who took me to the operating room. I remained in the hospital for five days, during which nurses, aides, and all kinds of people I didn't even know, who were AAs or Al-Anons kept coming in my room to visit and cheer me up. The emotional support was massive; that's the only word for it! At home, the support continued. It didn't taper off. That experience typified those whole nine years.

Joan confesses that since rotating off the board, she misses AA and her AA friends very much. She points out that the Class B Trustees continue attending their area assemblies and conferences, busy in their home groups. But the Class A's are, in effect, just dropped. They fade away from the AA activity to which they had become accustomed. They miss it.

"AA changed my life," Joan declares. "Not long ago, Stan and I were musing on 'roads not taken.' We asked ourselves, what if we had remained in Seattle. If we had taken that road, I had a career grant from public health, and I would still be Doctor Joan Jackson. By now I would have been opinionated, sharp, competitive.

"But having lived close to AA for forty years and having served on the AA Board for nine years, you have to live the program. As a result, I am much more tolerant and understanding of where the other fellow is coming from. I am a much mellower person, more happy and content."

Betty Ford

*To those who say that there is nothing spiritual going on in
their lives, I reply: "Telling your story to another human
being is sacred ground."*

(Source unknown)

THE WIFE OF THE THIRTY-EIGHTH PRESIDENT OF THE
UNITED STATES, ELIZABETH ANNE BLOOMER FORD, WAS
born in Chicago on April 8, 1918. Her parents were William
Stephenson Bloomer and Hortense Neahr Bloomer. She had
two siblings, Bill Junior, seven years older than she, and Bob,
who was five years her senior.

Her parents moved to Michigan, and Betty grew up in
Grand Rapids. After graduating from high school, she studied
modern dance at the Bennington School of Dance in Vermont.
Intending to make it a career, she became a member of Martha
Graham's noted concert group in New York City. Her dancing
career, however, was short-lived, and she returned to Grand
Rapids, where she became fashion coordinator for a department store, organized her own dance group, and taught dance
to handicapped children. She remembers that she always found
dancing exhilarating. It provided her with "the freedom to
express myself through my body."

In 1947 she began dating Gerald R. Ford, a practicing attorney
and a former University of Michigan football star. They were
married on October 15, 1948, in Grace Episcopal Church, while
he was waging an uphill campaign for Congress. The following
month Gerald Ford was elected as a Republican to the United
States House of Representatives, despite the landslide that
returned Harry Truman to the White House and gave control of

both houses to the Democrats. The Fords spent the next twenty-eight years in Washington, he as congressman, as vice president, and, with Nixon's resignation in 1974, as president; she as supportive wife and mother of their four children, Michael, John, Steven, and Susan. Betty Ford became an effective campaigner and worked at her husband's side during his long political career. She developed the necessary self-confidence to express herself candidly, with humor and forthrightness. When she became the first lady, she did not hesitate to state her views on such controversial issues as the Equal Rights Amendment (ERA) and women's right to abortion, both of which she supported.

As the years passed, one of her greatest strengths was her willingness to speak forthrightly on issues and subjects that affected her personally, which most people are reluctant to do. In doing so she affected literally millions of people. There are three principal instances in which this occurred.

Being the wife of a Washington politician was neither an easy nor an enviable task, particularly in the case of Gerald Ford, who was totally dedicated to his work and what he considered a genuine and privileged vocation. For three decades Betty's life was defined by her role as wife of an active and well-respected husband and by the strenuous task of raising four children, often with her husband absent for extended periods of time. This precipitated a bout with mental depression for which she sought psychiatric help. Later she spoke about it publicly before a national convention of psychiatrists, following which she received a standing ovation.

Of that period in her life she commented:

> Because so many people think it's shameful to confess that they can't make it alone, that it's an admission of something terribly wrong with them. There was nothing terribly wrong with me. I just wasn't the Bionic Woman, and the minute I stopped thinking that I had to be, a weight fell from my shoulders. (*The Times of My Life*, p. 139)

Little did she realize then that this same perspicacity would spill over into the way she dealt with her chemical dependency.

The second example of her forthrightness and its impact on people occurred shortly after her husband became president in July 1974, when she was unexpectedly diagnosed with breast cancer. She recalls that she received a great deal of credit for going public with the news of her radical surgery. In a way it was simply fate, as the press would not have come racing after her if she hadn't been the wife of the president of the United States. She remembers seeing on TV the lines of women queued up to go in for breast examinations because of what happened to her.

It is much the same story of what occurred when she went public with her illness of chemical dependency. Remembering the sacks of letters she had received, she decided to put her story into writing. She wrote *Betty: A Glad Awakening* to reach out to the many thousands who were reluctant, for whatever reason, to get help.

In 1978 Betty Ford became a classic example of two intervention processes—one that was a failure and one that was a success. For fourteen years she had been on medications for a pinched nerve in her neck, for arthritis, and for muscle spasms. Over the course of the years she had lost her tolerance for chemicals. In addition to that, a less dramatic but steady and continuous consumption of alcohol contributed to dependency upon this mood-altering chemical. Her daughter, Susan, was particularly anxious about Betty's deteriorating health. Susan sought the help of her gynecologist, Dr. Joseph Cruse, himself a recovering alcoholic and on the staff of the Eisenhower Medical Center, to accompany her to talk with the former first lady about her condition. Betty was surprised. As she recounts the story, her anger increased at her daughter and at the intrusion of this meddlesome doctor. As far as she was concerned, her life was going just fine. She remembers:

> So before he could finish Dr. Cruse was asked, not too politely—to remove himself from my presence, my

home, and my life. Dr. Cruse dusted himself off and went away—I retired to my sitting room to take another one of those wonderful little pills that made my life so pleasant. *(Eisenhower Seminar on Alcoholism)*

Fortunately for Mrs. Ford, her family and Dr. Cruse realized that her life was not "so pleasant," and they persisted in doing something about it. A short while after the first failed intervention, she found herself being confronted a second time, not only by her daughter, Susan, but also by her husband and other members of the family and a number of professionals, including Dr. Cruse, all of whom convinced her that it was time to wake up and do something about her life. The recollections of that successful intervention and her recovery process at the Alcohol and Rehabilitation service at Long Beach Naval Hospital, run by Captain Joseph Pursch, M.D., as well as her life after recovery are preserved in the last chapter of *The Times of My Life* (1978) and its sequel, *Betty: A Glad Awakening* (1987).

Treatment at the Long Beach hospital was a critical and painful juncture in the life of the former first lady. Going public upon entering treatment for her addiction to painkillers and then, halfway through treatment, for her dependency upon alcohol were two traumatic experiences. It wasn't quite the same as with depression and breast cancer. Despite some public education and enlightenment to the contrary, the public attitude for the most part was that alcoholism was a sign of failure, a moral weakness, and not an illness.

The *Washington Post* ran an editorial stating that her candor in publicly discussing her mastectomy had given hope and courage to others who were victims or prospective victims of breast cancer. In writing about her addiction to pills and alcohol the editorial commented, "Whatever combination of emotional stress and physical pain (she is arthritic) brought her to this pass, she is, characteristically, determined to overcome it. And she is unafraid and unembarrassed to say so."

On the contrary, Betty admitted to being greatly afraid and

greatly embarrassed. She recollects going through every possible emotion and suffering every possible mood—loneliness, depression, anger, and discouragement. But the fact of the matter is that she prevailed over every mood, and her perseverance provided immeasurable benefits to the field of chemical dependency.

The phrase *going public* simply does not capture the enormous expenditure of time and energy that Betty used over the years. It entailed not simply making a statement about her illness, but giving literally hundreds and hundreds of speeches and presentations throughout the United States. It entailed making endless appearances at public forums and on TV and granting innumerable interviews for reporters and other public figures. Because of her role and high profile as a first lady, she had a unique opportunity to "spread the message," to educate the public, and to lobby Congress for appropriate funding for the treatment of the illness of chemical dependency.

For example, her calendar for March 6, 7, and 8, 1944, included the following events and activities: *National Press Club*, live; *Larry King Weekend*, taped; NBC *Today Show*, live; CBS *This Morning*, live; *CNN Morning News*, live; editorial meeting with the *Washington Post;* dinner with Tipper Gore; a hearing testimony before the Senate Labor and Human Resources Committee; a private lunch with eleven leaders of the House of Representatives; and a meeting with Congressional/Cabinet Spouses Forum on Mental Health Issues. Estimated viewership for the TV appearances: more than twenty-five million people. Marty Mann herself could not reach in a lifetime the number of people who listened to Betty Ford in those three days.

Another essential part of Betty Ford's legacy is the treatment center that bears her name. She and Leonard Firestone, the former president of Firestone Tire and Rubber Company of California and past ambassador to Belgium, were the principal founders and promoters of the Betty Ford Center, which opened on October 4, 1982, in Rancho Mirage, California. One significant event prior to the opening needs to be mentioned.

Betty and Leonard Firestone wanted to provide quality care to as many alcoholics and drug-dependent people at the least cost possible. In other words, they wanted to build a treatment center that would be affordable. (It was never intended as a place for the rich and famous.)

As a result they went to the state capitol in Sacramento, determined to get permission for a relatively inexpensive facility, licensed as a hospital, but not a hospital, in order to be reimbursed by their clients' insurance companies. This was an extremely important step in the history of the Betty Ford Center as well as for treatment in general in the state of California. Betty Ford and Firestone contended that they could provide quality care at about one-third the cost being charged in acute care hospitals. President Ford contacted California Governor Jerry Brown and other key legislators, and a bill was passed in thirty days. The new license allowed for the building of chemical dependency recovery *hospitals*, of which the Betty Ford Center was the first of its kind.

Due to the reputation of the first lady and the quality care that the center provided, it quickly became one of the preeminent treatment centers in the United States. Situated in Rancho Mirage, California, on the property of the Eisenhower Medical Center, the attractive building and the beautiful landscaping, together with the formidable desert and majestic mountains in the background, promote and respond to the dignity and worth of each individual who goes through the center. The program itself is based upon the Minnesota Model, a self-help model inextricably interwoven with the principles and program of AA whose goals are abstinence and changed behavior. The Betty Ford program, however, is not a slavish imitation of the Minnesota Model but has its own discrete and distinct signature.

In the beginning Betty Ford wanted to be involved in everything: "I helped choose the chairs, the carpeting, the pictures on the walls, the colors of the bedspreads. I also helped hire personnel." (*Betty: A Glad Awakening*, p. 103) One board director observed that every nook and cranny of the facility had the Betty Ford signature on it. The patients loved to hear her lectures, which she gave once a month. They were delighted with her frequent, almost daily, visits to the campus and the dining hall. She cared deeply about the patients. When called upon by staff, she made herself available to coax the recalcitrant and straight-talk the arrogant.

From the beginning, Betty was especially concerned with the treatment of women. She made the decision to separate the men and women into different halls. Over the years the program has developed gender-specific services and characteristics with which the women are comfortable and can pursue their own special journeys to recovery.

Another unique service in the continuum provided by the center is the children's program for boys and girls between the ages of eight and thirteen, one or both of whose parents are chemically dependent. Besides recovery services for individuals and their families, the Betty Ford Center provides a variety of training and educational programs. Particularly significant is its educational and experiential program for medical students.

Betty has been, without a doubt, the heartbeat of the Betty Ford Center. As chairperson/president of the board from the center's inception, she has been its charismatic leader, an enviable fund-raiser, and its preeminent spokesperson. She has been instrumental in bringing together an outstanding board of directors. Over the years the board has been responsible for both the financial health of the organization and its planned expansion. When the hard decisions had to be made, she has been there to encourage the whole board to make them. Even with such a diverse composition of executives and entrepreneurs as the board exhibits, Betty Ford has had the ability to gain consensus.

In the arena of public policy, she has been relentless in her pursuit of the cause of the chemically dependent. Upon his election, President Bill Clinton had made it clear that the reform of health care would be his number one priority. In turn, Betty's number one priority was to see that chemical dependency benefits be included in whatever legislation Congress passed and the president signed. Part of the educational process would be to demonstrate that treatment was cost effective. And indeed, health care cost containment was a central issue in the 1992 campaign. When Clinton was elected, he pushed his agenda for universal coverage. As Hillary Clinton related to Betty Ford, he seemed to be sensitive to the issue of reimbursement for the treatment of chemical dependency.

Betty Ford traveled to Washington a number of times during the health care debate and was indefatigable in her lobbying efforts. She met with the president; the first lady; the wife of the vice president, Tipper Gore; and members of Congress on different occasions, emphasizing the positive cost benefits of treatment for the workforce in particular and for society as a whole. Once an individual has gone through treatment successfully, other illnesses, work-related accidents, and absenteeism drop dramatically.

She and former First Lady Rosalynn Carter joined forces to bring the mental health and chemical dependency message to various committees of Congress, reminding them that society has paid substantial costs for its failure to deal with serious and treatable mental disorders and substance abuse. It was a historic moment to witness the activities of this formidable pair, one a Democrat and the other a Republican, as they urged their listeners to move past the outmoded myths about mental health and substance abuse and to develop legislation that ensured access to the right treatment at the right time.

Largely due to the efforts of these two prominent leaders in the arenas of mental health and chemical dependency, before the collapse of the national health care initiatives in 1994 all the bills emanating from the various congressional committees contained benefits for mental health and chemical dependency in one form or another.

As Betty Ford began personally to experience the joy to be found in recovery she wanted to help others discover that same joy. Through her books, speeches, television appearances, and interviews she told the story over and over. The circles began to embrace and extend to millions of people—the curious, the skeptical, the wounded and suffering families, the recovering and the wondering, and those simply taken by the story and the woman unashamed and brave enough to recite it.

She was literally fulfilling Bill W.'s counsel that the best way to express thanks for one's personal recovery was to pass the message on to "the millions who still don't know." She was convinced that people could relate "to someone who has the same problems and who overcomes them. And I think God has allowed me—along with thousands of others—*to carry a message* that says, there's help out there, and you too can be a survivor. Look at us. Look at me." (*Betty: A Glad Awakening*, p. xv)

Indeed telling one's story to another person is sacred ground.

Mary Jane Hanley

IT SEEMS TO ME THAT TODAY, DESPITE OUR BETTER UNDER-STANDING OF ALCOHOLISM, MANY PEOPLE STILL BELIEVE THAT if someone's an alcoholic, he or she must have grown up in a family with alcoholism, or some kind of abuse, or *some* major problem, at least. That's simply not the case.

I'm an alcoholic, and my family life was wonderful. I had loving, generous, caring parents, and I couldn't have asked for a better childhood—the years of my youth were a happy time for me. I grew up in Carmel, California, in a family in which there was no alcoholism, at least none that I knew of. My mom and dad had an occasional social drink, but I don't think I ever saw either of them drunk.

My high school in Carmel was *lots* of fun. There was beer drinking in the high school, of course. My friends and I used to go down to the ocean, and the boys would bring some beer and Coca-Cola. I did drink some beer in high school, but I never got into any trouble with it, and I *never* drank any hard liquor. Actually, I didn't really like the taste of beer, but because everybody was drinking it, I taught myself to like it. The same thing happened with cigarettes. I didn't start smoking until I went to college, and it was nothing but peer pressure that made me begin. I can honestly say, however, that there were no problems with my drinking at that point in my life—in part because I didn't like it much!

My life and my feelings about alcohol began to change near the end of my final year of high school, which was, in my case, my junior year. For the first time, I found myself unhappy about things. This was a difficult time because, to begin with, World

War II had started. I had been running around with a group of kids who were a year ahead of me. My boyfriend was in the military and was going off to war, just like so many others.

I didn't want to finish up high school with all my friends gone. Since I only needed one and a half credits to graduate after completing my junior year, I decided to go to Lake Tahoe, where I could take the classes I needed to graduate in their summer school program.

Once in Tahoe, I met and began to run around with a group from Stockton. There was smoking and drinking, but I don't remember having any trouble. Frankly, I don't even remember drinking much at all. I do recall, however, going to Reno, Nevada, one night, where I had my first drink of hard liquor. At the time, I thought it was disgusting stuff! These new friends were all attending the University of the Pacific in Stockton, so when I returned home after finishing my classes, I told my parents that I wanted to attend the college there. At this time, the college was running what were called the v5 and v12 programs. These were programs in which the navy took male high school graduates and sent them to colleges and universities for training that would be useful for the war—radar, electronics, and so on.

As a result, many schools completely ignored their female students. We received no guidance or help in choosing classes, or a major, or anything else. No one really cared what classes we took or what we might want to become. We might as well have been invisible. What was worse, at age seventeen, I was younger than all my peers, and I'd never really been away from home, either. I *really* could have used some help and guidance.

These school years were fine, and I had a group of friends to run around with, but I wasn't learning much. It wasn't a particularly happy time, but I wasn't miserable, either. Life was just so-so—a big change for me. Because I wasn't happy and didn't have any direction or goal I could work toward, I decided to get into the school's junior college program, which allowed me to graduate after only two years.

By this time, my parents had moved from lovely little Carmel to the suburbs of Los Angeles in Beverly Hills. I decided to join them, but once again, I was in a new place where I knew absolutely no one. The few women friends I had left from high school were either away in college or in Carmel. I had to try to find another set of friends, something that wasn't easy for me to do.

Once in Beverly Hills, I went to work for the May Company's bookkeeping department—a menial job, to say the least! After I had worked there for a year or so, my mother decided that she had to get me out of there. She sent me to a secretarial school in Beverly Hills for the next two years. I met a lot of nice women there and had a nice time. I dated some of the boys I met—though there weren't many around since most were in the military. I drank a little then, but not much—to me it was just a social activity, something to do while on a date.

My life at this time was routine and unexciting. Then I met the guy who would become my husband. The war had just ended. Jack (John) Hanley had been in the navy for five years. He'd recently been hired by Procter and Gamble as a salesman in the Los Angeles area. Jack had grown up on the East Coast, so he wasn't someone I'd known before. We were introduced through a neighbor of mine, a man who was Jack's uncle. We met and started dating, and six months later, we were married in Beverly Hills.

Jack and I found a nice little apartment in L.A. For some reason, at this time in our lives, we were both drinking a lot. It wasn't unusual that Jack and I and some other folks headed down to the beach with a case of beer. We had a cocktail before dinner, a practice that soon became a habit. We were never drunk, but we always had the drink.

This period was a turning point in both our lives. Jack was becoming successful with Procter and Gamble and was moving up rapidly in the company. As a result, we were transferred a number of times in just a few years. We went from L.A. to Seattle, then six months later to Minneapolis, where we had our first child, John. We stayed in Minneapolis for just two years and then were off to Chicago, where our second child, Michael, was born. I was in my late twenties. Our stay in Chicago was also brief. Jack was soon transferred to Cincinnati, the location of Procter and Gamble's home office. Our third child, Suzy, was born not long thereafter.

While I was excited about Jack's rapid rise in the business world and happy for him, too, it made life difficult for me. I was at home, faced with the challenges of raising three young children. That's no easy task regardless of one's circumstances. But to do it with little, if any, support made it doubly difficult. All the moves we'd made because of Jack's transfers left me without any good friends to whom I could turn for help and support. Each move meant leaving fledgling friendships and again being thrown in with colleagues of Jack's whom I didn't know and into communities that were completely new to me. At this time, however, I wasn't drinking. Sure, Jack and I had the occasional cocktail at dinner, but it simply never entered my mind to drink more than that.

Our move to Cincinnati did provide, at last, some stability in our lives. Jack felt we'd be there for some years, so we built our first house. I was relieved, feeling that this house could actually become a home for Jack and me and our children.

In the ensuing years, my husband climbed quickly in the Proctor and Gamble world. Consequently, I found myself thrown in with people who were quite a bit older than me— people in their forties and fifties. Jack was by far the youngest man in the management group, and he was five years older than me too.

I'd always been on the shy side, and now here I was, at these big parties with a lot of people I didn't know, all much older than me. I had a hard time relating to them. They all knew each other, of course, since the men had been together for a while in the company. Jack was the new, young guy. It's sometimes hard for people who know each other and who are older to remember how a young woman in her late twenties from another part of the country might feel being thrown into a situation like this.

I was *very* uncomfortable. These were difficult situations for me. Jack and I were also expected to do a lot of social things, including civic activities. Being from a small town like Carmel, this was a whole new way of life and living for me. Again, I was uncomfortable with it.

It's important to remember the era in which this was all taking place. I keep referring to "the men" because there weren't many women working at executive levels in any company at that time. The "P&G wives" in the hierarchy were supposed to watch themselves and behave properly at all times. These were the days when a man's wife was important to his career—not for business skills or ability, however. No, it was important to be socially acceptable. At some point then, I discovered that if I had a couple of drinks, I felt much more outgoing and at ease with these situations. And *that's* how my drinking started.

After a few years in Cincinnati, Jack became the head of sales for P&G. This promotion meant a lot of travel to New York— and running into the fast advertising crowd there. These people drank like fish. It was unbelievable to me. We'd go, for example, to New York to spend weekends in the Adirondack Mountains with people from the big New York City ad agencies. These were social occasions—and the New York crowd drank all the time. I was trying to be accepted, to do the right thing, so when I was there, I went along with them. It's just what we did. Well, this was a bad scene for me.

Over a period of years, my drinking gradually increased. Having one drink went to two, two went to three, three to four, and on and on—until finally, it had become both a family problem and a problem for Jack in our social circle. Jack realized that I was getting bombed at these parties, and he was upset about it. He told me he didn't want me to drink anymore.

"Well," I thought, "who are you to tell me what I can or can't do?" I nevertheless made an attempt to drink less. My solution to the party drinking was to have a good shot of something before I went and then to try to limit my drinks once I was there, since I knew Jack would be watching.

I tried not to let my drinking affect my family and naively thought at the time that it hadn't. We had three children. Our oldest, John, was fourteen or so by then and attending school at Andover. We also had Michael and Suzy, who were still at home.

By now, too, we had hired Blanca, an Argentinean woman, to live with us to cook, clean, and help care for the children. This decision came about because of demands on us from Jack's responsibilities at work. There were regular events, meetings, and so on that Jack and I were both expected to attend, and they often involved travel to New York or other cities. At times, both of us had to be able to leave at the drop of a hat. In addition, Jack regularly had guests in town whom he had to entertain. Blanca was a great cook, and her contributions left both Jack and me free to entertain.

Blanca ran my house with an iron hand, which didn't help matters. With Blanca in our household, in a way, my jobs—cooking, cleaning, and so on—weren't mine anymore.

Quickly, I reached the point where I'd drink whenever Jack wasn't around at home and at our summer cottage. Blanca never said anything to me about my drinking, though she was certainly aware of it. I didn't think my kids knew, but I later found that they did, of course. John was attending school at Andover and then Stanford, so he wasn't around for much of it, but Michael and Suzy were the ones who knew—especially Suzy.

> Mom would be in a different mood when she was drinking. Later on, I began to recognize that the clinking of bottles meant she was drinking. I couldn't figure out why she would be drinking in the middle of the day. I remember many times when she'd take the car out, and I'd be scared that she'd be in an accident. I was always so relieved when I'd hear the garage door come up because that meant she'd made it home again safely. As all of us in the family now know, alcoholism doesn't

just affect the alcoholic in the family, it hits everyone.
—Susan Hanley-Meyers

Jack and I also had a cottage in Michigan where I and the children went in the summer. That's when my drinking really started to progress, because most of the time, Jack was in Cincinnati working. That left me at the cottage with the children. By now, they were old enough to look after themselves some, too, so I was able to enjoy my drinking there.

Jack had said not to drink, so I didn't—when I was around him. Otherwise, yes, I did. All of my drinking was done behind closed doors the last three or four years of my drinking—in my bedroom, or in the kitchen when no one was around, or wherever I could find the privacy I needed. Mind you, I didn't drink continually. I was what people call a periodic drinker. I could go several weeks without drinking, but once I started, I would be off for two or three days.

Our lives went on and on like this, with my drinking worsening, until, for the first time, Jack and I began to have problems in our marriage.

> In our case, neither of us understood that it was a disease that Mary Jane was suffering from. I certainly thought, and I think Mary Jane did too, that this was something she ought to be able to control. Well, she couldn't for some period of time. I know now that it's a disease, and you can't simply will it to end. And you end up not being able to control yourself, and eventually, you end up losing control of your life. It wreaks havoc on everyone involved.
> —John W. Hanley, cofounder,
> with Mary Jane Hanley,
> Hanley Family Foundation

Jack expected me to stop or at least control my drinking, but I couldn't and didn't, partly because I didn't believe that I was an alcoholic. Instead, my take on the situation was that it was Jack who wouldn't let me drink, and I resented him immensely for that. "Why won't he let me live the kind of life I want to live?" I thought. "What is so wrong with me? Why shouldn't I drink like other people? Why doesn't he just leave me alone?" Or I told myself, "If he wasn't gone so much, I wouldn't have to drink alone. I could drink with other people like everyone else. He's just too busy with work."

> I saw that there was a problem, and I spent not just one, but many nights lying awake all night wondering, "How do I cope with this?" I prayed to God for guidance and direction. I had no idea what to do. Eventually, though, we received the guidance we needed.
> —John W. Hanley

Finally one day, things began to break down. I'd been drinking at home, and when Jack came home from work, he realized it. We had a big row over this, and he left the house for a couple of days. Well, this scared the life out of me. Jack had never done anything like that before.

> By now, the children knew that there was something wrong with their mother. When I left the house that day, we were truly on the verge of splitting up as a family. That would have been a terrible tragedy, both for us and for the children. But it could have happened because neither of us yet knew how to get help.
> —John W. Hanley

> It was clear that their marriage was in jeopardy. Mom didn't want to lose Dad or us children, and that made her look inside and eventually seek treatment.
> —Susan Hanley-Meyers

I still loved my husband dearly, and I didn't want to lose him.

When he came back and said, "We have to do something about this," I agreed. We went to talk to our minister, a man who was also our personal friend.

Again, remember the time and the setting. When I say this, I don't want to sound snooty, but Jack was an important person in Cincinnati. He was active in the United Way, and his picture was in the paper all the time. By now, he was vice president of P&G and making a lot of money. Yet here he was with a wife who was clearly having a problem with alcohol. For a man of his social and corporate stature to have an alcoholic wife was a disaster, because we as a society weren't at all honest about this disease. Alcoholics were thought of as skid row bums, not wives of corporate vice presidents.

During our meeting, our minister said, "Well, Jack, because of your position in the community, we can do one of two things. Mary Jane could go to Alcoholics Anonymous, or we could send her to a psychiatrist." They chose the second option, recommending that Jack and I each go to separate psychiatrists. They chose that course of action because they felt there might be a stigma on Jack if I went to AA and word somehow got out.

Now there I was, sitting and listening to these two men decide what I was going to do. I was upset about this. Here were my husband and our minister making the decision—neither asked me what I wanted.

My drinking problem was now beginning to come to a head, but I still wasn't admitting that I was an alcoholic. I thought the psychiatrist plan was really stupid. I didn't think I had a problem, so why should I to go to a psychiatrist? I worried constantly the whole two days before my first meeting with this man. I didn't know what he'd be like, and I couldn't imagine what we'd discuss.

I went to that psychiatrist for a year, and during the whole time, never once did the subject of alcohol come up. It was never mentioned! I didn't bring it up because, of course, I knew I wasn't an alcoholic. But this counselor never brought it up, either. We never talked about it, and I never stopped drinking, of course. What's more, I remained peeved with Jack for making me see that man. It was just one more thing to blame him for and one more reason to continue drinking.

Finally, a year later while on the way home from the psychiatrist, I realized that we had sat together for a solid hour and had talked about his son and our daughter, and their experiences at the school they both went to. I thought, "This is ridiculous," and when Jack came home that day, I said, "I'm not going back."

But I told him, too, that I would go to AA. I thought perhaps that *something* was wrong and that this might be a good idea. I knew I had to do something, if at least to make my husband happy.

I went to those AA meetings, however, not because I thought I belonged in AA, because I didn't—I just had to get Jack off my back. It was a nice meeting in another neighborhood of Cincinnati in which no one knew me. I would sit in the back row and listen to the drunks tell their stories—and then I'd get up, go to my car, and drive home. That was it. I never once took a Step nor did I do anything else one was supposed to do, because I wasn't admitting I was an alcoholic.

Fortunately, those meetings did have one positive effect on me. Sitting there listening to all those people must have put something in my head because I stayed sober for nine months. I wanted to prove to myself that I wasn't an alcoholic.

During that ninth month, however, Jack and I were at the cottage in Michigan, hosting a big party, when I started to drink again. Jack found out, and he wasn't happy. I again told him I'd try to stay sober.

I did. I had heard about a little local AA meeting in Cincinnati just for women. Once there, I found that I liked some of the women. And for the first time, I asked for a sponsor. I also started to read some literature on alcoholism. I wasn't admitting I was an alcoholic yet, though I *thought* I was admitting. Looking back, it's easy to see that I still needed something more.

Through all these years of drinking, I seldom embarrassed myself or Jack. I was able to carry out my duties as the wife of someone like Jack. I never got out of hand. This observation became another piece of my denial. "We know lots of people who are drinking at the parties who really get out of hand," I told myself. What's more, I still blamed my drinking or any inappropriate behavior on Jack. He was forcing me into this situation, I thought. Looking back, I shudder to think of all the opportunities for disaster I dodged—driving kids in car pools, and so on—when I had been drinking.

> Eventually I realized that I had, in fact, been making the problem worse. I was picking at Mary Jane all the time. That made her angry and resentful, and then she drank again. But I couldn't seem to help it; I just couldn't control my anger, my concern, and my fears.
> —John W. Hanley

By this time, Jack had become one of two executive vice presidents, both of whom were aspiring to the top spot at P&G. But then the Monsanto Corporation came to Jack and wanted to hire him as their chairman, president, and chief executive officer. Jack decided to make the change.

Now here's a wonderful example of alcoholic thinking—the geographic cure. I told myself, "Now, Mary Jane, you're going to prove that you can give up drinking. You're going to move to a new city, meet new people, run into new situations, and you're going to stop drinking. You'll have a new life without alcohol."

Jack and I moved to St. Louis and started a new adventure. As part of Monsanto, we traveled all over the world. We had access to a company plane, a chauffeur—we had a luxurious life. I had made myself a promise, too, that if I started to drink again, I would do something about it.

One night, not long after we moved to St. Louis, sometime in 1973, I drank while Jack was out doing something else. When he returned, he simply said to me, "I left a number on your desk," and I knew that he knew. I went to my desk, and there was the name of a Monsanto doctor.

I called this man, Dr. Kelly, thinking that Jack wanted me to get back into AA. Dr. Kelly was wonderful, an older Irish man who was on the board of a place called Edgewood, a small treatment center on the outskirts of St. Louis. Dr. Kelly said, "Mary Jane, you may need treatment. But before we do that, I'd like you to call a woman I know, and she can take you to an AA meeting here. We have some good meetings in St. Louis."

I took Dr. Kelly's advice and attended that AA meeting. There I met some great gals who'd gone to Edgewood. They were so happy in their sobriety. I had lunch with them, and we all had a really good time. But I left feeling puzzled. Whenever *I* was sober, I was never really happy! I was so full of resentment, guilt, and all kinds of other garbage. How I could possibly be happy? But here were these women, alcoholics who were now sober, and they were happy. I thought, "Gee, I wish I could have what they have."

So I tried, I really tried at AA. I tried as conscientiously as I could to do the Steps. But I think that what I really needed was to get out of my environment for a while, because I did have a bad slip on a weekend when we had out-of-town guests.

The last drink I had was at that dinner. Everyone there was socializing at our house before dinner, when I walked into the kitchen to wait for our cook to arrive. I was just standing there when I noticed a bottle of wine on the counter. I never liked wine at all. Despite that, I went over and started drinking it. Straight out of the bottle. And from that moment on, I was gone. Out of it. I think they all knew I was drunk.

I realize now that when I went into that kitchen, I had no idea I was going to have a drink. I didn't go in there for one. I just went in to wait for the cook. That's when it dawned on me that maybe I really was an alcoholic. I guess that's when I hit my bottom. There were no more excuses. That was a huge shock to me—to realize that I just went in and drank that bottle of wine. I hadn't thought about drinking it. I didn't want to drink it. But I drank it anyway.

The following Monday, our guests were on their way back to their homes in Cincinnati and Jack was at the office, and I was sitting at home thinking, "Oh, God, what have I done now?" I was just crying and crying, when my husband came in the front door. Jack looked at me and said, "Mary Jane, I can't work."

When I saw the look on that man's face, I thought, "What am I doing to him?" I said, "Honey, I'm going to go into treatment," and I got up and went to the phone and called Edgewood. When they answered, I said, "Do you have room for me? I want to come." I had truly hit my bottom.

Unfortunately, they didn't have a place for me for three weeks, but during that time, I never had a drink. I was so scared. It had finally hit me that I really was an alcoholic.

The first shock I'd had came when I realized what I'd done with that bottle of wine two nights earlier. The other huge shock was looking at Jack, a man I dearly loved, and understanding at last what I was doing to him. I was destroying him. The last thing in the world I wanted to do was to hurt him. And for once, at last, I thought of Jack and how what I was doing was affecting him. I thought, "Well, maybe it's not all his fault. Maybe it's not his fault at all. Maybe it's all me! Or some combination of the two of us."

I was finally admitting to myself that I had a problem. I realized it that morning after the bad weekend slip. It had to be alcoholism that was ruining our marriage and making me do all these awful things I didn't want to do. I knew that to get better, I needed to be with other people who were just like me—to live with them.

> Mary Jane had struggled for a long time to find a solution to our problem. Finally, she realized what the solution was—that if she couldn't handle the alcohol problem, she would go to treatment. She found that treatment center and asked me what I thought. I said, "Fine, go to it." She came out a few weeks later, having acquired the tools that she'd use the rest of her life to live a good, godly, sober life.
> —John W. Hanley

During the three weeks I waited to enter Edgewood, I still struggled with the stigma that surrounded alcoholism. I knew if I went to Edgewood, there was a possibility that someone from our community would find out I was there for treatment. I didn't want anyone to know where I was, not for my sake, but for Jack's. I didn't want to hurt him anymore with something like this, so I offered him an alternative. I said, "You know, Jack, I've heard of a place called Hazelden up in Minnesota. Would you rather I go somewhere out of state for treatment?" To his credit, he said, "No, you go to Edgewood. That way I can be near you." That's an example of why I love this man so much.

Finally the three weeks passed. I got in a cab and went to Edgewood. I discovered that this center was an old, run-down motel out by the St. Louis airport. I discovered shortly after my arrival that the center was run by the Catholic Church and had been started by some Catholic families in St. Louis for priests and nuns. There were people from all walks of life—nuns and priests, truck drivers, and now the wife of a corporate executive. I began to realize how wrong the stereotype was that held that you had to come from a bad family to be alcoholic, and that alcoholics were all skid row bums.

One of my strongest memories of my time at Edgewood took place after I'd been there about three weeks. I was sitting out on the back lawn of the center, by myself, when all of a sudden, this enormous peace came over me. I said to myself, "Mary Jane, you are an alcoholic. You belong here. These are your people. This is where you should be." At that moment, I felt as though a great cloak had been lifted from my shoulders. It was an incredible feeling.

After about two weeks, I heard that Jack was coming to see me. That was a good sign. I realized that, yes, he was going to stay by me. Then I received a locket that Jack sent me in the mail, and I knew how much he loved me.

I stayed at Edgewood for five weeks. It was a great program, run by a man who had been through counselor training at

Hazelden. While there, I admitted at last that I was an alcoholic. During that time, I truly found myself. It was the most marvelous experience of my life. My sister came to see me from California, and, of course, my kids all came from all over the country to visit.

One of the best parts of the treatment was that, with help from Edgewood staff, Jack was able to understand what alcoholism was. He had never understood why I couldn't stop drinking. He thought it was lack of willpower on my part. He saw for the first time that this was a disease, that it wasn't all my fault, that this wasn't something I could just stop on my own, that I was alcoholic.

I realized that my drinking wasn't Jack's fault and that there was no point in blaming him for it. I was finally able to get rid of my resentments toward him. And I saw it wasn't just my fault, either.

The day I left treatment, a friend picked me up and took me to our home. Jack was at the office, and he came home early that day. Across from our apartment was a big park, and when Jack came in the door, he said, "Let's take a walk across the street." This was an uncomfortable time for both of us. We didn't know quite how to handle each other at this point. I had been in treatment for over a month, and we'd had little contact with one another. So in a way, we felt a little like strangers. Jack took my hand and we walked across the street and into the park. We didn't say too much. He told me he was there to help me in any way he could, to which I replied, "Thank you, dear. That means a lot to me."

Mom and Dad didn't desert each other; they decided to make it work. As a result, they have a wonderful gift, not just for themselves, but for many other generations.
—Michael J. Hanley

Our parents have one of the best marriages I'm aware of. It's because Mom got help that they became even closer. I admire that. There also came a peace in the family that hadn't existed before.

—Susan Hanley-Meyers

After Mary Jane went through treatment, our life together was so much better. In addition, I was able to do my work at Monsanto with considerably greater skill than I'd demonstrated up until that point. All of us, led by her example, started growing again. Of course, when you're growing, you're a happy camper.

—John W. Hanley

After I finished treatment, our love grew like crazy. I loved Jack like I'd never loved him before because of what he'd gone through. I think he felt a deep respect for me because of what I'd gone through too. Our love blossomed. It was like a second marriage. We've had a wonderful, wonderful marriage. I've been one of the fortunate ones. I haven't had a slip yet.

I didn't tell many people that I'd gone through treatment. I did write to four of my closest friends, however, people we'd done a lot of socializing with, people who I felt knew I had a drinking problem. I realized when I was in treatment how I had acted in certain situations and how I must have seemed to those around me. I admitted to these friends that I was an alcoholic and let them know I'd gotten treatment and wasn't drinking anymore.

While I and a group of gals who met in AA were pleased with the help we'd received at Edgewood, we all felt that St. Louis needed and deserved a bigger and better treatment center. All of us were married to men who were prominent in St. Louis, and we decided to work together and raise money to build a new treatment center, which became part of St. John's Hospital in St. Louis.

From this point on, Jack and I became committed to contributing to the field of chemical dependency—a commitment that soon became public. Until now, both Jack and I had kept my problems with alcohol private. We'd purchased a small condominium near North Palm Beach, Florida, where I spent the winters. Jack was still working and traveling back and forth between St. Louis and Florida but also thinking seriously about retiring. Our relationship continued to grow. Our children were doing well, and we were happy with life in general. Then, one day about six months before he was going to retire, Jack walked into our kitchen with a surprise.

> I woke up one morning with a message in my head. I don't know where it came from, but somehow I realized that if Mary Jane agreed, we were going to spend the rest of our lives helping other people find the same kind of return to God's grace that was given to our family. That's when I talked to her about this. Can we help alcoholics get into treatment? Can we help prevent alcoholism? Does southern Florida need a treatment center? If so, can we help build one? It was clear to me that this was what we ought to do. I frankly never questioned how that message came to me. It was so clear that I didn't have to question it. When I talked to Mary Jane about this, we decided to do it.
> —John W. Hanley

When Jack first spoke to me about all this, I didn't know what to think. I said, "Well, I've been going to AA meetings since we came to Florida, and I'll certainly ask these people." I did, and the response was overwhelmingly, "Yes! We certainly could stand a good one!" At the time, only two small centers were available to people who needed treatment.

After hearing that information, Jack wanted to know if I would be interested in working together to develop one—to raise money and so on. Well, this was a complete about-face on alcoholism for Jack. At first, he had tried to hide everything about alcoholism. What he was talking about now would mean that we'd both have to be public about what had happened to us. So I told him, "You know, Jack, what this would mean, don't you? We're going to have to go public about this, about our lives and how we've been affected by alcoholism." But, of course, Jack had already thought of this and had decided that he was ready to take that step too.

> We flew to Minnesota to visit Dan Anderson, the president of the Hazelden Foundation. We asked him if Hazelden would carry out the market research necessary to see if there truly was a need for a treatment center in southern Florida. According to Dan, Hazelden hadn't ever been approached to do something like this before, but he agreed to carry out the study. At the same time, we contacted the United Way in southern Florida and asked them to help with a similar study. Since I'd been the United Way's National Volunteer Director for two years, they knew me and knew that I was serious about creating a center if the need existed.
>
> When both studies came back confirming a substantial need for a center, Mary Jane and I returned to Hazelden and again spoke with Dan. We told him we'd raise the money and build the center, but we wanted Hazelden to run it. At first Dan declined, saying that Hazelden had never done something like this before, though he did offer Hazelden's help in running it. We felt that wouldn't be enough. Mary Jane and I had never run a treatment center and felt that Hazelden could do a much better job than we could. They were, after all, the leading experts in the field. After more discussion, Dan and the Hazelden board of directors agreed to accept our proposal.
> —John W. Hanley

The research we had carried out showed that 90 percent of the people in Palm Beach County had been touched in some way by alcoholism. It was clear that we were not talking about a foreign concept. Countless people had seen alcoholism affect their parents, siblings, friends, and children. We talked about how this could be an even better place to live and work and raise families if it had a world-class addiction treatment facility.

In carrying out this project, we would be responding to a definite community need. We knew, too, that other communities in the country had similar needs, so we decided to do this in a way that other communities could imitate if we were successful. What we were about to create came to be called Hanley-Hazelden. I am still amazed at this, and at Jack, when I look back on our work. The whole idea was Jack's—this man did a complete turnaround in regard to alcoholism. You have never seen such a change in a person.

> Mom is the one who's really behind Dad. She enables him to do what he does. She's very strong, with a powerful sense of right and wrong. When she's dedicated to something, she gives it her all. It's been the two of them working together who have accomplished all this. Most of the questions and attention may be directed toward Dad, but the answers come as much from Mom as from him.
>
> —Michael J. Hanley

We gave a substantial amount of money to get the ball rolling, but much more was needed. Jack was still a member of numerous corporate boards of directors at that time, and through these contacts we were able to raise a lot of corporate money.

In addition, Jack and I went out and did the "Dog and Pony Show." We felt that if we were going to ask people to help fund a treatment center, they had to know more about the problem of alcoholism and about the difference treatment can make, not only in the lives of alcoholics, but also in the lives of all those around them. How better to get that message across than for me to tell my story?

We decided to visit all the big country clubs in south Florida—Hope Sound, Country Club of Florida, and so on—the places that those with money in Florida frequent. We had decided that I would tell my story and Jack would explain what alcoholism was all about and the need for a treatment center.

The first talk I gave was at a club near the home we'd recently built. We'd been members at Lost Tree Village for about five years. The women I played golf with there knew I didn't drink, but they didn't have any idea I was an alcoholic.

We put up an announcement that we were going to do a talk about alcoholism. The day of the presentation, about 120 people showed up to hear us. I can tell you, this was the hardest thing I have ever done in my life. There were a lot of shocked people in that audience after I told my story. People came up to me afterward and said I was absolutely wonderful to do what I was doing.

> This was a great act of courage. At the time in our country when Mrs. Hanley went public with her addiction, people were only just beginning to be open about alcoholism. Mrs. Hanley stood up in front of peers, colleagues, and strangers to talk about her addiction. I was impressed by her passion for her program of recovery and her compassion for others. She clearly wasn't doing this for herself, but because she cared about others. She wanted others to have the gift she had been so fortunate to receive—the gift of recovery.
> —Doug Tieman,
> CEO, Caron Foundation
> and Hanley-Hazelden Center

I think Mom and I are alike in that we're both on the shy side when it comes to speaking in public. But part of the recovery process is wanting to help others. My mother is grateful for what she's learned, and she puts her fears aside to do what needs to be done.
—Susan Hanley-Meyers

I was sitting on the podium with Mary Jane, watching the audience while she spoke. There were 150 to 200 of her friends there. When she spoke, tears were streaming down the cheeks of men and women alike. Hers was the single most courageous act I have ever seen an individual take, outside of military service. She is one gutsy lady.

—John W. Hanley

While our talks were generally well received, some people were less than enthusiastic. After my first talk, two close friends who were in the audience ignored the subject completely afterward. They never mentioned it—and I never brought it up.

Another time, after Jack and I had finished talking at the Country Club of Florida, an old AA fellow in the audience got after Jack for doing what he was doing. He believed that we were breaking the anonymity rule. Jack and I both felt—and still do feel—that people will never understand what alcoholism is all about if we don't talk about it.

In my opinion, the anonymity idea has been the worst thing that has happened to alcoholics. In a way, it's treating alcoholism as though it's something shameful. It's not. But the anonymity idea reinforces that stigma—perhaps unintentionally, but it does. When you hide something, even with the best intentions, you're still hiding. Alcoholism was always seen as a shameful thing, and there's still a stigma to it, even though there shouldn't be.

Why do I want people to know my story? So they don't have to live it. It's that simple. I don't want their marriages to break up, which mine could have. I don't want their children to suffer because of alcoholism. I don't want them to be embarrassed by walking into a room drunk. I don't want them to have to go through what I went through.

We continued our work and eventually raised enough money to build Hanley-Hazelden—$5 million. We wanted the project to be a community effort, not a Hanley project. We wanted it to belong to the community, not to us.

During the new center's first three years or so, the bottom line came out in the red, so Jack and I had to help out. And Hazelden, God bless them, stuck by us. Now, however, it's a successful program. I am excited to say, we recently completed an addition for the older adults' program—a program that is receiving national recognition.

> This was a family project right from the beginning. Before we began, we sat down with our three children and said, "Here's what we are thinking about doing. People will know how this addiction affected our family. It will be public. It will take our family's resources, and that will affect you directly. Is that okay?" And they all said, "This is so important to our family, we have to do it." They were totally behind what Mary Jane and I wanted to do.
>
> We are making a difference in the lives of people who are involved in Hanley-Hazelden, as well as through all the other activities our family is involved in regarding the disease of alcoholism. These activities continue to be deeply rewarding to our family.
>
> We believe that having a passion about something is important in making your life worthwhile. I see others who are retired and who have means—people who could do something more with their lives but don't. That's unfortunate. I do recommend that people find something that they can do that will contribute to others.
>
> —John W. Hanley

We have also started a foundation that is dedicated to teaching people about alcoholism and its treatment. We founded it just after Hanley-Hazelden got off the ground, and we're happy to say that it now has resources of about $7 million. Jack and I know we've been fortunate in our lives, and we want to share that good fortune. This foundation is something that will carry out our work after we're gone, and each of our children is active in it.

My brothers and I have a great responsibility. We're the second generation, and we need to carry forth the good work our parents began in the 1980s. That's no easy task. But with the resources they have, there will be more grants. We're working hard to develop a board that can carry forth their passion for the work they're doing now. It's also a wonderful opportunity and a privilege to have the chance to tap the resources at hand and to match them with appropriate causes and organizations that can have a dramatic impact on people in the future. Our family got whole and well again, and now we're working as a family to help others have what we have now.

—Susan Hanley-Meyers

To Mom and Dad, I would just say, "We thank you for having the courage many years ago to address the problem. It's meant everything to the family, and we'll do the best we can to carry forward and to fulfill the dream you had when you created this foundation."

—Michael J. Hanley

Jack and I will work in this field for as long as we're able. Jack works on a national level to educate doctors about the disease, and he stays busy with that. This is our life. I say today that God made me an alcoholic to give Jack something to do when he retired!

I'm so grateful for what's happened to us, and so grateful that there was an Edgewood Treatment Center when I needed it— when I was ready for it. We want to make sure that people have good treatment available to them if they need it too.

Help yourself first, be true to yourself. If you're true to yourself, and you're an alcoholic, you'll admit it. Then, help others—

that's what will help you the most. You'll find great reward in helping other people, especially if you've walked down their path.

Hanley-Hazelden opened its doors September 29, 1986. Since then, nearly nine thousand people have received treatment there for chemical dependency.

In spring 1999, Mary Jane Hanley marked twenty-five years of sobriety.

SOURCES:

Hanley, Mary Jane. Interviews by Joe Moriarity. June 1998.

The International Alcoholics Anonymous Women's Conference (IAAWC): The Language of the Heart

"I'm never going to this conference again!" That's what I said the first time the conference was held in Chicago. Six of us bused together from Kansas, and everyone slept in one room. We had things all over the place. Somebody's makeup was over here, and you had to step over somebody's body to get whatever you were looking for. And we kept saying we were never going to do this again. But, then the next conference time comes around, and there's always somebody asking to room with me, and I go ahead and do it again. I've been to sixteen conferences in a row now.

Philomena R., Wichita, Kansas,
twenty-seven years sober

IT IS A CONFERENCE LIKE ANY OTHER, WITH A TIGHT AGENDA AND LOTS TO ACCOMPLISH ON THE SIDELINES: WORK, HUSTLE, going from session to session, and meeting wonderful women sitting next to you during the speaker sessions. Every woman attending this conference is exceptional, because each one is recovering from alcoholism.

Among the women is much smiling, comfortable chatting, friendly hellos, occasional shrieks of delight as old friends recognize one another from previous conferences, and a rush to hug. After three days of immersion in the conference, to see a man seems strange.

The conference is hallmarked by two subtle but distinct

differences: the use of the restroom and the bar. The women's restrooms on all floors have an absence of women. There is no loitering, no extended conversations, no vanity displayed before the mirror with makeup or hair, an absence of concern with appearance. Instead, women rush in and out, quickly returning to the speaker sessions or ongoing conversations. At this conference, topics range from practicing the Twelve Steps to general sessions on sex, love, sobriety, and AA on-line recovery. This schedule gives everyone plenty of choice in finding just the right recovery topic, in an atmosphere of complete comfort and sharing.

The bar is empty. It is dark. Women sit on chairs outside the bar. No one sits inside. No one carries drinks in the hallway. No one is drunk.

A sound in the lobby, elevators, hallways, and throughout all the floors of the conference hotel is unmistakable: the sound of busy women having a happy time.

> We chartered a bus to Oklahoma City, only three hundred miles away from Wichita, Kansas. While on the bus, we really had a lot of AA. We kidded each other about one thing and another. We were able to laugh about it, instead of getting angry. And that was new behavior for some of us. I find that women who go to women's meetings can really do this more easily than women who go to mixed meetings. They seem to be able to tease each other more and not get angry. They're more comfortable with themselves, about opening up and talking about their problems. All of this has been experienced and practiced in meetings. It's easier to talk about problems in a women's meeting.

This hum increases as women arrive from all parts of the United States, Canada, and a few foreign countries. Gestures abound. Drama is everywhere. There are shrieks of recognition, shouts to a friend down the hall, laughter popping up as a constant staccato throughout the crowded hallways. Arms are slung over one another. Small groups of three, four, and five walk arm in arm, a unit within a unit. And everywhere smile . . . hugs . . . laughter . . . talk.

A slowly increasing intensity reaches a crescendo on Saturday, when all of the twenty-five hundred women have arrived, and weariness begins to show by Saturday evening.

The bustle of the twenty-five hundred women belies what is going on at the individual level. Within minutes of meeting, women quickly drop down to a deeper sharing that permeates the group until the individual units become united into one. It is a time of transition and transference, when the larger conference becomes the embodiment of an individual AA group meeting. It is a place where the persona and language of the street quickly change to those most familiar in intimate AA meetings: openness, vulnerability, and healing. The superficial greetings quickly become warm hugs, eyes meeting, souls connecting, two people exchanging at a profoundly deep level.

> I just really didn't realize there were that many women alcoholics. I found out I wasn't the only one. I think it was from this point on I started opening up and talking about myself. Because at first I didn't want anybody to know me.
>
> For example, at AA speaker meetings, I would turn to my husband with the worst face and say, "He's telling my story!" My husband would turn to me and say, "He's telling my story, too!" From that repeated experience, I learned that we all walk the same road, only some of us took different paths to get on that road.
>
> Philomena R., Wichita Kansas

Opportunities abound to meet women. Openness is the rule. Wherever there is a woman, you can expect her to be another recovering AA woman. A quick glance at her name tag will reassure the doubtful. Only last-name initials are used on the name tags. But still, some women who treasure their anonymity feel the conference name tag is a bit like wearing a scarlet *A* in a public place, until the discomfort is healed by the warmth from the eyes of another woman wearing a similar name tag. Additional comfort comes from knowing there are "only us women here," and the hotel staff is exceptionally kind, courteous, and helpful.

Especially comfortable for women attending the conference alone are the hospitality suites for relaxing longer conversations, one for smoking, one for nonsmoking. Each suite is filled with huge coffee urns, snacks, and a smiling hostess who immediately approaches as you enter the room, asking, "Would you like a cup of coffee?"

> I learned a lot at the women's conference. I feel different about myself and my recovery. It made me see that I can be sober and happy with it if I choose to.
>
> I also have had a very hard time getting along with women because all the women I have had in my life hurt me, and I truly feel they didn't like me at all. Now I can see that all women are not that way and I can have a good, honest relationship with women. I am very privileged and blessed to have been able to take part in the women's conference. I have walked away a better person than I was when I went in.
>
> Danielle D., Salt Lake City
> conference, 1996

The conference consists of speaker and topic meetings, Friday and Saturday banquets, entertainment during the Saturday banquet, Sunday breakfast, Sunday spiritual program, hospitality suites, raffles, and souvenirs. Throughout all are women coming for the sharing, unity, fellowship, and love. Marathon AA meetings are held for those who want to attend a "real" meeting with women around the country. Tapes of conference speakers are available for purchase, to bring home a little bit of the conference.

Also available in an unofficial way are hotel rooms turned into retail sales outlets for every type of recovery item, from pins, shirts, and bookmarks, to recovery books and tapes. Most women find themselves drawn to these rooms at least to look.

The evening banquets are extraordinary places to talk easily with women at your table. It is a time to make friends and ask questions about how AA is practiced in different parts of the country. When personal problems begin to be discussed, as they quickly are with women, hearing the same AA slogans and Steps offered as suggestions for solutions is profoundly reassuring. This is one of the many ways in which the universality of AA is reinforced again and again through participation in the conference.

Dining in the banquet hall with a thousand women is a unique experience. A businesswoman sits at her assigned banquet table and sensing the difference in the room, asks herself when was the last time she was in a conference room with a thousand people. Then she wonders when was the last time she was in a conference room with a thousand women. With a thousand sober women? The answer is—never! The difference is staggering. Everyone is calm, serene, talking pleasantly. The volume of noise reflects the active presence of a thousand women, but no tension is in the air. No one is hustling business cards. No one is making frantic connections. No one is running to the bar.

A glimpse around the room shows a mixture of clothing styles, most dressed up for a special event. Among the most beautiful are African-American ethnic dresses, like a field of flowers, irresistible to women unused to ethnic minorities in their hometowns. Some dresses are breathtaking in their chic and are worn with aplomb. Many hats dot the room. One particularly stunning black woman in an eye-catching dress, molded to a beautifully fit body, with saucy, cocked hat to match, holds the eye of everyone as she walks onto the stage to begin the evening's announcements. As she saunters up to the microphone, the crowd erupts in whistles and catcalls and spontaneous applause, sounding for all the world as though it were a roomful of men. Seizing the moment, she tosses her head, squares her shoulders, and says to the crowd, "Eat your heart out!"

This is not a place for young women only. Most are over thirty, and many are in their seventies. During the sobriety countdown, it seems that more than half had more than ten years of sobriety. These women have come from all but two states in the United States, each province of Canada, and a few foreign countries. Their sobriety ranges from twenty-four hours to forty-seven years.

The Saturday banquet is the highlight of the conference. There is a gourmet feast, sobriety countdown, state roll call, raffle, introduction of the next year's conference committee chair, announcement of the location of the conference in two years, speaker meeting, and entertainment. During the state roll call, applause punctuates the announcement, each state trying to outdo the other with enthusiasm as they are introduced. Then it is over for the night as women leave in groups to talk quietly or to attend the ongoing marathon meetings.

> We are two women talking intently after the banquet, seated on the sidelines of this enormous banquet hall, searching for something in one another's eyes. We have found each other. Twenty years separate us, yet we share the same alcoholic experiences, the same soul. I, the younger, ask questions of her with the beautiful face and dress. I see nothing but her eyes and the crystal chandeliers and mirrored walls behind them. I am telling my story to this woman I just met and sharing my most painful secrets. Nothing else exists for me. The wait staff silently remove dishes and tables and themselves. It is midnight. Not a soul is in the room but us. Nothing moves, but our eyes and mouths as we talk through the problems I came with. The room is kept open for the two of us . . . to finish this sacred business . . . which everyone recognizes.
>
> Joan Z., Chicago conference, 1997

It is easy to meet people at the speaker sessions where the women sitting around you nod their heads in agreement with the speaker and share warm looks and a "knowing" glance with those nearest to them. The hallways are a constant stream of animated talkers, as is the conference registration line and the small tables and chairs lining the hallways. There is no end to the possibilities and places to have a conversation about AA recovery with women who have "been there, done that."

> Being new to AA, the IAAWC gave me courage, strength, and hope. I feel privileged to be able to attend the conference, and I learned that my life depends on AA unity.
> Jamie, Salt Lake City conference, 1996

Meanwhile, in concurrent sessions in smaller rooms open to anyone interested, the actual business of the IAAWC and its future is being carried on by the advisory committee. This group of sixteen women has the responsibility of ensuring that the conference runs smoothly from year to year.

Each year there are many memorable moments at each conference, but some are especially memorable:

1976, San Antonio, Texas: The female mayor of San Antonio gave the welcoming speech to the IAAWC.
1983, Phoenix, Arizona: Over fifteen women with more than thirty years of sobriety were in attendance.
1990, Kansas City, Missouri: Twenty-fifth anniversary "coming home"—returned to the same city in which the conference began.

How Did the IAAWC Start?

The first women's conference was held on February 14, 1965, at group No. 1, 6125 Troost Street, Kansas City, Missouri. This date was chosen to honor Bernadette O'K.'s sobriety birthday. The first conference was attended by forty-five women, mainly local Kansas City women.

Bernadette O'K. and other AA women in Kansas City, Missouri, began talking about a conference just for women in AA. Such a forum would be aimed at providing sharing of experiences common to women alcoholics, discussions of problems of particular interest to all women AA's, and opportunities to hear AA women speakers from many areas.

So enthusiastic was the reception of the first conference, plans were made to make it an annual event. February was chosen as conference month because this was Bernadette's AA anniversary month; it was also traditionally the month of love, and most everyone welcomes a break in the winter doldrums.

Founder: Bernadette O'K.

To female members of AA in Kansas City, Missouri, Bernadette was a legend in her time. The following description of her life and times comes from the *History of the IAAWC:*

> She was 5'1, weighed 155 lbs., had piercing black eyes that could see right through you and was always there when anyone, anywhere needed help. She was ahead of her time having graduated from the University of Michigan in Engineering. She had 14 years of sobriety

in 1963, after sobering up in the late 1940's.

Starting the women's Conference was only one of many things that Bernadette did to promote AA in the area. Her typical day consisted of her regular work; then stopping by Group #1 (located at 6125 Troost Street, Kansas City, Missouri) to see if anyone needed help or a 12 Step call. She would have dinner with one of the many women she was sponsoring in the program. Then off to another meeting. She was always helping someone.

She used to say that she was a traveling drunk. So when she sobered up, she also traveled quite a bit to various Round Robins or other AA functions through the Midwest. It was not uncommon for her on three-day holidays to travel as far as Michigan or Texas. On other three-day holidays, she organized all-day AA functions that brought families together. Women were in the kitchen skinning chickens for dinner while meetings or other recreational activities were going on. She was a great delegator. Marie B. was one of the main women behind the scenes who was there to implement the work that was inspired by Bernadette.

In the early 1960's, Bernadette helped to organize the first women's group at Group #1 at 6125 Troost in Kansas City, Missouri. It met once a week. *That meeting continues today.*

Bernadette helped AA to grow in Kansas City. Since there were no halfway houses for women in the fifties and sixties, she started one in her home, known as the Winona Simmons Home. She helped to promote the first treatment center in the area at St. Joseph Hospital in St. Joseph, Missouri.

Bernadette's last Conference, prior to her death was held at the Muehlebach Hotel in downtown Kansas City, Missouri in 1968. About two weeks after the

Conference, Bernadette traveled to California to make an amend to her former husband, whom she had not seen for more than 20 years. Although he was not anxious to see her, she was able to tell him a little about what she had been trying to do with her life. So he finally agreed to see her. After she had made her amend, her former husband invited her to dinner to meet his wife and family. As she was crossing the lobby to meet him, she suffered a massive stroke and died a few hours later. It is one of those many stories we often hear around AA which once again reaffirms how spiritually-guided our program truly is.

According to her friends, she came forward when the stigma for women alcoholics was much greater than it is today. Bernadette stood for honesty and was a firm believer in the basics of the Twelve Step Program. Today, the women on the Advisory Board of the IAAWC carry on Bernadette's tradition.

Maybe the women's Conference would have gotten started without Bernadette. But many are grateful she was the promoter and instigator for what has become one of the truly beautiful experiences within women's sobriety.

Bernadette was good friends with Marty Mann, one of the first women in AA. Marty helped to promote the Conference from her position in New York. However, knowledge of the existence of the woman's Conference occurred by word of mouth. That simple tradition continues today, given a very limited promotion budget.

THE CONFERENCE GROWS

Held for the first five years in Kansas City, the conference started out as local. Its popularity caused many women in other places to ask for the conference to be held in their cities. Following Bernadette's death, the location became movable. The conference moved to St. Louis in 1970, becoming regional. It became national by moving to Des Moines, Iowa, in 1974. At that time, it became the tradition to move the conference to various parts of the country, finally returning to its roots in the twenty-fifth year back in Kansas City.

Many women continued to lobby for the expansion of the conference to their part of the country. A handful of Canadian women attended the conference in 1991. They appealed to the Advisory Board to expand the board composition to include Canadian representation. The board agreed. Consequently, the name had to be changed from National to International Alcoholics Anonymous Women's Conference. The name change also reflected a growing awareness of globalism and the universality of AA. This immediate change in definition cleared the way for women of Canada to bid for future conferences, and they were successful. The conference became "international" with the 1993 conference held in Vancouver, British Columbia.

There was initial disagreement over the definition of the term *international*. Many Advisory Board members felt that the title of the conference should reflect the attendance, which had always been from the North American continent and never truly international in scope. Although there had always been a few visitors from other countries, these women were usually visitors who happened to be in the area and hear of the conference. Information about the conference had always been limited by a small promotion budget and the traveling location of the conference.

However, the communication barrier quickly dropped with

the rise of the Internet and AA on-line meetings. Information about date and place of the conference now travels throughout the world in seconds, not dependent on the limited promotion budget of the IAAWC. Therefore, one can anticipate the next conference being widely attended by women throughout the world as they become aware of its existence and its value.

The conference has been held in these cities:

Year	City
1965–69	Kansas City, Missouri
1970	St. Louis, Missouri
1971	Wichita, Kansas (Conference became movable)
1972	Oklahoma City, Oklahoma
1973	Little Rock, Arkansas
1974	Des Moines, Iowa (Conference became national)
1975	Minneapolis, Minnesota
1976	San Antonio, Texas
1977	Chicago, Illinois
1978	Cleveland, Ohio
1979	Denver, Colorado
1980	New York, New York
1981	Costa Mesa, California
1982	Oklahoma City, Oklahoma
1983	Phoenix, Arizona
1984	Atlanta, Georgia
1985	Denver, Colorado
1986	Philadelphia, Pennsylvania
1987	Albuquerque, New Mexico
1988	Dallas, Texas
1989	Kansas City, Missouri
1990	Minneapolis/St. Paul, Minnesota
1991	Orlando, Florida
1992	Reno, Nevada
1993	Vancouver, British Columbia (Conference became international)
1994	New York, New York

1995	Omaha, Nebraska
1996	Salt Lake City, Utah
1997	Chicago, Illinois
1998	Cleveland, Ohio
1999	San Jose, California

STRUCTURE IS NEEDED

With the rapid growth of the conference, the consensus was that some organizational structure was needed. A business meeting was held the Saturday morning of the 1972 conference and after much discussion, an Advisory Board was formed. There were to be two delegates from Oklahoma and Missouri, one each from Kansas, Arkansas, and Texas, and two "at-large" delegates.

The original elected delegates were

Bertha C.	Kansas City, Missouri
Emma G.	Springfield, Missouri
Elizabeth E.	Tulsa, Oklahoma
Jeanne F.	Oklahoma City, Oklahoma
Olga M.	Hoxie, Kansas
Mary P.	Little Rock, Arkansas
Kate R.	San Antonio, Texas

At-large delegates were

| Laura L. | Chicago, Illinois |
| Marie B. | Grafton, Ohio |

After the general business meeting, the nine delegates met and elected Jeanne Fleetwood as chair and Olga Moon as secretary.

> We set sail on uncharted waters. We made mistakes and we corrected them.

We had no money to begin, and if you have ever taken on such a task you know what it takes. A post office box must be rented, flyers and registration forms printed, and mailings done *before* any money arrives! Our AA state committee gave us some money, and several individuals advanced us a loan.

We sent flyers to all women's groups, clubhouses, intergroups, and state offices listed in the eastern and western AA directories. We made tote bags, "Big Book" felt covers, and felt bookmarks for all attendees. The efforts resulted in 225 attendees in 1972!

We literally "talked" Little Rock into hosting the 1973 conference (no one else bid on it)! We were able to give Little Rock $100 to get started. This was the beginning of "seed money" for the next conference site. Today the seed money is up to $5,000 for the next year's conference.

A lot of growing has taken place since 1972, but at least the Advisory Board and conferences are on solid ground. It has been my privilege to be part of this growth.

> Jeanne F.,
> Oklahoma City
> (Chair of the IAAWC
> Advisory Board, 1972)

THE IAAWC ADVISORY BOARD

Today, the Advisory Board has sixteen women: two representatives from each of six U.S. and two Canadian regions. The IAAWC areas are grouped to correspond with General Service Office (GSO) areas.

East Central:	Illinois, Indiana, Michigan, Ohio, Wisconsin
Northeast:	Connecticut, Delaware, Maine, Maryland, Massachusetts, New Hampshire, New Jersey, New York, Pennsylvania, Rhode Island, Vermont, Washington, D.C.
Pacific:	Arizona, California, Idaho, Nevada, Oregon, Utah, Washington
Southeast:	Alabama, Florida, Georgia, Kentucky, Louisiana, Mississippi, North Carolina, South Carolina, Tennessee, Virginia, West Virginia
Southwest:	Arkansas, Colorado, Kansas, Missouri, New Mexico, Oklahoma, Texas
West Central:	Iowa, Minnesota, Montana, Nebraska, North Dakota, South Dakota, Wyoming
Eastern Canada:	British Columbia, Alberta, Saskatchewan, Manitoba
Western Canada:	New Brunswick, Newfoundland, Nova Scotia, Ontario, Prince Edward Island, Quebec

The board meets annually during the conference, where new board members are chosen during regional meetings.

The purpose of the Advisory Board is to ensure the continuity of the annual conference. It suggests policies and guidelines, selects conference cities, and assists conference committees. The board members also publicize the conference in the area they represent. The Advisory Board meets annually during the conference to consider ideas and problems and to suggest guidelines gleaned from experiences, and always in accordance with AA Traditions.

Requirements for board membership are five years' continuous sobriety, ability to attend the annual board meetings (held during the conference) for the three years of her term, and willingness to fulfill obligations of the job, including publicizing the conference in her locality.

Board members serve three-year terms. When a board vacancy exists, it is announced at the conference. Those in attendance from the area where a replacement is needed are asked to hold a caucus in regional meetings and select a nominee to represent their area on the board. The nominee is introduced to the board at the annual business meeting and then announced to the conference during the Saturday evening banquet.

IAAWC CONFERENCE
SITE SELECTION

City committees wishing to host the conference present their bids to the Advisory Board during the current conference. These committees should have already selected their conference chair, a hotel, and a date. They present comprehensive information on facilities, room, and food costs, accessibility to airport, and the all-important feature of every conference—cost of coffee. Also, they should have an indication of willingness on the part of local groups to host the conference and have enlisted the support of local AA women and the local AA office.

Each conference committee adheres to a list of twenty-six "suggested" guidelines, including

— International AA Women's Conference decisions and actions adhere to AA Traditions.
— February is conference month; a change would require board action.
— Each conference host city committee is responsible for conference costs.
— Each conference committee receives rotating seed money, so preconference bills can be met prior to receipt of registration fees. (Amount: $5,000)

Presentation by members of cities bidding for the conference is made at the Advisory Board meeting on Saturday morning—limiting time to ten minutes. Conference location is set for two years ahead. These highly professional presentations are open to any interested conference attendee and are a joy to watch. The enthusiasm of each committee member for her city becomes a mixture of cheerleader, hostess, professional salesperson, and devoted AA member.

When the announcement of the chosen city, two years forward, is made Saturday evening of the current conference, it is greeted by thunderous applause and delighted cheers by the chosen city committee. The committee then has two years to plan and prepare for the conference. This practice provides the necessary time for planning, recruiting committee workers, and securing the best locations and date.

A conference has never run a deficit, always bringing in more income than expenses. The use of any "leftover" money is determined by the local city conference committee; however, the conference committee is restricted to donating such proceeds to an AA-related enterprise. This is often the New York GSO, but occasionally some committees have chosen to help support Dr. Bob's house in Akron and other similar AA-related local enterprises.

Each host committee feels similarly to the group from the 1981 Conference in Costa Mesa, California:

> Our most important job on this weekend is to make you feel welcome and at ease in "our place" and to let you experience the hospitality and friendliness of AA in this part of the country. Let us make this weekend a glorious celebration of our sobriety, individually and collectively. May each of us leave this conference with the feeling that we have taken away with us something special for ourselves, and left something special for another.

The Conference Is an
Official AA Meeting

The IAAWC falls under the GSO category of a "meeting" rather than a "group." The difference between these AA entities is spelled out on page 33 of Pamphlet 16, *The A.A. Group.*

> Some A.A.'s also attend meetings that are not a function of any established A.A. group . . . specialized gatherings . . . men's, women's, gays', young people's, doctors', priests', deaf people's, etc. . . . hold meetings where *only recovery from alcoholism through the A.A. program is discussed.* . . . Meetings of all these types have proved valuable for many A.A.'s as an adjunct to, but never as a substitute for, the regular meetings held by A.A. groups.

The IAAWC is planned and carried out in this AA spirit, according to the GSO's *AA Guidelines: Conferences & Conventions.*

Statement of Purpose of the IAAWC

The Women's Conference is a bridge to better understanding of AA philosophy and way of life because of our special needs in sobriety as women. We are survivors who have found a way to bring meaning, depth and responsibility into our lives. This was born of desire, decision, determination and spiritual guidance. Our goal is an "elevated sense of belonging" augmented and expanded by the services and answers to particular needs provided by our Women's Conference.

> (Adopted by the Eighteenth Annual Women's Conference in Oklahoma, City, Oklahoma, February 6, 1982)

The Conference Today and Tomorrow

The Thirty-third Annual International Women's Alcoholics Anonymous Conference was held in Chicago on February 13–16, 1997. More than twenty-five hundred women attended this conference, the largest group to date.

Hundreds of Chicago-area women, soul sisters in sobriety, participated in the conference and provided a strong force to welcome women AA's from virtually every state. For more than two years, the committee planned and prepared. All AA women in the host city were sought and asked to help with the many final preparations, especially in the final weeks, as well as throughout the conference.

Those women who have attended previous conferences have often expressed great enthusiasm for the joy experienced in gaining new insights into AA recovery and fellowship at the national level. Sharing their experience, strength, and hope with others throughout the country reinforced the potent and miraculous power of Alcoholics Anonymous. Each February since 1965, the conference theme has been "The language of the heart is spoken here."

> From the beginning, communication in AA has been no ordinary transmission of helpful ideas and attitudes. It has been unusual and sometimes unique. Because of our kinship in suffering, and because our common

means of deliverance are effective for ourselves only when constantly carried to others, our channels of contact have always been charged with The Language of the Heart.

Bill W. (*AA Today*)

And now, hundreds of AA women attend each year this special weekend. From the steadily increasing interest, the conclusion is plain: The IAAWC beautifully fills a need in AA women's lives. A note of caution: This can be habit forming!

> My very first IAACW WOW! What an experience. I never felt so high in my life. Drugs have never come even close to this. I feel it was a turning point for my recovery. The love, power, and serenity was just awesome. It gave me so much hope to see so much recovery. I want to be a part of these women's lives. I want to be part of AA.
>
> Mary Ann (twenty days sober),
> Salt Lake City conference, 1996

For nearly two years, our committee has worked to make this twentieth annual NAAWC a memorable experience for everyone. We hope that you will have a wonderful time during your visit to Atlanta and that you will find here something very special. AA is like a bountiful fruit tree, giving to all who will take and growing ever stronger with the giving.

While you are here, we will share the sweet fruits of AA and still have plenty left to share with our groups when we return.

And, as we each travel our separate paths to "happy destiny," we hope that each of you will remember us with love and a smile . . . as we shall remember you.

Until next year, go with our love and the very special
promises of your private miracle.

> The Committee, IAAWC Twentieth
> Annual Conference, Atlanta,
> Georgia, 1984

FURTHER REFERENCES:

Thirty-sixth IAAWC Conference, P.O. Box 723964, Atlanta, GA
31139. IAAWC@geocities.com

In Memory of

Marty Mann

MARTY MANN (1904–1980), ONE OF THE FIRST WOMEN TO MAINTAIN CONTINUOUS SOBRIETY THROUGH AA, WAS THE FIRST to "go public" about her alcoholism—to talk about her disease in public and with the media.

In 1944, when she'd been sober for five years, Marty became overwhelmingly frustrated at "the dark fog of ignorance and misconception" about alcoholism. She felt "smothered by the stigma surrounding us, and what we in AA were trying to do," she later told *Guideposts* magazine.

Marty dreamed of starting a nationwide educational program about alcoholism—to remove the stigma from the disease and find ways to let all alcoholics and their families know that help was available. She also wanted to stimulate public interest in providing nationwide diagnostic, counseling, and treatment facilities.

She sold her dream to a group of scientists at the Yale Center of Alcohol Studies, including Dr. H. W. Haggard, Dr. E. M. Jellinek, and Dr. S. D. Bacon. In October 1944 the National Committee for Education on Alcoholism (NCEA—now called the National Council on Alcoholism and Drug Dependence) officially opened in New York City. Board members included Bill W. and Dr. Bob S., cofounders of Alcoholics Anonymous. Also on the advisory board were actress Mary Pickford and writer Dorothy Parker.

To spread NCEA's educational message, Marty shed her AA anonymity. The October 1944 issue of the *AA Grapevine* reported, "As Marty said in an interview with us yesterday, 'I'm going to lecture to non-alcoholics on alcoholism. I could be much more convincing, and give them much more understanding, by speaking as an alcoholic—from the inside. . . . That left me with two choices. To say that I was an alcoholic and had recovered, period. And not to mention AA. Or to give AA full credit for my recovery and break the anonymity rule. I couldn't conceive of not publicly giving AA all the credit.'" AA at the time was only nine years old and the Tradition of anonymity at the public level had not yet been finally adopted.

As an openly recovering alcoholic, Marty Mann was a curiosity who attracted press coverage all over the country. "Mrs. Mann became the first woman member of Alcoholics Anonymous," reported the Louisville *Courier-Journal* when she gave a 1946 speech in that city. "The daughter of a socially prominent family, she explains that she married an alcoholic and became one herself."

The *New York Times* in 1946 described Marty as "an attractive, smart-looking woman in her thirties [she was actually forty-two]. Her clear complexion, her alert blue eyes and her manner bear no trace of years of hard drinking."

Marty's "fervor carried her 24,000 miles in a year," reported *Dallas News* that year, "seeking to convince a nation that alcoholism is a disease . . . and the scientific way of handling it is the establishment of information centers, clinics for diagnosis, admission to hospitals for sobering up and rest centers for long-term treatments."

Marty Mann's dreams came true. Alcoholism is officially recognized as a disease today. NCEA has 184 affiliates from coast to coast. There are hundreds of other alcoholism agencies, hundreds of alcoholism treatment centers, and thousands of trained alcoholism counselors.

Although she continued lecturing until three weeks before she died—often two hundred speeches a year—and discussing her own alcoholism, Marty changed her stance after two years and stopped talking about her AA membership. "No one was ever happier to resume that protective cloak," she wrote years later.

A true pioneer, Marty continues to be an inspiration to women the world over.

OTHER TITLES THAT MAY INTEREST YOU . . .

The Little Red Book
50th Anniversary Edition

This special anniversary hardcover edition features the original 1946 text with an introduction that chronicles Dr. Bob's influence on the writing of *The Little Red Book*.
110 pages
Order no. 1029

Practice These Principles and *What Is the Oxford Group?*

The Oxford Group, which existed before Alcoholics Anonymous, is where Bill W. and Dr. Bob first met. The latter used its Four Absolutes as the foundation for the Twelve Steps. This comprehensive, historical text of the AA fellowship explores the early years of AA.
Two-book volume, 164 pages
Order no. 1059

Not-God
A History of Alcoholics Anonymous
by Ernest Kurtz

This book is a comprehensive, candid, and truly definitive history of the creation, development, and legacy of Alcoholics Anonymous.
436 pages
Order no. 1036

For price and order information or a free catalog, please call our telephone representatives or visit our Web site at **www. hazelden.org**

Hazelden
1-800-328-9000 (Toll-free U.S. and Canada)
1-651-213-4590 (24-hour fax)